ESSAYS ON THE THEORY AND PRACTICE OF CRIMINAL JUSTICE

Robert M. Rich
Criminologist

University Press of America™

University Press of America™
division of
R.F. Publishing, Inc.
4710 Auth Place, S.E., Washington, D.C. 20023

Printed in the United States of America

ISBN: 0-8191-0235-0

CONTRIBUTORS

Ibtihaj Arafat, Ph.D.

Matthew R. DeZee, Ph.D.

Finn Hornum, Ph.D.

Mary S. Knudten, Ph.D.

Richard D. Knudten, Ph.D.

Kathleen McCahery, M.A.

William F. McDonald, D. Crim.

Gordon E. Misner, D. Crim.

F. X. Ribordy, Ph.D.

Robert M. Rich, Ph.D.

Frank Stavish, Ph.D.

TABLE OF CONTENTS

*adapted from Reduction of Robberies and Assaults of Bus Drivers, U.S. Department of Transportation Demonstration Project, Final Report, Volume II, 1970, Chapter IV.

PREFACE

This book consists of selected original essays on the theory and practice of criminal justice. The text is designed for students of criminology, criminal justice, and law and society programs from the police officer to the full time student.

The essays written for the book are by a number of criminologists who have been interested in either theory or the practical application of theory. Since most criminology and criminal justice texts are both theoretical and general in orientation, this book examines theory and attempts to relate it to specific practical application.

Topics from the areas of sociology of law, crime control, and crime prevention are presented. The theory section of the book consists of two essays on sociology of criminal law, three on crime control, and one on crime prevention. The practice section consists of essays on clients of criminal lawyers, victims of crime, criminal offenders, the role of the patrol officer, the role of the prosecutor, and crime in public transport.

My thanks to May Thompson and Doris Suttlehan for their understanding and persistence at the typing task. Also thanks to Pam Caldarone, Maria Thomae, and Lucy Brennan for their work as proofreaders.

Robert M. Rich, Ph.D.
Alexandria, Virginia
1977

The Sociology of Criminal Law: Toward a Paradigmatic Perspective

Robert M. Rich

Sociology Paradigms

According to Ritzer, there are currently only three basic paradigms in sociology. These are the social facts paradigm, social definition paradigm, and social behavior paradigm.[1] A paradigm is defined as "a fundamental image of the subject matter within a science. It serves to define what should be studied, what questions should be asked, and what rules should be followed in interpreting the answers obtained. The paradigm is the broadest unit of concensus within a science and serves to differentiate one scientific community or sub-community from another. It subsumes, defines, and interrelates the exemplars, theories, and methods/tools that exist within it."[2]

Criminology and its subdivision, sociology of criminal law, must fit into one or more of these paradigms if Ritzer is correct in his analysis. Consequently the purpose of this analysis is to examine the theories of the various classical and contemporary sociologists of criminal law to see which paradigms they adhere to and in what theoretical direction they are moving. In order to accomplish this task, one will first have to define the various applicable paradigms and describe their theories. Briefly the social factist is interested in the development of grand, abstract theory. Institutions and social structures are the basic type of facts of interest to adherents of this paradigm. Lastly social factists concentrate on the social group.[3] Social definitions are concerned with debunking myths about society and devote themselves to changing various things that are regarded by them as detrimental to society. Social definitions are basically social interactionists concerning themselves with the relationship between individual and social group.[4] The social behaviorists accept both the need to develop theory and use sophisticated quantitative methods of analysis. The adherents to the social behavior paradigm concentrate on the individual.[5]

Social Facts Paradigm

The social facts paradigm is composed of two theories, structural-functionalism and conflict theory. Structural-functionalists feel that structures and institutions can contribute to the maintenance of other social facts and can also have negative consequences for them (i.e., utilize the concepts of function and dysfunction). Followers of this theory justify the status quo and tend to have a conservative societal orientation (i.e., emphasize order in society and de-emphasize conflict and change).[6] In particular structural-functionalists are oriented toward the analysis of social structures and institutions. Concern is with relationships between structures, between institutions, and between structures and institutions. The individual is largely controlled by social facts that are external and coercive. Functionalists view society as static or in a state of moving equilibrium. They strongly emphasize the fact that society is orderly; that every societal element contributes to stability; and that society is kept together informally by norms, values, and common morality.[7]

Conflict theory for the most part is simply a series of positions directly antithetical to structural-functionalist ideas according to Ritzer. Thus conflict theorists are oriented toward the study of social structures and institutions like functionalists but perceive society as based on conflict and consensus emphasizing the role of power in maintaining societal order.[8] In particular conflict theorists see every structure and institution of society subject to change, conflict ridden, and riddled by dissension. Whatever order there is in society stems from the coercion of the powerless by those in authority. Differential authority is an attribute of various societal positions. Authority does not reside in individuals but in these positions. Thus the individual is concerned with societal positions and the differential distribution of power among these positions. Hence the structural origin of conflicts must be sought in the arrangement of social roles endowed with expectations of domination or subjection (i.e., authority implies both superordination and subordination). Finally the identification of various authority roles within society is the primary focus of conflict theorists.[9]

Both theories of the social facts paradigm tend to be holistic (i.e., look at society as composed of interrelated parts with an interest in the interrelationship between the parts); both theories ignore each other (i.e., one emphasizes societal integration while the other emphasizes societal conflict); both share an evolutionary view of social change; and both are basically equilibrium theories.[10]

Social Definition Paradigm

The social definition paradigm is composed of three theories, action, symbolic interactionism, and phenomenology. Action theorists (ala Weber) view the individual as possessing a dynamic, creative, voluntaristic mind. They see Weber's verstehen concept as a method for gathering data on social institutions and social structures, not as a method for understanding the mental process. The action theorist attempts to put himself in the place of the actor, not in order to comprehend the person but to understand the cultural and societal milieu in which the actor exists.[11] Social action theorists examine the problem solving process through the minds of the actor under study. They examine the actor's means to ends whether both are valued in the same manner or differently utilizing the verstehen concept (i.e., empathy and reliving the experiences of the actor). The feelings, emotions, and habits of the actor are sometimes receptive to analysis using this concept (i.e., interpretive understanding).[12]

Symbolic interactionism theory deals with covert aspects of behavior. Theorists view behavior as a process of interpretation inserted between the environmental stimulus and response of the actor. Social facts are not viewed as things controlling or coercing the individual but only as the framework within which symbolic interaction takes place. Individuals fit their actions to those of others through a process of interpretation. Through this process actors form groups, the action of the group serving as the action of all actors within it. The world of the actor is found in the process of interpretation or orientation of himself vis-a-vis the group. The mind is a process in which the individual interacts with himself and others through symbol utilization.[13]

Phenomenological theory is more philosophical than sociological. These theorists state that man constitutes and reconstitutes what is real (i.e., objective social reality is not independent of the individual). Thus to define a situation as real makes it real. Phenomenologists try to comprehend the meaning that the actor's behavior has for him by both studying the process through which social facts are created by the actor rather than the social facts themselves and by examining the ongoing process of reality construction in society as social facts do not possess an objective existence. By uncovering the processes through which social order emerges from the negotiative behaviors of everyday life, phenomenologists hope to learn how people engage in the process of creating the social facts that are coercive on them. Order and meaning cannot have an objective existence since people impose order and meaning on themselves through manipulation and molding of norms. Reality is what one makes of it. Thus order and social reality have a tenuous existence according to this theory.[14]

Social Behavior Paradigm

Sociology of criminal law theorists tend not to be oriented toward the social behavior paradigm by definition if one goes according to Sutherland. He states that this division of criminology "is an attempt at systematic analysis of the conditions under which criminal laws develop."[15] The crime causation and crime control divisions of criminology appear to be primarily concerned with the social behaviorist paradigm as they tend to be individual oriented. On the other hand, sociology of criminal law is theoretically both group and individual-group oriented since it deals with people on the basis of laws and legal institutions, not on the basis of individual behavior patterns. Thus sociology of criminal law theorists would tend to either fit into the social facts or social definition paradigms. Therefore one will not deal with the theories of the social behavior paradigm in this paper (see Ritzer, Sociology: A Multiple Paradigm Science, Allyn & Bacon, 1975, Chapter 4, pgs. 145-177).

A Paradigmatic Persepctive of Sociology of Criminal Law

At this point in the presentation, one can ask whether sociology of criminal law can be divided into one or more paradigms. Ritzer answers that there is no way that one can be sure that sociology of criminal law is divided into the social facts or social definition paradigms.[16] Obviously Ritzer cannot prove the viability of his classification of paradigms although the evidence for his case is impressive. But he points out that one should not "reify" these paradigms as they are only constructs for understanding sociology and its divisions. Paradigms should be used as a means to examine social reality, in this particular case, sociology of criminal law.[17]

It is the author's contention that sociology of criminal law theorists for the most part "fit" into the social facts paradigm. This paradigm in particular states that the individual, his social behavior, and social activities are largely determined by the social structure and institutions of society (i.e., social roles, institutional patterns, social processes, cultural and subcultural patterns, social norms, group organization, social values, etc.). The person is perceived as totally determined by the broader social structure (i.e., a victim of the social world). Thus he is controlled by and responds to societal values, norms, and social control agencies. Social structures and institutions act as a static set of coercive social facts (i.e., man is viewed as a complex, normative programmed automaton). Therefore external social constraints determine the actor's behavior.[18]

Sociology of Criminal Law Theorists

Let us now examine the statements of the various theorists to determine whether or not most sociologists of criminal law tend to be social factists or social definitionists. Data from the following theorists has been analyzed: Beccaria, Bentham, Tarde, Durkheim, Hall, Allen, Jeffery, Turk, Hills, Chambliss, Quinney, Reasons, Akers, Shur, and Gibbs.

Beccaria

Cesare Beccaria indirectly defines criminal law through his reliance on the social contract theory of Rousseau which was partially an expansion of the writings of Hobbes and Locke. According to this theory, laws result from the combination of men who agree for mutual protection to surrender individual freedom of action. Thus the government must rest on the consent of the governed.[19] Therefore legislative law is more important than judge-made law since only those creating statutes can alter them since the legislative body represents the will of the governed.[20]

The essence of social contract to Beccaria is that it is constituted by the meeting of persons who relate to each other in value-attitudes, life-styles, and behavior patterns. Societal laws apply to everyone on an equal basis since all accept the social contract doctrine.[21]

Sociology of criminal law to Beccaria is an analysis of the effect of environmental stimuli upon the actions of the individual. The individual through proper "legal" education learns to deal with and respect the rights of others. Thus punishment should have both crime prevention and control functions. Continuous clarification of the criminal law serves as a framework for the individual in which to choose his course of action.[22] Therefore through the mechanism of the social contract theory, Beccaria states that all members of society perceive the law as pertaining to each individual equally and equitably with no variations on the basis of age, sex, or social status. Beccaria can be placed in the social definition paradigm as a social interactionist on the basis of the facts presented.

Bentham

The cofounder of the sociology of criminal law with Beccaria does not directly define law. The criminal law is a method of making the interests of the individual coincide with those of the community. Thus it is to the community's interest that one abstain from theft, but only to one's interest where there is an effective criminal law.[23] Bentham would probably concur with the statement that behavior is not criminal unless it is prohibited by the criminal law which in turn is considered as a body of specific rules regarding human conduct made known by the government on behalf of the community.[24]

Bentham deals with the concept of social control and feels that only explicit social controls keep the average person from becoming a criminal. He states that individuals are to be punished by the criminal law in order to maintain order and prevent feuding. But punishment should be certain to be effective.[25]

Sociology of criminal law to Bentham is an analysis of the behavior of individuals in relation to their socio-psychological environment. People learn to fit their actions to those of others through application of the pleasure-pain principle (i.e., one state of affairs is better than another if it involves a greater balance of pleasure over pain or a smaller balance of pain over pleasure).[26] Thus his theory of crime control is based on the philosophy of utilitarianism. Bentham's sociology of criminal law is quite similar to that of Beccaria. He is a social definitionist who is an advocate of social interactionist theory.

Tarde

Tarde does not directly define criminal law but sees crime as related to value-attitudes of one's reference group (i.e., crime results from the influences of one's social environment). One's orientation to the criminal law is dependent upon the influence of primary and secondary group standards upon the individual.[27] Crime is explained as a socially acquired conduct (i.e., learned through imitation or the product of the socialization process).[28]

Crime to Tarde is a social-psychological product and represents the relation of the criminal's social self to his cultural and subcultural environments (i.e., concept of moral responsibility). Tarde noted the causal relationship between the individual and his degrees of freedom in a given environment.[29] His laws of imitation constitute his basic theory (i.e., behavior patterns or laws of fashion, custom, and substitution). As Schafer states Tarde never clearly explains why the first offender committed his crime which sets the imitative patterns in operation or why only a small percentage of the general population imitate criminal types.[30]

Sociology of criminal law to Tarde is an analysis of the interaction of the individual with others. Thus crime is a social product and represents conduct that is socially acquired. The individual fits his actions to those of others (i.e., criminal or non-criminal) through application of the laws of imitation. Through the laws of imitation, the individual seeks out others eventually forming a criminal group which serves as the focal point for all individuals in the group. The socio-psychological world of the individual becomes his orientation towards other group members, both symbolically and behaviorally.[31] Tarde can be placed in the social definition paradigm as a social interactionist.

Durkheim

Durkheim explains law as the expression of a basic social fact. He makes a distinction between repressive law (criminal law) (i.e., those laws that repress antisocial conduct) and restitutive law (civil law) (i.e., laws that prescribe remedies for wrongs).[32] Durkheim states that law is a measure of the type of solidarity or unity in a society (i.e., homogeneous society = mechanical solidarity = repressive law; heterogeneous society = organic solidarity = restitutive law).[33] Thus he reaches the conclusion that crime is a necessary component of society, and its presence allows the criminal law to evolve.[34]

According to Durkheim, in a homogeneous undifferentiated society, punishment is meant to protect and preserve social solidarity. Punishment is a mechanical reaction to preserve solidarity and there is no thought of correction of the offender. The wrongdoer is punished as an example to the community.[35] In an advanced and differentiated urban society, punishment is centered upon the individual and deals with restitution and reparations. Crimes are thought of as acts which offend others and not the total community. Punishment is evaluated in terms of what is good for the individual and is applied to the offender in order to reform him.[36]

The concept of anomie is utilized by Durkheim to explain crime in gesellschaft type societies. Heterogeneity and increased division of labor weaken traditional societal norms and the resultant social changes loosen traditional social controls upon people ultimately creating an environment producing crime and deviant behavior on a large scale.[37]

Sociology of criminal law to Durkheim is an analysis of the culture, its values and norms and their conflict which increases the potential for crime in society. He feels crime is a fundamental part of societal life and is a normal part of every culture. Durkheim feels that crime is a product of societal structural weaknesses as there are inconsistencies in the social structure and uneven distribution of values, means, goods, and rewards.[38] Thus Durkheim deals with social structures, processes, and institutions and can be placed in the social facts paradigm as a structural-functionalist.

A Clarification

A few early contemporary criminologists have opposed the Positivistic concept (i.e., non-legal) of crime. These theorists are Hall, Allen, Jeffery, and Turk to name just a few. A summarization of their main conclusions at this point will help reduce repetition later in the essay. All believe crime should be studied within the framework of the criminal law. The criminologist must account for the definitions by which specific behavior is considered criminal or deviant. Most importantly, the sociology of criminal law must study how the criminal law is formulated and administered in society. This is necessary since the legal definition of behavior determines what society regards as criminal.[39]

Hall

Hall has attempted to determine the relationship between legal changes and value changes in society through an analysis of the law of theft. He expresses four theories concerning sociology of criminal law: (1) the functioning of courts is related to accompanying cultural needs. This applies to both procedural and substantive law.

(2) Legal change follows a definite order. First a lag occurs between the substantive law and the social needs of society followed by an attempt by judges, officials, and the laymen to make adaptations (i.e., use of legal fictions). The last step in legal change is the enactment of new legislation to eliminate the lag. (3) Technicality and legal fiction function both to link the old law to the new and as indexes to solutions of societal legal problems between social orders. (4) Sociology of criminal law is represented by the "law process" of the norm-oriented and directed conduct of large sectors of a societal population.[40]

Sociology of criminal law to Hall is an analysis of social structures, processes, and institutions of society. Criminal law represents a sustained effort to preserve important social values from serious harm and do so not arbitrarily but in accordance with rational methods directed toward the discovery of just ends.[41] Hall has analyzed the effects of legal and socio-economic change upon society and has demonstrated how changes in society are possible without rapid alterations of the law. He can be placed in the social facts paradigm where one can classify him as an adherent to the theory of structural-functionalism.

Allen

Allen feels that the concentration of interest on the nature and needs of the criminal law has resulted in an absence of concern in the nature of crime. The behavioral scientist has all but forgotten how to deal with the types of behavior that should be declared criminal.[42] Allen states there has been a systematic lack of attention to the substantive criminal law which is due to the Positivist bias against authoritative rules in any form and even challenges the reality of such rules.

Instead of considering the law as a set of rules or authoritative norms, Positivists have considered the law as a process according to Allen.[43] Interest has shifted from dealing with substantive law problems and definition of crime to dealing with procedural law and enforcement problems. Thus the systematic disconcern in the law of crimes has not stopped the enthusiastic enactment of penal laws which has created the problem of overcriminalization in our society. Allen refers to both offenses that affect or are believed to affect the security of the state as well as those crimes created by legislatures in large numbers to effect certain objectives of economic regulation or public welfare (i.e., regulatory offenses).[44]

Sociology of criminal law to Allen is an analysis of authoritative normative facts. He is concerned with social structures and institutions of society. Thus Allen is a structural-functionalist who can be placed within the social facts paradigm.

Jeffery

The law is a measure of social rather than individual responsibility and assumes that individuals are responsible for their actions. The law is utilized to evaluate behavior and establish norms of conduct. The offender is one who has been judged by the social group to have violated the code of conduct and is punished accordingly.[45] Jeffery rejects the argument that criminology be independent of the criminal law. He has resurrected the views of the Classical school that the sociology of criminal law should be an essential and necessary part of criminology.[46]

There is a basic dilemma between the Classical (i.e., legal reform) and Positive (i.e., scientific criminal study) schools of criminology.

The Classical school defines crime in legal terms and examines it as a legal entity while the Positive school examines crime as a psychological entity. What Jeffery is alluding to is that most positivistic theorists are adherents of the social behavior paradigm while most classical theorists are social factists. The Classical school defines crime within the strict limits of criminal law while the Positive school attaches the legal definition of crime and replaces it with sociological definitions of crime.[47]

The rejection of the legal definition of crime has left many theorists with no agreement as to the definition of crime. The positivists confuse crime and criminal behavior since they reject the legal definition of crime and try to explain criminal behavior without explaining what is crime. It is Jeffery's contention that positivists are not interested in the sociology of criminal law since they are crime control oriented and concerned with social problems solution.[48]

The positivists believe that crime should be defined as anti-social behavior. In particular they have substituted scientific categories of behavior for legal categories (i.e., accept deviant behavior as criminal, not one who violates a criminal statute).[49] Positivistic theorists seek an explanation of crime in the criminal, not in the criminal law. They seek a universal category of behavior that can be explained in terms of behavioral theory, not in terms of legal definitions of crime.[50]

The positivistic position consists of several basic postulates. It rejects the legal concept of crime; rejects criminal law study; rejects the concept of punishment.[51] Positivists by ignoring the criminal law have abandoned the traditional legal safeguards of society (i.e., law protects society against the individual and the latter against arbitrary state actions). Thus legal process by which crimes are created is ignored by positivistic theorists. Finally positivism's entry into criminal law has created an untenable position wherein the legal rights of juveniles, alcoholics, addicts, and the mentally ill have been ignored in the name of treatment.[52]

Sociology of criminal law to Jeffery is an analysis of social norms and behavior patterns. He is concerned with social institutions and social structures. Jeffery is interested in the interaction process between the law and other societal institutions. He is a social factist who utilizes structural-functional theory.

Turk

Turk accepts the conflict perspective on the law as the most relevant for sociology of criminal law. He perceives legality as an attribute of whatever words or deeds are defined as legal by those able to use to their advantage the machinery for making and enforcing rules. Political power then determines legality.[53] Law is directly related to social conflict in society according to Turk. A law is a set of words about behavior, either describing what people actually do or specifying what they ought to do.[54] Legality depends upon the ability of some social groupings jointly to seize upon the mechanisms for creating, maintaining, changing, and destroying laws. For those powerful enough to have some impact on the legal process, law will be viewed as compromise. For those who have no power in the struggle to control legal mechanisms, law will assume the form of edicts.[55]

The focus in sociology of criminal law should be upon patterns of conflict (i.e., overt and covert). This focus is between different kinds of social groups who manifest different value-attitude systems. Society is composed of authorities (i.e., those holding dominant, decision-making positions) and subjects (i.e., those holding subordinate positions). Legal norms vary in regard to the proportion of a population affected according to Turk. Thus subjects can be distinguished from authorities by their inability to influence the processes of norm creation or enforcement.[56]

There is an attempt by Turk to construct a theory about authority-subject conflict over legal norms and about the conditions under which subjects are likely to be criminalized in the course of conflict. He states that the study of criminality is the analysis of relations between the statuses and roles of legal authorities (i.e., creators, interpretors, and enforcers of right-wrong standards in society) and those of subjects (i.e., acceptors or resistors but not makers of such standards).[57]

The legality of norms according to Turk depends upon how they are defined by authorities. A norm is a law if the authorities say that it is (i.e., they are prepared to use force to make people comply). The ultimate legal norm is the rule that the final decision of the authorities is binding. If the expectations of the authorities regarding their legal treatment of subjects is unclear, there is room for normative conflict to arise.[58]

In an authority relationship the control ordering of the parties should be clear as both authorities and subjects should continue to perform their roles in a way that the relationship does not become either too coercive or too consensual. Obvious and repeated failure by the authorities to sanction violators of any legal norms constitutes inadequate role performance and contributes to weakening the authority structure over time.[59] The increasing estrangement of authorities and subjects can be reversed only if the authorities exercise restraint in dealing with the norm-violators. The law is an instrument of order no matter how receptive the authorities are to making legal changes. Should the authorities fail to achieve conditioning of norm violators, there will be an eventual dissolution of the social order, a period of explicit power struggles, and establishment of a new social structure in which new groupings have emerged and take their places in the new power struggle.[60]

Crime is taken as an indicator of the failure or lack of authority in society. Sociology of criminal law to Turk is an analysis of social norms and authority structures in society. He accepts the conflict theory of societal functioning and is a social factist.

Hills

Law is not defined by Hills who accepts the conclusions of interest-group theorists that criminal laws change as the interest-power structure of society changes. Thus criminal law definitions change and adapt themselves to the changes of the societal social order.[61]

Hills states there are two competing major theoretical perspectives to the sociology of criminal law: the value-consensus and interest-group theories. The value-consensus position states that criminal laws reflect those societal values which transcend the immediate, narrow interests of various individuals and groups, expressing the social consciousness of the whole society. The legal process thus regulates, harmonizes, and reconciles all conflicting claims to enhance the welfare of the social order.[62]

The interest-group position states that criminal laws will change with modification in the interest-power structure of society. As societal social conditions change, the criminal law will adapt to these changes in the distribution of power of various interest groups. Interest-group theorists emphasize the ability of particular groups to shape the societal legal system to serve their needs and safeguard their interests.[63]

Sociology of criminal law to Hills is an analysis of conflicting moral codes and interests caused by an absence of societal consensus which is kept alive by strong and powerful interest groups which influence legislation and its application on a society-wide basis.[64] Thus Hills adheres to the social facts paradigm and is a conflict theorist.

Akers

The central theoretical issue in the study of law and society is the nature of interrelationships between law and other institutions and normative systems in society.[65] In examining law in the political state, Akers reviews what he calls the two major models or theoretical approaches to understanding modern politically organized society (i.e., consensus or conflict). The first of these theories states that the law evolves from normative consensus in society and serves the broad interests and functions of society as a whole. The second theory views law as formed out of the conflict of values and actions of various groups in society and reflects the narrow interests of societal groups which wield economic, social and political power.[66]

After a review of the literature that includes the writings of several theorists, Akers states that most evidence is in support of the conflict model. He notes that the law supports the norms of groups who have been politically successful in society. Accepted as fact is that the law is most often the outcome of group conflict. More important to Akers is whether the nature of group conflict can best be described as due to either the power elite or pluralistic concepts.[67]

Akers states that neither the pluralistic nor power elite concepts deny the importance of power, domination, and conflict in society. He also feels that either model (i.e., pluralistic or power elite) more closely fits reality than a consensus model. But admitting the primary importance of power and conflict should not deny a place for the consensus model of law in society. Akers states there can be little doubt that the core of the criminal law is designed to protect the life and property of everyone although differentially enforced against the less powerful in society. He concludes that powerful groups in society make the law reflect their interests to a great extent but the law also reflects the views of all of society at any given time.[68]

Sociology of criminal law to Akers is an analysis of the consensus and conflict approaches to society. In particular he deals with the conflict model where he reviews both pluralistic and power elite concepts. He concludes that the societal legal system reflects both special interests as well as areas of concern to everyone (i.e., victimless crimes, public interest laws, and regulatory statutes). Akers feels that law is both shaped by and has an independent impact on society; grows out of, is influential upon, and is consistent with conspicuous normative structures.[69] Akers' approach is structural-functional and fits the social facts paradigm.

Chambliss

Law is defined by Chambliss and Seidman as not merely a body of rules but as a dynamic process involving every aspect of state action, for this action involves either creation of a norm, adjudication about its content, adjudication that has been violated, or a sanctioning process. This set of processes comprises the law.[70]

In his writings, Chambliss refers to the consensus model or theoretical approach to law and society as the value-expression hypothesis and to the conflict model as the interest-group hypoesis.[71] In 1971, he renamed the two models of law and society value-consensus and value-antagonism.[72] In 1973 Chambliss refers to the models as positivist (i.e., functionalist) and conflict.[73] In 1975 he has updated his 1969 theoretical viewpoint and reutilizes the terms consensus and conflict models in reference to the legal system of society.[74] Here Chambliss refers specifically to both structural-functional and conflict perspectives.[75]

Sociology of criminal law is presently dipolar in theoretical orientation according to Chambliss. The functionalist view states that acts are defined as criminal because they offend the moral beliefs of society. Those who violate the criminal law are punished according to prevailing mores of society. Individuals are labeled criminal because their behavior exceeds tolerance limits set by the community. The lower classes are more likely to be arrested because they commit more crimes. Criminal law becomes more restitutive rather than repressive (i.e., penal) as society becomes gesellschaft. The conflict view states that acts are defined as criminal because it is to the interest of the ruling class. Ruling class members are able to violate the laws while members of the subject classes will be punished. Individuals are labeled criminal because it is in the interest of the ruling class and regardless of community tolerance. The lower classes are labeled criminal more often because the bourgeoisie's control of the state protects them from stigmatization. As capitalist society becomes more gesellschaft and the gap between the bourgeoisie and proletariat widens, penal law will expand in an effort to coerce the proletariat into submission.[76]

With respect to the sociology of criminal law, the consensus and conflict models of society present quite different fundamental assumptions according to Chambliss. The consensus model emphasizes the shared interests of everyone in society and the consensus over fundamental values which this shared interest creates. The conflict model emphasizes the role of conflicts between social classes and interest groups as the moving force behind the creation and implementation of criminal laws.[77]

Chambliss lists the theories derived from the consensus perspective. There are theories that see the law as a reflection of "perceived social needs" which all reasonable men agree must be met if society is to continue; theories that see the criminal law as an expression of what is in the "public interest"; theories that perceive the law as a reflection of the "moral indignation" of a particularly influential segment of society; and theories that see the law as an expression of the most fundamental values that are inherent in society.[78] Chambliss also lists the theories derived from the conflict perspective. There are theories that emphasize the role of "moral entrepreneurs" (i.e., groups that organize to achieve legal changes which they think are essential for societal well-being); theories that emphasize the importance of bureaucratic interests in the rationalization of problems that are inherent in society; theories that emphasize the conflicts that inhere between interest groups competing for the favors of state power; and theories that emphasize the inherent conflicts between those who rule and those who are ruled and who perceive the criminal law as incorporating rules for enforcing the interests and ideologies of the ruling classes.[79]

The structural-functional perspective has dominated sociology of criminal law for many years according to Chambliss. The basic assumption of this perspective is that the criminal law is a set of rules stipulated by legislatures and courts which reflect societal beliefs. This perspective also sees the criminal law as fulfilling certain basic societal needs. The problem with this perspective is its failure to specify whose interests, views, and needs are being satisfied by the societal legal system. The emergent perspective in sociology of criminal law is the one emphasizing social conflict as the moving force behind the criminal law in action. The social relations which are part of the class, labor, and productive system of capitalist societies are viewed as more important in determining the content and functioning of the criminal law process than are societal values, norms, and beliefs.[80]

Sociology of criminal law to Chambliss is an analysis of social and normative conflict. He is a conflict theorist who can be placed in the social facts paradigm.

Quinney

The most significant developments in criminology today are awareness of the criminal law and inquiries into its formulation, enforcement, and administration. Criminal law is established to govern the lives and affairs of members of politically organized society. Behind all law formulation are special interests groups. The criminal laws are formulated to promote the interests of certain societal groups. Thus the criminal justice system caters to special interests and is influenced by socio-economic considerations.[81] Quinney believes that law is both a social product (i.e., developing its own internal logic and proceeding along its own lines) and a social force (i.e., operating simultaneously as a reflection of society and influence on society).[82]

Quinney's sociological theory of interests provides a theoretical perspective for comprehending the sociology of criminal law. The theory of interests postulates that law is created by interests; assumes a conflict-power model of society; and proposes a conceptual scheme for analyzing the law-interests relationship. Quinney's conceptual scheme consists of several propositions. The law consists of specialized rules that are created and interpreted in politically organized society; such a society is based on an interests structure; this structure is characterized by unequal distribution of power and by conflict; and the law is formulated and administered within the interest structure of society.[83]

Sociology of criminal law accepts and supports the legal order as it exists and studies the legal system in terms of the existing social order. Thus there is no critique of the capitalist legal order in the sociology of criminal law. The source of crime is not located in the person who violates the law but in the authority structure that defines behavior as criminal. The state is not the ultimate crime control agency of society but a source of crime according to Quinney.[84]

A critical theory of criminal law based on a Marxist understanding of and orientation toward the legal order is presented by Quinney. Law in capitalist society gives political recognition to powerful social and economic interests. The legal system provides the mechanism for the forceful and violent control of the majority in society as the state reflects and serves the needs of the ruling class.[85]

Sociology of criminal law theorists neglect the state as a focal point of inquiry, thus ignoring the fact that the civil society is secured politically by the state which serves an economic elite. The American state is based on an advanced capitalist economy which is organized to serve ruling class interests. Thus the criminal law is an instrument of the ruling class used to maintain and perpetuate the existing socio-economic order. Crime control is accomplished by a government elite in order to establish domestic order for the ruling class, thus keeping the subordinate classes oppressed through utilization of coercion and violence supplied by the criminal justice system. Only the replacement of capitalist society with socialist society can resolve the crime problem according to Quinney.[86]

Sociology of criminal law to Quinney is an analysis of socio-economic conflict. He offers a critique of American sociology of criminal law from a Marxian perspective and must be placed in the social facts paradigm as a conflict theorist.

Reasons

It is important to analyze the criminal law as there is a definite need for data dealing with the emergence of criminal statutes within a sociohistorical context.[87] Theorists have not been concerned with laws but with crime control. There is nothing inherent in criminal behavior since criminality is a status conferred upon specific behavior by the state's political apparatus.[88] Crime may be viewed as phenomena created by individuals in concern who wish their definitions of rightness to triumph and become the laws of society according to Reasons.[89]

Reasons creates what he calls three major paradigms for the field of criminology. The "kinds of people" paradigm asserts that the causes of criminality is in the characteristics of the criminal (i.e., positivistic view).[90] The "kinds of environments" paradigm asserts that crime is a product of the social system (i.e., social deterministic view).[91] Both these paradigms accept a legalistic definition of crime (i.e., behavior violating criminal laws) according to Reasons.[92] The third paradigm, power/conflict recognizes the importance of power, politics, and people in creating, sustaining, and shaping conditions conducive to criminality.[93]

The three paradigms proposed by Reasons fit into the three paradigms proposed by Ritzer which has been expounded upon in a previous section of this essay. Reasons' "kind of people" paradigm can be placed in part in both the social behavior and social definition paradigms. His "kinds of environments" and "power/conflict" paradigms can both be placed in the social facts paradigm. It is possible that if Reasons knew of the work of Ritzer before creating his paradigms he would have utilized the concise system devised by the latter rather than the vague descriptions he uses that in actuality overlap with two paradigms or are part of the same paradigm.

Sociology of criminal law theorists should look at behavior patterns which violate other norms which transcend the political state (i.e., basic concepts of humanity and justice) rather than a continuation of analyzing those behaviors which are officially prohibited by state laws according to Reasons.[94]

To comprehend the law, power/conflict theorists want to demystify the misconceptions concerning the nature and function of the law. The law must be understood in the context of power, politics, and people.[95] Legal system personnel hold values, attitudes, and orientations which influence their professional actions preventing them from operating in a value-free intellectual atmosphere. The law is an instrument of those in power who use it to maintain their positions of high status and privilege in society through utilization of interest groups whose function is to put pressure on legal system personnel.[96]

The power/conflict paradigm demystifies the traditional conception of the criminal and non-criminal which pervades contemporary criminological thought. By focusing on the political nature of criminal definitions, their application, and enforcement - the power/conflict perspective asserts that crime is a product of current power differentials and conflicting world views. Crime is a definition of behavior made by officials of the state and is not inherent in an act. Those behaviors which are offensive to the establishment will be made crimes. Rather than focusing on the crimes of the common criminal, this paradigm places emphasis on the lawless behavior of the state and those in power positions. When attending to common crimes and criminals, paradigmatic emphasis is placed on the oppressive, arbitrary, and self-serving nature of the criminal justice system and its injustices from the offender's perspective.[97]

Sociology of criminal law to Reasons is an analysis of the concepts of social power and conflict in society. He offers a paradigmatic perspective of the sociology of criminal law based on social conflict. Reasons is a conflict theorist who is a social factist.

Schur

Schur thinks it would be a mistake to single out any one definition of law and label it "the definition." The closest he comes to a definition is his statement that the criminal law consists of the rules established by the legislatures and courts, and backed up by sanctions imposed by the courts.[98]

Criminal law theorists have noted that those criminal laws that do not have the support of the dominant social norms of society have limited effectiveness. Attempts to utilize the criminal law in order to regulate private morality causes problems for both the legal system and other societal institutions. Theorists should concern themselves with what the criminal law should be and place the burden of justifying applications of the law on those who seek to impose their conception of the criminal law on the behavior of all societal members.[99]

For example, there is a growing recognition among theorists that the criminal law is the inappropriate means to use in dealing with deviance and that social, medical, and psychological services are more appropriate means.[100] Schur states that some criminal laws are so ineffective and unenforceable that they are of criminological significance because of conflict of interest and value inconsistencies. These unenforceable laws (i.e., crimes without victims) attempt to legally proscribe the willing exchange of socially disapproved but demanded goods or services (i.e., homosexuality, drug addiction, prostitution, gambling, etc.). These types of crimes involve a consensual transaction or exchange and no direct and clear harm is inflicted by one person against another so no legal complaint is made by either party.[101] Further our reliance upon a criminal law solution to most social problems leads to overcriminalization of situations that really do not concern the criminal justice system. Thus there has been overcriminalization in the area of deviance (i.e., sexual behavior, vice, drugs, and political activity) in our society that leads to a doubting of the effectiveness of our legislative process and criminal justice system.[102]

Sociology of criminal law to Schur is an analysis of the effectiveness of law in society, especially in the area of victimless crimes. Schur feels that the criminal law generates a distinctive and coherent, though changing set of roles, norms and structures which interact with other societal institutions. Schur is a social factist whose theoretical orientation is structural-functionalist.

Gibbs

Theorists tend to employ a statutory criterion of criminality which Gibbs criticizes (i.e., the idea that crime is an act so designated by a statute). But as inadequate the statutory conception of crime appears to be, alternative conceptions have not been easily formulated largely because many of the attributes commonly ascribed to criminality are of doubtful nature.[103]

Some of the alternatives to the statutory conception of crime are examined by Gibbs. Sellin's proposal that criminology abandon the soncept of criminal law and study norms of conduct is rejected by Gibbs. The social evaluation of crime (i.e., reaction to behavior that is publicly considered criminal) proposal is also rejected by Gibbs.[104] Using Sutherland's definition of crime as any conduct which is contrary to the criminal law, one can formulate an analytical definition of the criminal law. Thus the criminal law can be defined from politicality, penal sanction, specificity, and uniformity (i.e., the criminal law's four characteristics). Gibbs accepts this definition as applied to modern industrial society.[105]

Gibbs states that any definition of criminal law should recognize that crimes are acts contrary to criminal law and not laws in general.[106] A law then is an evaluation of conduct held by at least one person in a social unit. Further there is a high probability that one or more people in a special status on their own initiative or at the request of others will attempt by noncoercive or coercive means to prevent, rectify, or revenge behavior that is contrary to the evaluation with a low probability of retaliation by individuals other than those at whom the reaction is directed.[107] Gibbs can be placed in the social facts paradigm as a structural-functionalist.

Conclusion

This paper has been written in an attempt to determine whether sociology of criminal law theorists fit into the paradigms proposed by Ritzer, and in what theoretical direction theorists are moving. Fifteen classical and contemporary theorists have been selected for analysis. For the most part the theorists analyzed are representative of the sociology of criminal law field.

It has been the author's contention that sociology of criminal law theorists are adherents to either the structural-functionalist or conflict theories which would place them within the social facts paradigm. Three of the classical theorists are social definitionists (i.e., Beccaria, Bentham, and Tarde) with only Durkheim as a social factist. All twelve contemporary theorists are social factists. All the theorists who fall within the social definition paradigm are social interactionists. Durkheim as a classical theorists is the only one who is an adherent of the social facts paradigm where he is classified as a structural functionalist.

All contemporary theorists are adherents of the social facts paradigm. Six are structural-functionalists (i.e., Hall, Jeffery, Allen, Schur, Gibbs, and Akers) while five are conflict theorists (i.e., Turk, Hills, Chambliss, Quinney, and Reasons). The trend appears to be toward acceptance of conflict theory if one considers that both Jeffery and Akers are quite aware of this theoretical orientation.

According to Taylor et al., the causes of crime must be intimately bound up with the form assumed by the social arrangements of the time. For crime to be abolished, then those social arrangements themselves must also be subjected to fundamental social change.[108] The new criminology must be able to bring politics into the discussion of issues and must be normatively committed to the abolition of inequalities of wealth and power and in particular of inequalities in property and life-chances.[109] Reasons adds that the "power/conflict" paradigm will increasingly gain attention and legitimacy from criminological theorists in the future.[110] Finally Chiricos and Waldo examine the conflict perspective in criminology stating conflict criminologists have generally failed to establish precise links between their criminological propositions and the more general sociological propositions or concepts which they reflect.[111] Hopefully this essay is a step in the right direction.

Notes

1 George Ritzer, Sociology: A Multiple Paradigm Science, Boston: Allyn and Bacon, 1975, pg. 24.

2 Ibid., 189.

3 Ibid., 24.

4 Ibid., 24-25.

5 Ibid., 25.

6 Ibid., 48-57.

7 George Ritzer, Sociology: A Multiple Paradigm Science, The American Sociologist, 10 (August, 1975), pgs. 159-160.

8 George Ritzer, Sociology: A Multiple Paradigm Science, Boston: Allyn and Bacon, 1975, pgs. 57-67.

9 George Ritzer, Sociology: A Multiple Paradigm Science, The American Sociologist, 10 (August, 1975), pg. 160.

10 George Ritzer, Sociology: A Multiple Paradigm Science, Boston: Allyn and Bacon, 1975, pg. 63.

11 George Ritzer, Sociology: A Multiple Paradigm Science, The American Sociologist, 10 (August, 1975), pgs. 161-162.

12 George Ritzer, Sociology: A Multiple Paradigm Science, Boston: Allyn and Bacon, 1975, pgs. 86-87; George Ritzer, Sociology: A Multiple Paradigm Science, The American Sociologist, 10 (August, 1975), pg. 162.

13 George Ritzer, _Sociology: A Multiple Paradigm Science_, Boston: Allyn and Bacon, 1975, pgs. 96-115; George Ritzer, Sociology: A Multiple Paradigm Science, _The American Sociologist_, 10 (August, 1975), pg. 162.

14 George Ritzer, _Sociology: A Multiple_ Paradigm Science, Boston: Allyn and Bacon, 1975, pgs. 96-115; George Ritzer, Sociology: A Multiple Paradigm Science, _The American Sociologist_, 10 (August, 1975), pg. 162.

15 E.H.Sutherland and D.R. Cressey, _Criminology_, Philadelphia: J.B. Lippincott Company, 1970, pg. 3.

16 George Ritzer, _Sociology: A Multiple Paradigm Science_, Boston: Allyn and Bacon, 1975, pg. 196.

17 _Ibid_., 200.

18 George Ritzer, Sociology: A Multiple Paradigm Science, _The American Sociologist_, 10 (August, 1975), pgs. 158-160.

19 Henry C. Black, _Black's Law Dictionary_, Minnesota: West Publishing Company, 1968, pg. 1561; Elio Monachesi, Cesare Beccaria, In _Pioneers In Criminology_, Hermann Mannheim (ed.), Montclair, New Jersey: Patterson Smith, 1972, pgs. 38-39.

20 Elio Monachesi, Cesare Beccaria, In _Pioneers In Criminology_, Hermann Mannheim (ed.), Montclair, New Jersey: Patterson Smith, 1972, pgs. 39-40.

21 Julius Gould & William Kolb (eds.), _A_ Dictionary of the Social Sciences New York: Free Press, 1964, pg. 650; Elio Monachesi, Cesare Beccaria, In _Pioneers In Criminology_, Hermann

Mannheim (ed.), Montclair, New Jersey: Patterson Smith, 1972, pgs. 41-44.

22 Elio Monachesi, Cesare Beccaria, In Pioneers In Criminology, Hermann Mannheim (ed.), Montclair, New Jersey: Patterson Smith, 1972, pgs. 45-47.

23 Bertrand Russell, A History of Western Philosophy, New York: Simon and Schuster, 1959, pag. 775.

24 Edwin Sutherland and Donald Cressey, Criminology, Philadelphia: J.B. Lippincott, 1970, pg. 4; Stephen Schafer, Theories in Criminology, Random House, New York, 1969, pg. 33.

25 Gilbert Geis, Jeremy Bentham, In Pioneers In Criminology, Hermann Mannheim (ed.), Montclair, New Jersey: Patterson Smith, 1972, pgs. 53-66; Bertrand Russell, A History of Western Philosophy, New York: Simon and Schuster, 1959, pg. 775.

26 Bertrand Russell, A History of Western Philosophy, New York: Simon and Schuster, 1959, pg. 775.

27 Margaret Vine, Gabriel Tarde, In Pioneers In Criminology, Hermann Mannheim (ed.), Montclair, New Jersey: Patterson Smith, 1972, pgs. 292-295; Stephen Schafer, Theories In Criminology, New York: Random House, 1969, pg. 75.

28 Stephen Schafer, Theories In Criminology, New York: Random House, 1969, pg. 238.

29 Margaret Vine, Gabriel Tarde, In Pioneers In Criminology, Hermann Mannheim (ed.), Montclair, New Jersey: Patterson Smith, 1972, pgs. 296-299; Stephen Schafer, Theories In Criminology, New York: Random House, 1969, pg. 239.

30 Stephen Schafer, Theories In Criminology, New York: Random House, 1969, pg. 239.

31 Margaret Vine, Gabriel Tarde, In Pioneers In Criminology, Hermann Mannheim (ed.), Montclair, New Jersey: Patterson Smith, 1972, pgs. 300-302.

32 Roscoe Pound, Sociology of Law, In Twentieth Century Sociology, Georges Gurvitch and Wilbert Moore (eds.), New York: The Philosophical Society, 1945, pgs. 316-319.

33 F. James Davis, Law As A Type of Social Control, In Society and the Law, F. James Davis et al., New York: Free Press, 1962, pgs. 41-43; Roscoe Pound, Sociology of Law, in Twentieth Century Sociology, Georges Gurvitch and Wilbert Moore (eds.), New York: The Philosophical Society, 1945, pgs. 318-319; Georges Gurvitch, Emile Durkheim, In Sociology of Law, London: Routledge and Kegan Paul, 1947, pgs. 83-96.

34 Walter Lunden, Emile Durkheim, In Pioneers In Criminology, Hermann Mannheim (ed.), Montclair, New Jersey: Patterson Smith, 1972, pgs. 390-391; Stephen Schafer, Theories in Criminology, New York: Random House, 1969, pg. 243.

35 Walter Lunden, Emile Durkheim, In Pioneers In Criminology, Hermann Mannheim (ed.), Montclair, New Jersey: Patterson Smith, 1972, pgs. 392-393.

36 Ibid., 394-395.

37 Ibid., 396-397; Stephen Schafer, Theories In Criminology, New York: Random House, 1969, 245-246.

38 Stephen Schafer, Theories In Criminology, New York: Random House, 1969, pg. 244.

39 Richard Quinney, Toward A Sociology of Criminal Law, In Crime and Justice In Society, Boston: Little, Brown and Company, 1969, pgs. 13-17.

40 Jerome Hall, Theft, Law and Society, Indianapolis: The Bobbs-Merrill Company Inc., 1952, pgs. xii-xiii.

41 Jerome Hall, General Principles of Criminal Law, Indianapolis: The Bobbs-Merrill Company, Inc., 1947, pg. 1.

42 Francis Allen, The Borderland of Criminal Justice: Essays in Law and Criminology, Chicago: University of Chicago Press, 1964, pgs. 29 & 31.

43 Ibid., 125.

44 Ibid., 126-130.

45 C. Ray Jeffery, Criminal Justice and Social Change, In Society and the Law, F. James Davis et al., New York: Free Press, 1962, pgs. 264-269.

46 Ibid., 270-275.

47 Ibid., 276-281.

48 Ibid., 282-284.

49 Ibid., 285-288.

50 Ibid., 289-294.

51 Ibid., 295-301

52 Ibid., 302-304.

53 Austin Turk, Criminality and Legal Order, Chicago: Rand McNally, 1969, pgs. 30-32.

54 *Ibid.*, 36.

55 *Ibid.*, 32.

56 *Ibid.*, 33.

57 *Ibid.*, 35.

58 *Ibid.*, 37-38.

59 *Ibid.*, 43 & 45.

60 *Ibid.*, 46-48.

61 Stuart Hills, Crime, Power, and Morality: The Criminal-Law Process in the United States, Scranton, Pennsylvania: Chandler Publishing Company, 1971, pg. 5.

62 *Ibid.*, 3-4.

63 *Ibid.*, 4-5.

64 *Ibid.*, 6.

65 Ronald Akers & Richard Hawkins (eds.), Law and Control in Society, Englewood Cliffs, New Jersey: Prentice-Hall, 1975, pg. 41.

66 *Ibid.*, 43-44.

67 *Ibid.*, 47.

68 *Ibid.*, 48-49.

69 *Ibid.*, 41.

70 William Chambliss & Robert Seidman, Law, Order, and Power, Reading, Massachusetts: Addison-Wesley Publishing Company, 1971, pg. 9.

71 William Chambliss (ed.), Crime and the Legal Process, New York: McGraw-Hill Company, 1969, pgs. 8 & 10.

72 William Chambliss & Robert Seidman, Law, Order, and Power, Reading, Massachusetts: Addison-Wesley Publishing Company, 1971, pgs. 17, 40, 45-46, 53-54.

73 William Chambliss, Functional and Conflict Theories of Crime, New York: MSS Modular Publications, Module 17, 1973, pgs. 1-23.

74 William Chambliss, (ed.), Criminal Law In Action, Santa Barbara, California: Hamilton Publishing Company, 1975, pgs. 5-6.

75 Ibid., 476-477.

76 William Chambliss, Functional and Conflict Theories of Crime, New York: MSS Modular Publications, 1973, Module 17, pgs. 1-23.

77 William Chambliss (ed.), Criminal Law In Action, Santa Barbara, California, Hamilton Publishing Company, 1975, pg. 5.

78 Ibid., 6.

79 Ibid., 6.

80 Ibid., 476-477.

81 Richard Quinney, Toward A Sociology of Criminal Law, In Crime and Justice in Society, Boston: Little, Brown and Company, 1969, pgs. 1-10.

82 Ibid., 11-20.

83 Ibid., 21-30.

84 Richard Quinney, A Critical Theory of Criminal Law, In Criminal Justice In America, Boston: Little, Brown and Company, 1974, pgs.8-13.

85 Ibid., 14-20.

86 Ibid., 21-25.

87 Charles Reasons, Law and the Making of Criminals, In The Criminologist: Crime and the Criminal, Pacific Palisades, California: Goodyear Publishing Company, 1974, pgs. 99-100.

88 Ibid., 101-102.

89 Ibid., 103-104.

90 Charles Reasons, Social Thought and Social Structure: Competing Paradigms in Criminology, Criminology, 13, no. 3, November, 1975, pgs. 336-337.

91 Ibid., 337-339.

92 Ibid., 342.

93 Ibid., 342-343.

94 Ibid., 344.

95 Ibid., 346.

96 Ibid., 346-347.

97 Ibid., 348-349.

98 Edwin Schur, Law and Society: A Sociological View, New York: Random House, 1968, pgs. 4-13.

99 Edwin Schur, Unnecessary Crimes: The Peril of Overlegislating, In Our Criminal Society, Englewood Cliffs, New Jersey: Prentice-Hall, 1969, pgs. 191-197.

100 Ibid., 198-201.

101 Ibid., 219-223.

102 Ibid., 224-227.

103 Jack Gibbs, Crime and the Sociology of Law, In Crime, Criminology, and Contemporary Society, Richard Knudten (ed.), Homewood, Illinois: The Dorsey Press, 1970, pgs. 397-398.

104 Ibid., 399.

105 Ibid., 400-401.

106 Ibid., 402.

107 Ibid., 403-404.

108 Taylor, Walton, and Young, The New Criminology: For A Social Theory of Deviance, New York: Harper and Row, 1973, pg. 281.

109 Ibid., 281.

110 Charles Reasons, Social Thought and Social Structure: Competing Paradigms in Criminology, Criminology, 13, no. 3, November, 1975, pg. 354.

111 Theodore Chiricos and Gordon Waldo, Socioeconomic Status and Criminal Sentencing: An Empirical Assessment of a Conflict Proposition, American Sociological Review, 40, no. 6, December 1975, pg. 770.

"Stop and Frisk: An Historical and Empirical Assessment"

William F. McDonald

"The danger of unbounded liberty and the danger of bounding it have produced a problem in the science of government which human understanding seems hitherto unable to solve."

— Dr. Samuel Johnson

Introduction

For centuries in Anglo-American legal history the compromise between bounded and unbounded liberty has revolved around the notion of probable cause. A citizen could not be seized and searched unless there existed facts and circumstances within the knowledge of the arresting official which are "sufficient in themselves to warrant a man of reasonable caution in the belief that"[1] an offense has been, is being; or is about to be committed. In America this criterion has incorporated into the Fourth Amendment of the Bill of Rights.[2]

Any compromise between liberty and oppression is never wholly satisfactory. Wherever the balance is struck some will believe they are paying too high a price for liberty while others will see it as too high a price for security. The probable cause standard has not escaped this problem. As America became increasingly urbanized and crime rates increased concomitantly the pressure to lower this threshold requirement grew.[3] Legal theorists searched for ways around it while in practice the police circumvented it through the use of legal subterfuges such as arrests for vagrancy or on the grounds that an ancient provision of common law authorized "stops and frisks" on grounds less than probable cause.

The situation began to crystalize into open debate in the 1920's. On June 10, 1968 a milestone in the ensuing debate was reached when the Supreme Court rendered its decision in Terry v. Ohio.[4] It was the first time the Court addressed the meaning of the Fourth Amendment as it bears on "the confrontation of the street between the citizen and the policeman investigating suspicious circumstances."[5] The court held that "in justifying a particular intrusion the police officer must be able to point to specific and articulate facts which, taken together with rational inferences from those facts, reasonably warrant that intrusion. . . Anything less would invite intrusions upon constitutionally guaranteed rights based on nothing more substantial than inarticulate hunches. . . .[6] It held further that when nothing in the initial stages of an investigative encounter with a suspect served to dispel a police officer's reasonable fear for his own protection and others in the area it was permissible for the officer "to conduct a carefully limited search of the outer clothing of such persons in an attempt to discover weapons which might be used to assault him."[7] Thus, the time-honored standard of probable cause was lowered to "reasonable suspicion." Justice Douglas dissented warning that the decision represented "a long step down the totalitarian path."[8] In contrast supporters of the decision believed it would make the police more, not less, lawful.

The purposes of this paper are to review the debate on "stop and frisk" and to report some empirical findings related to the opposing claims.

Method

The empirical research was done in Washington, D.C. in the summer of 1972 and involved approximately 500 hours of accompanying the police on patrol to observe their use of their stop-and-frisk practices. The official purpose of the researchers was that they were making observations of drug enforcement. Most officers did not appear to be affected by the presence of the researchers especially when responding to rapidly unfolding events where field stops might be involved.

It was not possible to employ a probability sampling design in selecting the units of observation. Numerous accomodations to the administrative necessities and restrictions of the police department had to be made. Most observations were between 6 p.m. and 2 a.m. in the higher crime districts.

The History of Stop and Frisk

The Origin of the Debate

In the 1920's a continuous series of unprecedented mass inquiries into the administration of criminal justice occurred.[9] Legal scholars came to realize the vast discrepancies between the law in action and the law on the books. They believed these discrepancies could be reduced by attacking the problem from both ends. Lawlessness should be reduced not only be reforming the officials but also by reforming the law. The Wickersham Commission put it this way:

> "It is of the first importance that the officers charged with the enforcement of the law themselves obey the law. But it is no less important to have legal rules governing their actions consonant with the practical extigencies of enforce ment, so that they shall not be driven to

exceeding their powers in order to do what is expected of them, or subjected to harrassing liabilities in the practical execution of their duties. Not the least cause of non-observation of law is to be found in the screwing up of legal requirements beyond the limits of practicable observance. The rules applicable to arrest and its incidence should be restated with reference to the conditions in the cities of the present century."[10]

The idea that the law needed to be changed because society had changed became a mainstay in the arguments of those who sought to increase police power. The law of arrest had been derived from common law rules developed in the 18th century and contained numerous and chaotic distinctions.

The Commission concluded that the lack of clarity in the law of arrest had undesirable consequences. It resulted in the failure of the police to act because their legal authority was unclear and they feared civil liability for false arrest; and it resulted in the police exceeding the legal limits of their authority and being allowed to do so by magistrates in the supposed interest of law and order. Both of these problems could be solved in part by clarifying the law and by giving the police more power. In its survey of police practices in fifteen cities, the Commission had found extensive lawlessness.[11] But, in Boston it found that the general level of police lawlessness seemed much lower. It attributed this to the existence of two statutes which did not exist in the other cities it studied. The statutes authorized the arrest of suspicious persons on less than probable cause. One provides for the arrest of a person abroad at night whom the police have reason to suspect of unlawful design if he cannot give a satisfactory account of himself.[12] The other made it legal to arrest as a vagabond any person known to be a pickpocket, thief, or burglar, if acting in a suspicious manner in various public streets and places.[13]

In other cities the Commission had found that the police regularly held suspicious persons for several days and subjected them to the "third degree" in order to justify, by confession, the illegal arrest. Boston seemed unusually free of such abuses. Therefore, the Commission concluded that "when the detention for investigation is lawful in its beginning it is more likely to end lawfully. On the other hand, if it begins illegally the time of ending may depend on the whim of the police."[14] It further concluded that the legalizing of suspicion arrests and vagrancy arrests under proper limitations and control was "one of the really effective methods of preventing the third degree in Boston."[15]

The Commission also approved of authorizing the police to dispose of cases without the approval of a magistrate. A Philadelphia study had shown the benefits of such a reform. Under common law and by statute in Pennsylvania a police officer did not have the legal authority to release a suspect once an arrest had been made. He was required to take the defendant to a committing magistrate for a hearing. In practice this legal requirement was not being strictly adhered to and the study had concluded that if and when it were it "would interfere with efficient police work."[16]

The historical context in which the Wickersham Commission and other law reformers were writing is significant. Four factors converged in the 1920's to bring pressure for changing the law of arrest: (1) the growth of the cities with their increasing anonymity and possibilities for criminals to hide from the law; (2) the proliferation of hand guns and the increasing number of people in the city carrying weapons; (3) the passage and enforcement of the 18th Amendment and the National Prohibition Act; and (4) the existence of the exclusionary rule, by which evidence that was obtained in violation of constitutional guarantees against unreasonable searches and seizures is not admitted into court. The Wickersham Commission was established primarily because of the law enforcement problems created by Prohibition.[17] The advocates of Prohibition were pressing for more latitude for searches and seizure. This led directly to an attack on the exclusionary rule and the probable cause standard. The exclusionary rule was involved because most of the cases in which it was applied involved liquor.[18] The Wickersham Commission, however, did not agree that the probable cause standard should be diluted to achieve more effective enforcement of Prohibition. It argued that "... the limitations upon search and seizure have undoubtedly hampered investigators and special agents in every connection. But apart from constitutional questions, too much resentment and irritation is likely to be provoked by changes which would give to enforcement of national prohibition greater latitude than is permitted with respect to other laws. We do not think it advisable to alter the federal law with respect to search and seizure, assuming it would be possible."[19]

But when the issue changed from alcohol control to gun control other reformers felt the danger justified a lower standard of arrest. Professor John B. Waite led the attack. He found particularly disturbing the rule that arrest may be unlawful even though the arrestee is guilty of the felony for which arrested so long as the officer did not have reasonable ground to suspect. This was a "strange" principle by which a person who is in truth guilty, and guilty even of the particular felony for which the arrest was made, does not justify the arrest.

> The arresting officer may be quite right, may have apprehended a felon who for the sake of society should have been apprehended, may have made the arrest without undue violence and with all the requisite formality, and may nevertheless be guilty of an unlawful arrest. The rule is that an officer may lawfully arrest even an <u>innocent</u> person when he believes and has reasonable ground to believe that person guilty of a felony. But, for some inenubilous reason, it is not the law that he may lawfully arrest a <u>guilty</u> person whom he suspects of felony but whom, the court opines, he had not reasonable grounds to suspect.[20]

This rule is a hardship for several reasons, he argued. What constitutes reasonable ground is an indefinite matter that cannot be clearly and specifically stated in advance; but rather is determined in each instance after the fact by a court. Thus, the policeman is left to do his job without clear guidance. If he errs he is liable to civil suit for damages. In some cases the officer attempting to arrest was killed and the determination as to the lawfulness of the arrest directly affected the criminal liability of the killer. He may have been guilty of felony, may have merited arrest; but if he could raise sufficient doubt as to the reasonableness of the officer's belief in his guilt, he could successfully assert at least a limited privilege of resistance and could avoid the charge of murder.

Furthermore, he produced data report that showed that, "one-fourth of the 'gun-toters' discovered and arrested in Detroit during [a particular] year escaped punishment not because they were innocent, but solely because the courts thought the arrest unlawful."[21] At one time Waite had argued that the solution to the problem was to statutorily authorize arrest without a warrant where a felony had in truth been committed, whether or not the officer had reasonable ground to believe so.[22] Later he suggested that legislatures should see how far they could go in declaring an arrest to be "lawful" in a way that the exclusionary rule would not apply.[23]

In 1938 Professor Jerome Hall responded to some of the proposed reforms. He felt that experience clearly indicated that it was absurd to continue to require policemen to make on-the-spot determinations of whether an offense was a misdemeanor or felony. But he did not believe that most of the proposed reforms were clearly desirable. "How to evaluate them, how to rest their validity upon a sounder basis than mere opinion, is the general problem of greatest concern to students of human affairs."[24] Included among "them" was the recommendation "to provide a simple and legal method of interrogating suspected persons."[25]

Hall presented additional documentation of extensive police illegality. Although the law clearly required the police to bring every arrestee before a magistrate, Hall estimated that one of every persons arrested was released by the police without being brought before any judicial officers. This problem was especially acute regarding "suspicion", drunkenness, gambling, crimes against property, and traffic violations of all sorts. In some instances, especially for gambling, "suspicion", and drunkenness, more arrestees were released than held for prosecution. "Suspicion" arrests were widely used to hold a person long enough for the police to investigate a matter. Vagrancy arrests were being used similarly as well as to harass notorious criminals whom it was impossible to convict for major offenses.

Hall concluded that the great disparity between the rules and the practices relating to arrest "may be regarded as symptomatic of difficult social problems. In this view, the practices result, in part at least, from inadequate legal provision for coping with the social need."[26] He felt it was dangerous to allow the situation to continue indefinitely. "As between strict adherence to outmoded rules, and practices at odds with such rules, the latter may well be the lesser evil. But, that alternative, as a deliberate policy, cannot in a society constructed upon law, be a permanent one....[27] The elimination of illegal and abusive practices by police [is] the essential prerequisite to the enlistment of public support, and hence to efficient detection and arrest.[28] . . . .In the long sweep of events, abuse by police is at the expense of the protection by police."[29]

The Doctrine of the Night Prowler

Professor Andrew Bruce recommended a revitilization of the "doctrine of the night prowler."[30] Their reference is to a special exception to the law of arrest at common law. Ordinarily, a warrantless arrest is lawful only if the person making the arrest - whether he be a constable or a private person - is able to show both that a felony has been committed and that there is probable cause to believe that the party arrested committed it. However, some authorities had indicated an exception to this rule in the cases of nightwalkers.[31] This exception was apparently well known among legal scholars and practitioners but until the 1930's it had not become a focal point for expanding police power.

The origin of the exception goes back in English history to the Ordinance of 1233 which instituted night-watchmen, and directed them "to arrest those who enter vills at night and go about armed."[32] Later the Ordinance of 1252 mentions "disturbers of our peace."[33] The Statute of Winchester, 13 Edw. 1, c, 4 (1285) instructed the "Night Watch" to arrest any strangers until morning. By a somewhat later statute (5 Edw. 3, c. 14 1331) watchmen may "search . . . for night walkers and persons suspicious either by night or day. . . ."[34] Hale states: "[Watchmen] have power to arrest such as pass by until the morning, and if no suspicion, they are then to be delivered [released], and if suspicion be touching them, they shall be delivered to the sheriff."[35] Hawkins reports: "It is holden by some, that any private person may lawfully arrest a suspicious night-walker and detain him till he make it appear that he is a person of good reputation."[36] In a later chapter he states that the watch clearly had such power.[37] Blackstone says: "Watchmen . . . may virtute officii arrest all offenders, and particularly night-walkers, and commit them to custody till morning."[38]

This ancient right of watchmen to stop and investigate suspicious persons was recognized by the courts. A frequently cited case, Lawrence v. Hedger,[39] involved an action of trespass and false imprisonment. Lawrence had been passing through the streets of the city of London with a bundle in his hand around 10 P.M. when he was stopped by a watchman and taken to the watchhouse, where Hedger, a beadle, was in attendance and asked him what he had in his bundle and who gave it to him. He replied to both questions that he did not know, but was carrying it to his sister in St. George's Fields; and gave the beadle an address there at which he might check his story. But the beadle did not send anyone to make inquiries;

instead he had Lawrence held until the next morning when he was brought before the sitting alderman and discharged.

Lawrence sued Hedger for the detention and imprisonment on the grounds that Hedger was not a constable as defined by an act passed 10 Geo. 3 in which constables were given the power to apprehend malfactors and suspected persons. However, "Mansfield C.J. was of opinion that, without the aid of this act, any watchman might detain the Plaintiff, and carry him to a constable; and that it would be the constable's duty to secure him when so apprehended."

On appeal, Heath J. upheld Mansfield's view saying, "It would be extremely mischievous if it were not so. At every Old Bailey session numbers of persons are convicted in consequence of their being stopped by watchmen while they are carrying bundles in this way."[40]

Chambre J. said, "The case of Samuel v. Payne, Doug 359, was an arrest even in the day time, which was much stronger: but in the night, when the town is to be asleep, and it is the special duty of these watchmen, and other officers, to guard against malefactors, it is highly necessary that they should have such a power of detention. And, in this case, what do you talk of groundless suspicion? There was abundant ground of suspicion here. We should be very sorry if the law were otherwise."[41]

A much earlier case[42] sheds light on both the matter of the requisite level of suspicion required by the courts for making these arrests and the practice of arresting "night-walkers". The case involved a constable who had arrested without a warrant one Ann Dekins between eight and nine at night in the Parish of St. Paul's Covent Garden in the street between the playhouse and the Rose Tavern. He had had her in his custody in the past for being a disorderly person and he apparently suspected her to be a disorderly person on the present occasion.

The argument against the lawfulness of this arrest was, in part, that she had been "very decent at the time, and there was no cause of suspicion; but they should have found her to be a night-walker, as is usual in such cases."[43] With regard to taking up a suspicious person, it was further urged that "it must appear that there was a just cause of suspicion: as when a man is taken up for felony, if a felony has been committed, it is cause of suspicion, for the cause of suspicion is traversable."[44]

The court ruled ". . . it is not a constable's suspecting, that will justify his taking up a person, but it must be just grounds of suspicion, for that is traversable, 2 Inst., 52, as if a felony be done, it is good cause of suspicion, that is, if I suspect a person where a felony is done, it is warrent enought for me to arrest him; but it would be hard, that the liberty of the subject should depend on the will of the constable, and shall his not liking a woman's looks be any cause of suspicion?"[45]

The doctrine of the night prowler was not limited to England. It was carried over to America implicitly in the common law tradition and explicitly by statute in Massachusetts and New Hampshire.[46]

Two points are especially noteworthy about Bruce's proposal to revitalize the doctrine of the night prowler. It was written at the suggestion of the Chicago Crime Commission; and it was being advanced as a gun control measure. In contrast to Waite's proposals for getting around the exclusionary rule by tampering with either the concept of probable cause or the definitions of arrest, Bruce argued that by virtue of the doctrine of the night prowler the police already had the legal authority they needed.

Bruce had hoped the Illinois Supreme Court would apply the night prowler doctrine [47] in a case whose facts are similar to those on which the Terry vs. Ohio decision were eventually based. On July 6, 1933, at 10:40 o'clock at night, three Chicago policemen, while riding in a squad car, saw the defendant walk away from a gas station and join another man. They testified that because of numerous recent robberies of such stations, their suspicions were aroused and they therefore stopped the men, although they had no knowledge that a crime had been committed or that these men were about to commit one. One of the officers, with no knowledge that the defendant had a weapon, then put his arms around the defendant, apparently as part of a search for a weapon. At this, the defendant made a movement which revealed the existence of a concealed revolver. The defendant was convicted of the crime of carrying concealed weapons -- which at the time was only a misdemeanor. For Bruce the case presented three questions:

> "(1) Should evidence wrongfully obtained be admitted in a case where the gist of the action is the carrying of concealed weapons and the weapon itself is conclusive evidence of guilt?
>
> (2) In the Macklin case, was the evidence in fact illegally obtained? Has not an officer a right to arrest or detain for interrogation a man whom he finds at 10:40 at night in a place which creates a suspicion and, if so, . . . does not such right of interrogation

involve the right to search the person, and, though the attention of the officer was first called to the person on account of a suspicion of robbery or attempted robbery alone, to use a weapon which has been thus discovered as evidence in a prosecution for carrying concealed weapons?

(3) Is there a distinction between the procedure which is or should be adopted in a case where human life is involved and one in which a sumptuary law merely is sought to be enforced or evidence obtained which may help in a prosecution for its violation? Is there a clear distinction between the discovery of a pistol. . . and the discovering of liquors or documents or even narcotic drugs. . .? Is not the menace of the gunman too great a menace to be trifled with?"[48]

Yes to the first question would be a repeat of the Waite proposal to alter the concept of probable cause. The second question represented Bruce's solution. Once a legal arrest is made, it should be permissible to make a protective search for a weapon. His third question reveals his interest in gun control and implies a last-ditch legal tactic that might be used if all else fails to get around probable cause, namely, distinguish gun cases from all others and permit a special exception for them on the grounds of overriding social need.

The Uniform Arrest Act

A decade after the Wickersham Commission, the Interstate Commissioners on Crime asked Professor Sam Warner to conduct a first-hand study of police arrest practices "in order to determine the possibility of drafting a model act to reconcile the law as written with the law in action."[49] Once again the solution of the problem of police lawlessness was approached in terms of changing the laws rather than the police. The Commissioners were of the opinion that "in nearly all, and probably in all, American cities the police regularly violated the law in making arrests, and they hazarded the guess that over 75% of all arrests are illegal in some particular. [But] they wondered if this was not necessarily so, because strict compliance with the law would hamstring the police in their efforts to protect society."[50]

Warner felt it was. He concluded that if the inadequacies of the law of arrest were eliminated the more serious forms of police lawlessness would probably be greatly reduced. Warner had found that "the great majority of arrests by police officers are illegal in their inception, continuation, or termination.'[51] But, this was not in his opinion a bad reflection upon the police. Rather it was "the result of the antiquated law on the books. This illegality is hardly their (the police's) fault for they cannot fulfill both their duty to obey the law and their duty to protect the community."[52] Furthermore, he reasoned that

> If the police are, practically speaking, forced continually to violate the law of arrest, that would seem to be an explanation of the serious violations of personal liberty which they occasionally commit as well as of much of the public hostility toward the police.
>
> Certainly one way to make the police more law-abiding. . . is to instill in police officers a strong feeling that they, as guardians of the law, should obey it. This feeling cannot easily be instilled in officers who find that in many of the ways in which the law touches their duties, it is ridiculous, and that they cannot follow it and protect the

> public. Hence legalizing proper police practices should prove a great help in eliminating improper ones and in building up an espirit de corps in police departments.[53]

In Warner's view one of the most pressing inadequacies of the law of arrest was in regards to the modern needs for questioning and detaining suspects. He felt that an American common-law right to question and detain suspects had not been established. Therefore he recommended that authority to do so be expressly provided by legislation. He argued that "every day large numbers of persons are questioned by police officers. A man climbing into a window late at night may be the householder who forgot his key or may be a burglar. The teenager who looks around furtively; tries the door of an expensive automobile; gets in and seems unfamiliar with its mechanism may or may not have a right to drive the car. An officer observing these circumstances should have a right to question the suspicious behavior."[54]

Legalizing the questioning of suspicious persons would be advantageous, for all parties concerned. It would resolve the police officer's dilemma between investigating a possible crime at the risk of being sued for false arrest; or not intervening in suspicious situations unless he had probable cause but risk being charged with dereliction of duty. The public would receive greater protection because the police would not fear to act. Suspects would be less inconvenienced because police would be able to release them without bringing them before a magistrate.

Based on Warner's recommendations the Uniform Arrest Act was drafted.

It provides:

> (1) A peace officer may stop any person abroad whom he has reasonable ground to suspect is committing, has committed or is about to commit a crime, and may demand of him his name, address, business abroad and wither he is going.
>
> (2) Any person so questioned who fails to identify himself or explain his actions to the satisfaction of the officer may be detained and further questioned and investigated.
>
> (3) The total period of detention provided for by this section shall not exceed two hours. Such detention is not an arrest and shall not be recorded as an arrest in any official record. At the end of the detention the person so detained shall be released or be arrested and charged with a crime.
>
> A peace officer may search for a dangerous weapon on any person whom he has stopped or detained to question, as provided in section 2, whenever he has reasonable grounds to believe that he is in danger if the person possesses a dangerous weapon. If the officer finds a weapon, he may take it and keep it until the completion of the questioning, when he shall either return it or arrest the person. The arrest may be for the illegal possession of the weapon.[55]

The kind of search contemplated here is known as a "frisk", which according to Warner, is often required by "good police practice."[56] In his view the benefits of this provision are several. He believed that police officers would always be governed by the instinct for self preservation and hence will frisk for weapons even if they are never given lawful authority to do so. Thus, authorizing frisks would probably have "no effect" on police practices, but it would have other benefits.

> "First, it is undesirable to have the law tell officers not to do something their instinct for self-preservation requires them to do. The existence of one common situation in which it is obviously necessary to violate the law reduces their respect for all law and increases the likelihood of violations in less justified circumstances. Second, legalizing 'frisking' prevents a suspect who has been 'frisked' from suing the officer for damages. And the innocent person who is 'frisked' is less likely to feel that he has been unjustly treated and be unwilling to cooperate with the police. Third, if 'frisking' is legal, then resistance to 'frisking' is illegal, and therefore less likely to occur. Fourth, it is important that underworld characters carrying concealed pistols be punished. If 'frisking' is illegal, such convictions are difficult in states having the federal exclusionary rule preventing the admissibility of illegally obtained evidence, since the pistol discovered by a 'frisk' before arrest, that is, an illegal search, would not be admissible."[57]

The Uniform Arrest Act did not address the issue of what should be done if a frisk turns up evidence of crimes other than unlawful carriage of a weapon, such as drugs, alcohol, gambling, burglary, or theft. However, it might be inferred that Warner did not intend that frisks should be legal for these kinds of crimes. His support for authorizing stops and frisks is based on his view that gun-carrying represents a special menace in modern society and an exception to the law of arrest should be allowed to cope with this unique problem. He believed the courts had already been moving towards such a position. In practically all the cases he examined which expressly denied the right to search except as incident to an arrest, the search of the person was directed at the discovery of contraband other than firearms, or the search was of the suspect's house. Consequently, he believed that "a distinction having its genesis in the potential menace of concealed weapons should point the judicial path towards holding a search to disarm to be reasonable."[58]

Vagrancy, Disorderly Conduct and Arrests on Suspicion -- The Subterfuges

Some police authorities believed that common law or statutory authority existed for stopping, frisking, and detaining suspicious persons on less than probable cause. But, most policemen did not worry about it. They regularly circumvented probable cause by a little legal chicanery. When there was no probable cause the police could always charge the catch-all crimes of vagrancy or disorderly conduct or arrest "on suspicion." This practice has been developed to a fine art among the American police. Its use was so versatile -- solving everything from petty to heinous offenses -- it perhaps deserved acknowledgement in the police textbooks as the major weapon against crime. It was the answer to every city's problems of dealing with the presence of that large class of homeless, unemployed men and women who represented a nuisance and a potential source of criminals. They were locked up or forced to leave town under the threat of being locked up.[59] It was also the answer to the presence of serious criminals. If not convictable, they could always be harassed with disorderly conduct charges.[60] Similarly unpopular political groups and minorities could be harassed and controlled.[61] The subterfuges provided a means of "freezing" a situation while the police conducted their investigations.[62] They also protected the police from civil suits for false arrest. Contrary to the speculations of the Wickersham Commission and others, researchers found that the fear of civil suits for false arrest did not ordinarily prompt policemen to sit idly by while desperate crimes occurred around them.[63] On the contrary, they intervened and made arrests. They knew they could always cover their actions later through the use of the legal subterfuges. If the arrested suspect turned out to be innocent, and there had been no legal grounds for the arrest the police could always protect themselves against civil actions by "improving" the legal grounds. They regularly charged such people with vagrancy or disorderly conduct, even though the innocence of the suspect was fully apparent to the police officer. It had become almost standard police procedure for preventing civil suits.

The Criminal Law Revolution of the 1960's

If that law of arrest could be "modernized" -- that is, if the police could be authorized to make arrests without probable cause -- the lawlessness, inefficiencies and patent injustices caused by the inadequacies of the existing law, would be greatly reduced and in some cases eliminated. By 1950 this line of argument had become conventional wisdom. The Yale Law Journal confidently predicted that if the stop and frisk provisions of the Uniform Arrest Act were adopted, the practice of charging innocent persons with vagrancy-type statutes merely to foreclose suits for false arrest would end.[64] This would happen even if vagrancy-type laws continued to exist. But the Uniform Arrest Act was never widely adopted[65] and by the end of the decade additional studies of police practices made it evident that the police use of vagrancy-type laws continued to flourish.[66] In 1960 Justice William O. Douglas observed that while there were no such crimes as "suspicion of robbery" or "suspicion of burglary", police arrests statistics revealed that thousands of persons were being arrested on such grounds.[67] The reform movement seemed to have become moribund.

When the Supreme Court imposed a Fourth Amendment exclusionary rule on the states in 1961[68] and then imposed a Fifth Amendment exclusionary rule to bar admissions obtained without certain warnings in 1966,[69] the old issues were given new life. The need for clarifying the policeman's authority to stop; interrogate; search; and temporarily detain people without probable cause suddenly became more urgent. A flurry of activity and comment on the subject occurred.[70] In 1964 the state of New York adopted a statute entitled "Temporary Questioning of Persons in Public Places; Search for Weapons", which came to be known as the "stop and frisk" law.[71] Two years later, the American Law Institute published the first draft of <u>A Model Code of Pre-Arraignment Procedure</u> which favored giving the police the authority to stop and frisk under certain conditions.[72] A year later, the President's Commission on Law Enforcement and the Administration of Justice followed suit and recommended that the police be authorized "to stop suspects and possible witnesses of major crimes, to detain them for brief questioning if they will not voluntarily cooperate, and to search such suspects for dangerous weapons when such a precaution is necessary."[73] However, also at this time there was increased concern about police abuse of power. The civil rights movement had increased popular concern for the rights of minority groups. Urban race riots began to occur focused attention directly on the relationship between the police and minority groups. The cutting edge of this relationship was the street encounter between the policeman and the citizen.

The President's Crime Commission found that these street encounters were "causing serious friction with minority groups in many localities" and were regarded by minority group leaders as "a principal problem in police-community relations".[74] Criticisms of police field interrogations included the following: (1) they are used disproportionately against racial minorities, the poor, juveniles, and persons whose clothing, hair, and walking mannerisms are unconventional; (2) the style and manner of the police during encounters is unfriendly, abusive, offensive, and no explanation is given by the policeman for his actions; and (3) the interrogations are often conducted with little or no basis for suspicion.[75]

Despite these findings the Commission still recommended that the police be given stop and frisk powers. But it also recommended that arrests for investigation, arrests for harassment, and arrests for minor crimes such as vagrancy, disorderly conduct, loitering and curfew violations be eliminated or greatly curtailed.

In summary then, on the eve of the Terry v. Ohio decision after forty years of studies and discussion, the anticipated effects of giving the police clear authorization to stop and frisk suspicious persons on less than probable cause were as follows. In the advantages column were: (1) because the police would no longer be forced to act unlawfully in order to fill the gap left by an inadequate law of arrest, they would develop a greater respect for law and would therefore act more lawfully in general. (2) This means that not only petty police lawlessness would diminish but the grosser forms of abuse such as the third degree and other police brutality would also decline. (3) There would be less concern among the police about civil suits for false arrest. (4) Therefore, they would be less likely to sit idly by while crime was being committed fearing to act because of uncertainty about whether sufficient probable cause existed. Thus, crime would be reduced to some extent. (5) Not fearing civil suits also meant the police would no longer deliberately arrest and prosecute people who at first appeared to be clearly innocent. (6) The number of arrests for vagrancy, disorderly conduct, and other minor offenses as well as for "suspicion" or "investigation", would decline. (7) The police would be more effective in controlling the problem of citizens carrying guns. (8) Because the police would be authorized to release suspects who had been temporarily detained and found innocent of any wrong doing, the costs and inconveniences of a trip to the courthouse and awaiting release by a judicial officer would be avoided by both the police and the citizen.

The expected adverse consequences of legalizing stop and frisk were: (1) the police would over use it in two ways: (a) many stops would be made where there was very little, if any, grounds for suspicion and (b) the police would not limit themselves to frisks but would conduct full blown searches; and (2) the use of this authority would fall disproportionately against racial minorities, juveniles, and persons displaying unconventional clothing, hair styles and walking mannerisms. It was not claimed that legalizing stop and frisk would <u>increase</u> the frequency of such stops or of the discourteousness of stops. Legalizing such stops was only giving the law's blessing to a practice which was already widespread. The opponents of legalizing stop and frisk could only argue that such an action would <u>increase</u> the number of stops (and all of the consequences of such, e.g., increased police-community tensions) if the police were effectively prevented from making such stops by any other means.

Findings

Ideally, an analysis of the impact of the Terry v. Ohio decision would involve subjecting each of the claims and counterclaims for legalizing stop and frisk to rigorous empirical testing. But research is the art of the practical. The grand questions behind public policy usually cannot be answered with a high degree of confidence, if at all. Realizing this, the researcher either goes no further; or proceeds on the assumption that answers with a low degree of confidence are better than none at all; or that there are other lesser, related questions which can be answered and are worth answering. The present research proceeded on the last two assumptions.

In regard to whether the police developed a greater respect for the law and collaterally became more law abiding as a result of their being legally authorized to stop and frisk, it is impossible to draw any firm conclusions. A few limited observations can be made. Police officers who began their careers in the 1940's and '50 report a drastic change in police practices and attitudes between then and now. The shift has been in the direction of more law-abiding behavior and greater respect for the law. The grosser abuses are, generally, unthinkable today. As for lesser forms of abuse of power which would not have given policemen of the forties and fifties pause to think are today at least recognized by policemen as problematic. Whether this is due to Terry v. Ohio, or the "criminal law revolution" of the 1960's, or other social changes is impossible to say. For instance, a white sergeant from Arlington, Virginia, recalled an incident that occurred in the fifties. He discovered a reputable black minister parked in lover's lane with a younger white woman who was not his wife. The sergeant decided to scare the minister. He cocked his gun and put it to the minister's head. After the minister had begged not to be killed and had sworn he would never fool around with white women again, the sergeant let him go. "Today," the sergeant said, "you couldn't get away with that." Whether the sergeant's hesitation to repeat that type of conduct today was due to the Supreme Court decisions of the sixties or the increased vigilance of civil rights groups or other factors cannot be determined. It is not clear that this sergeant's conversion represents a step in the direction of increased "respect for law." He may not abuse his power as he did before but his motive seems more to avoid trouble than to honor the abstract principle of respect for law.

The comments of a younger police captain who was the commanding officer of a large drug investigation unit made this point even clearer. He eschewed illegal police tactics but only because it "wasn't worth it." He did not want to risk hurting his career over an arrest for "some lousy drug addict who would be back on the streets in a minute anyhow." As for the idea of respect for law, the captain had nothing but contempt. "These lawyers say you have to play fair, by the rules. That's a lot of crap. This isn't no game we're playing. Those guys aren't playin' by any rules. Why should we?"

Reports of older policeman that police today are more concerned about acting lawfully than they were two decades ago do not, of course, establish the truth of such claims. Even if the police are more concerned about acting lawfully it does not mean they are actually doing so. It may mean they have to be more clever in getting around the law. While there is room for such cynicism, there is also some reason to believe that some changes have occurred. But what changes and to what extent?

One indirect measure of the impact of _Terry v. Ohio_ is its effect on the number of arrests for vagrancy, disorderly conduct and arrests on "suspicion." Since these charges were frequently used to cover situations where the police did not have lawful authority to act, one would expect to find a substantial decline in arrest statistics for these offenses beginning in 1968. As Table 1 indicates there was a decrease in the frequency of those arrests between 1968 and 1974. The decrease is most apparent for vagrancy and suspicion arrests where it amounts to about a 66% reduction. One might be heartened by these statistics if it were not for the fact the 29,000 arrests for suspicion in 1974 represents arrests for a crime that does not exist and the combined total of 540,000 arrests for all three offenses that year is higher than in any year from 1940 to 1959 -- a period when the police openly admitted to the use of these charges as a substitute for stop and frisk powers.

With regard to the matter of the fear of civil suits for false arrest, it does not appear that _Terry v. Ohio_ has had the predicted effect. Even with stop and frisk powers the police continue to worry about their civil liability; and they continue to make arrests in situations where they know the defendant is innocent. They arrest him in order to protect themselves from civil liability. The following incident was observed. Two policemen spotted a middle-aged black man in work clothes driving a beat-up old volkswagon in the southeast section of D.C. on a week day around 7 p.m. They did not suspect any particular crime but they felt it was the type of situation that called for a "spot-check." They pulled the man over and asked for his license and registration. He informed them he was a government official and made it clear he did not appreciate being stopped. They called the car registration and defendant's name and license number into the police computer. The check came

Table 1.

Trends in Arrests for Vagrancy, Disorderly Conduct and Suspicion. 1940-1974.*

Totals	Year	Vagrancy	Disorderly	Suspicion
130,052	1940	48,952	25,739	55,361
107,848	1945	33,488	38,304	36,056
140,236	1950	48,604	45,438	46,194
327,566	1955	63,936	193,119	70,511
765,028	1960	153,201	475,502	136,325
766,884	1965	120,416	570,122	76,346
782,237	1968	99,147	593,104	89,986
768,037	1969	106,269	573,503	88,265
760,908	1970	101,093	589,642	70,173
755,611	1971	80,180	621,057	54,374
679,668	1972	55,680	582,513	41,475
513,320	1973	41,635	441,598	30,087
539,860	1974	28,624	482,352	28,884

* Source: Federal Bureau of Investigation, Uniform Crime Crime Report (for years specified).

back positive. There was an outstanding arrest warrant for the defendant. One of the officers got out of the police car and went forward to talk to the suspect. Shortly after he left the car, a call came in over the radio that a mistake had been made. The man was not wanted. Upon hearing this the second officer got out of the car; went forward; and took the first officer aside for a quiet conversation. A few minutes later the suspect was arrested for changing lanes without signalling.[77]

In many jurisdictions there is indirect but suggestive evidence of the police tendency to rely on arrests to protect themselves from civil liability. It is the high rate of rejection by the prosecutors of cases referred to them by the police for prosecution. In 1975 in St. Louis City, Missouri, sixty percent of the cases referred by the police were rejected by the prosecutor. The chief prosecutor explained that because of civil rights actions against the police in that city, the local police department had adopted a policy of bringing all cases to the prosecutor and dropping none on their own initiative.[78]

As for the claim that the police would sit idly by and allow crime to occur if they did not have clear authority to act, our findings were similar to those of other researchers who found this fear unwarranted. At no time during our period of observation did it appear that police were reluctant to investigate an apparent crime because their legal grounds for acting were unclear. If anything the opposite was true. They took action in situations where it is doubtful that even the most generous interpretation of "reasonable suspicion" could have supplied them with legal justification. In the northeast section of Washington, D.C. around 4 p.m. a policeman suddenly stopped his car and began chasing two youths who were running along a sidewalk in a mixed residential and commercial neighborhood. He caught and questioned them and then released them. Later, he explained to the researcher that he had seen the two boys running and had thought that the bigger boy was trying to beat up the other one. There had been no display of weapons; no cries for help; nor any other specific facts which the researcher was able to observe or which the policeman reported to him which might have supported the inference that one youth was about to assault the other.

With regard to gun control the Terry v. Ohio powers do not appear to have served as an effective instrument. Eight years after Terry gun control is still an unsolved problem. No doubt some criminal cases involving guns have resulted in conviction which would have been lost before Terry; but they have not stemmed the tide of gun offenses. What is more, the police do not regard their Terry powers as something to be used as a gun control measure per se. Their "aggressive patrol" tactics, which they do justify in terms of large number of unlawful weapons seized, operate under a different kind of legal authority than that provided by Terry; the tactics involve the stopping of motor vehicles for spot checks. The police justify these stops not on the basis of suspicious behavior but on their authority to inspect motor vehicles. If there is any doubt about the validity of such authority, the police officers will follow the vehicle they want to search until the driver makes a minor traffic violation -- which never takes too long. He is then stopped, questioned and searched.

A study of stop and frisk in San Diego, California, attempted to determine the specific types of crimes that could be suppressed by stop and frisk practices. While its analysis was not conclusive, the indications were that stop and frisk did not seem to emerge as a gun control measure. The types of crimes most influenced (i.e. suppressed) by stop and frisk practices were burglary, petty theft, and malicious mischief/ disturbances -- crimes frequently committed by two or more juveniles or young adults.[79]

With respect to the frequency of use of the stop and frisk powers, the findings of our study were in agreement with those of the San Diego study. Both studies observed relatively few field interrogations. During about 500 hours of actual time on the street the present study observed only 16 encounters which it regarded as encounters which if justified at all were justified on Terry powers and not some other legal grounds such as probable cause or traffic inspections. Similarly, the San Diego study observed only 79 "field interrogations" in approximately 625 hours of observation.[80]

The Georgetown and San Diego studies at first glance appear to suggest that the police use stop and frisk methods sparingly. Sixteen incidents in five hundred hours of observation does not seem like much. But, when this rate is multiplied by the total number of police hours on patrol per day, the problem assumes more serious proportions. In 1973 there were an estimated 3,992 hours of real patrol time per day by the Metropolitan Police Department.[81] That suggests a rate of 128 stops and frisks per day or an annual rate of 46,720 stops and frisks per year. Such an order of magnitude is not unrealistic. In 1967 the New Orleans Police Department reported that from April 15 to December 31 its patrol, tactical, and canine units combined made 47,834 stops of citizens of whom 25,230 were frisked, resulting in a frisk rate of 53 percent and an arrest rate of 17 percent.[82]

In addition to the Georgetown and San Diego studies, the research of the National Commission on Marihuana and Drug Abuse provides some insight into the police use of stop and frisk powers since Terry vs. Ohio. The Commission conducted two national studies, one of the enforcement of marihuana laws in 1970 the other of the enforcement of other drug laws in 1972. Both studies suggest that in the enforcement of these laws the police are making substantial use of stop and frisk practices as well as their contemporary version of the old police legal "dodges" of vagrancy, namely, vehicle checks. What is more, the old "dodges" apparently continue to be employed. Vagrancy, loitering, and curfew violation type offenses are the specific grounds given by police for searches that have resulted in drug-related arrests in a substantial minority of cases.

Of 3,071 arrests for marihuana in 18 jurisdictions, 39% were vehicle-related arrests, 31% occurred outdoors and 29% occurred indoors. The cause most commonly indicated by the police for the vehicle stops was "suspicious circumstances" (28%). The most commonly indicated (by the police) causes for arrests after the vehicle was stopped were visibility of marihuana (39%), "furtive gestures" (27%) and the officer smelling marihuana (12%).[83]

Of the 878 outdoor arrests nearly all (91%) were on-view arrests with no prior police investigative activity. The most common reason given by police for outdoor searches was "suspicious behavior" (34% of those searched). Other reasons for searches were: officer saw marihuana (24%); officer smelled marihuana (9%); suspected loitering (9%); drug paraphernalia seen (8%); suspected theft (3%; marihuana bought (2%); suspected curfew violation (1%); and suspected vagrancy (1%). Unlike the vehicle and the outdoor arrests, the basis for most of the indoor arrests did not involve "suspicious circumstances" associated with Terry-type arrests.

It is also relevant to point out that the Commission found that arrest location was associated with ultimate disposition. "Terminations"[84] were more common among persons arrested in vehicles (50%) and arrested outdoors (52%), than among persons arrested indoors (41%). Since these two categories are the ones in which many arrests were based on suspicious circumstances, it suggests that the Terry-type arrests are more likely to drop out of the criminal justice process short of conviction.[86] To put it another way, arrests based on this Terry-type grounds may be less efficient in producing convictions than arrests based on firmer grounds.

The Commission's second study was based on data on 16,466 arrests in six jurisdictions for drug crimes other than marihuana-related offenses.[87] It found that 44% of the arrestees were arrested "spontaneously" i.e., arrests "which result from direct police-arrestee contact, often fortuitous or non drug-related without prior investigation.[88] The Commission was not able to learn the specific grounds for many arrests but did establish that at least 800 of the 16,466 arrests for drug offenses other than marihuana were based on suspicious behavior or furtive gestures by the arrestee (or someone in the group of arrestees). It also established that at least 414 drug arrests grew out of arrests for loitering and vagrancy.

In regard to the Commission's marihuana study, it was found that the Terry-type i.e., suspicious behavior or furtive gestures, was the basis for a substantial proportion of the arrests of persons in connection with vehicle stops (28% of 1,185) and a substantial proportion of the arrests of persons searched in public areas (approximately 35% of 878 or 298 arrests). It was also found that vagrancy, loitering, and curfew laws were used as the grounds for searching some proportion of the persons arrested in public areas and searched (approximately 10% of 878 or 88 arrests).[89]

Conclusion

The claims and counterclaims made on behalf of legalizing stop and frisk practices are difficult to test empirically. Limited evidence suggests that both sides of the controversy have oversold their arguments. The anticipated benefits have not been delivered. While there may have been a decrease in the grosser forms of police lawlessness, abuses still occur. Contrary to predictions the police still make use of the legal subterfuges of disorderly conduct, vagrancy, loitering, curfew violations, and arrests on suspicion. Similarly, they rely heavily on vehicle stops for minor traffic violations as an additional means of circumventing the probable cause standard despite the existence of Terry powers. They also continue to fear civil suits for false arrest; and they will arrest innocent people to protect themselves from such suits. What is more, the crimes which seem to be most susceptible to being affected by stop and frisk practices are not the terrible crimes of murder, rape, and robbery but the lesser crimes of burglary, petit larcency, vandalism, marihuana possession, and possession of other drugs. Thus, one wonders whether the trade-off between freedom and control was worth it. Should the probable cause standard have been abandoned for the sake of suppressing these crimes?

On the other hand, the dire predictions about the police running amuck with these powers and race riots being continually provoked. From the perspective of the individual police officer on an eight-hour shift, stop and frisk is used rarely. But, from the broader perspective of the sum total of all stops and frisks by all officers in a department over a year's time, the estimated frequency of use of this police tactic is substantial, possibly as high as 42,720 or higher per year in a city like Washington, D.C. Despite this order of magnitude, however, the race riots of the 1960's have not reoccurred.

The problem of finding a proper balance between the citizen's interest to be free from governmental interference and society's interest to be safe from crime has not been solved by Terry v. Ohio. Rather, a new compromise has been struck, and it too is not wholly satisfactory.

Notes

1 Carroll v. United States, 267 U.S. 132, 162 (1925).

2 R.A. Rutland, The Birth of Bill of Rights 1776-1791, (1962).

3 Such pressure peaks at times when the community faces particular problems of crime, including generalized, longterm problems like the carrying of hand guns, see p. 21 infra; and the prohibition of alcohol, see p. 13 infra; and also more localized, short-term crime threats such as mass murders or kidnappings. This occurred, for example, in connection with the "Zebra" killings in San Francisco. Over the course of five months 12 white persons were killed in random street shootings by one or more blacks. The police responded with "wholesale stops and indiscriminate searches" of more than 600 blacks who fit a loose description of a suspect in the murders. R. Joffee, Zebra Killer Manhunt: Judge Ends Wholesale Searches, The Washington Post, April 26, 1974, at A28.

4 392 U.S. 1 (1968).

5 Ibid., 4.

6 Ibid., 21-22.

7 Ibid., 30.

8 Ibid., 37-38.

9 G. Meuller, Crime, Law, and the Scholars, 96 (1969).

10 U.S. National Comm'n on Law Observance and Enforcement, Report on Criminal Procedure, 21 (1931). [Hereinafter cited as Wickersham Commission, Criminal Procedure.]

11 U.S. National Comm'n Law Observance and Enforcement, Report on Lawlessness in Law Enforcement (1931). [Hereinafter cited as, Wickersham Commission, Lawlessness in Law Enforcement.]

12 Massachusetts Annual Laws Chapter 41, Section 98 (1975).

13 Massachusetts Annual Laws Chapter 272, Section 68 (1975).

14 Wickersham Commission, Lawlessness in Law Enforcement at 109. The Commission also notes that a judge in Denver recommended "a similar law." Ibid., 109, n. 50.

15 Idem.

16 Ibid., 113.

17 Note the emphasis in the legislative statement of purpose of the Commission: "thorough inquiry into the problem of the enforcement of prohibition under the provisions of the Eighteenth Amendment of the Constitution and laws enacted in pursuance thereof, together with the enforcement of other laws. U.S. National Comm'n on Law Observance and Enforcement, Report on the Prohibition Laws of the United States 1 (1931). [Hereinafter cited as Wickersham Commission, Prohibition.]

18 Atkinson, Prohibition and the Doctrine of the Weeks Case, Michigan Law Review Vol. 23, p. 748 (1925).

19 Wickersham Commission, Prohibition, p. 66.

20 Waite, Some Inadequacies In the Law of Arrest, Michigan Law Review, Vol. 29, p. 448, 453 (1931) (emphasis in original).

21 Waite, Public Policy and the Arrest of Felons, Michigan Law Review, Vol. 31, pp. 749, 765. He further observed that "the rule affirmatively creates unlawful practices instead of checking them. When the police are unable to prosecute arrested bootleggers and piggers in the courts, because the arrest is without such 'reasonable cause to believe' as will satisfy the judicial rule, they do not refrain from making the arrests. They simply take into their own hands the punishment which the courts will not impose. That procedure has at least the virtue of checking bootlegging to some extent and of mitigating the criticism for incompetency which the press directs at the police. There are no data compiled to prove this, but any first-hand observation of police activities will demonstrate it." Ibid., p. 766 n. 36.

22 Waite, "Some Inadequacies in The Law of Arrest," loc. cit. pp. 457-459.

23 Waite, "Public Policy and the Arrest of Felons," loc. cit., p. 766.

24 Hall, The Law of Arrest in Relation to Contemporary Social Problems, University of Chicago Law Review, Vol. 3, pp. 345, 374 (1936).

25 Idem.

26 Ibid., 366 (emphasis in original).

27 Idem.

28 Ibid., 372-373.

29 Ibid., 373 (emphasis in original).

30 A Bruce and S. Rosmarin, The Gunman and His Gun, J. Criminal L.C. & P.S., pp. 521, 537 (1933-1934).

31 See 1 Chitty, The Criminal Law 14-20 (1847); F. Bohlen & H. Shulman, Arrest With and Without a Warrant, University of Pennsylvania Law Review Vol. 75, p. 485 (1926). "Until the case of Carroll v. U.S., 267 U.S. 137 (1925), the statements both of judicial decisions and textbooks were substantially unanimous to the effect that there was no privilege to arrest without a warrant for a misdemeanor other than a breach of the peace, except in the case of a few misdemeanors such as "night walking" and "riding armed" for which authority to arrest without a warrant had been given by statutes so ancient that the statutory origin of the privilege had been forgotten and the privilege regarded as substantially one of common law." It is noteworthy that the Bohlen and Shulman article from which this excerpt was taken was in substance the brief on questions discussed in the commentaries prepared for the American Law Institute Torts Restatement. However, it was not until 1966 that the A.L.I. returned to this "exception" to justify its proposal to give the police the authority to stop suspicious persons. See A Model Code of Pre-arraignment Procedure, Tentative Draft No. 1 p. 93. It is of further interest to note that while legal scholars were rediscovering the "doctrine of the night prowler," a noted police expert and chief of police, August Vollmer, described that authority as something which was unremarkable and virtually taken for granted in the police world. In his renowned work, The Police and Modern Society, he deals with the matter under "Personnel: Routine duties." He writes, inter alia that "the routine

duties of all police departments are pretty much the same. . . . patrolmen must be constantly on the alert for street walkers, not only in order to remove such persons from the street and protect pedestrians and others from insult and annoyance, but also because from these underworld denizens they gather information which is especially useful in the solution of crimes. Patrolmen are also required to question persons who may be suspected of having committed a felony, and at night time, according to the law in many states, they have the power to demand of suspicious characters that they give an account of themselves, including the nature of their business, their residence, destination, and any other details that the occasion warrants. Persons observed carrying goods between sundown and sunrise under circumstances which strongly indicate that the property has been stolen may rightfully be questioned, and it is the policeman's duty to make such inquiries." Vollmer, Police and Modern Society pp. 217-218. (1936). Vollmer's lack of critical comment on the legality of the practices is particularly significant in light of his strong concern for lawful police actions. He and theDean of the University of Southern California Law School co-founded the Southern California Academy of Criminology. The Academy brought together police, social workers, lawyers and others to debate criminal justice related issues. These debates were in part responsible for the information of the Committee on Constitutional Rights of the Los Angeles Bar Association. The purpose of the Committee was to check police lawlessness of various specified forms including "illegal arrests without a warrant." Wickersham Commission, Lawlessness in Law Enforcement p. 144-145. Vollmer apparently based his statement more on his knowledge of existing practices than on his knowledge of the law because the law in most states did not explicitly provide the authority he describes. Professor Sam Warner found that in states where the authority to arrest suspicious persons abroad at night was not specifically provided by statute police departments assumed a common law basis for it. For example, Rule 465 (6) of the Rules and Regulations of the Police Department of the City of Chicago (1933) read in part, "A person shall be arrested who is found prowling around at night, who is unable or refuses to give a satisfactory explanation of his conduct under such circumstances, or who has in his possession dangerous weapons or instruments ordinarily used by housebreakers." Warner, "The Uniform Arrest Act" Virginia Law Review, Vol. 28 p. 319 (1942).

32 2 F. Pollack & F. Maitland, The History of English Law p. 583. (1899).

33 Idem.

34 2 Hale, Pleas of the Crown p. 97 (1 Am. ed. 1847).

35 Ibid. 96.

36 2 Hawkins, Pleas of the Crown. Chapter 12 Section 20 (6th ed. 1787).

37 Ibid. Chapter 13, Sections 5 and 6.

38 4 Blackstone, Commentaries p. 292 (1902).

39 Lawrence v. Hedger, 3 Taunt. 13, 16 (1810).

40 Idem.

41 Idem.

42 The Queen v. Tooley, 2 Ld. Raym. 1296 (1709).

43 Ibid. (emphasis added). "They" apparently refers to the jurors.

44 Idem.

45 Ibid. p. 1301. This case suggests that a distinction existed at common law between the right to stop "night walkers" and the right to stop other persons at night. The defense argument suggests that it was legally acceptable and common practice to arrest certain persons who were on the street at night even though they were not acting in any disorderly, indecent, or suspicious manner so long as they were "night walkers."

Of course, it would be helpful to know what is meant by the term, "night walker." Unfortunately, the definition of this term is not entirely clear. Historically it seems to have had two meanings. One usage had it synonymous generally with being a stranger abroad at night. For example, in 1643 Dalton wrote: "Night-walkers, being strangers, or suspected persons, watchmen may arrest them till the morning. . . yea, every man may arrest such Nightwalkers, for it is for the good of the common wealth." Dalton, The Country Justice p. 416 (6th ed. 1643). No doubt it is this definition of the "nightwalker," or as they put it, the "night prowler," that Bruce and Rosmarin had in mind in recommending the revitalization of this legal authority to arrest suspicious persons.

However, the second and much more common usage of the term, both historically and today, refers to the prostitutes and the business of soliciting for prostitution. In the 1707 case cited supra it is a reasonable inference that the "disorderliness" of Ann Dekins refers to solicitation for prostitution. A century later in Lawrence v. Hedger that is clearly the definition of the term. There one of the justices remarked, "A woman walking up and down the streets to pick up men, a night-walker, may be apprehended: yet there is a much less offense than is here suspected." 4 Taunt at 15-16.

In America a similar use of the term to denote a specific category of persons -- probably prostitutes -- as opposed to the more general category, "all strangers abroad at night," is clearly inferred in various legislative enactments. In the Code of 1648 the General Court of Massachusetts ordered "that everie Constable within our Jurisdiction shall henceforth have full power to make, signe and put forth Pursutes or Hue-and-Cries after Murtherers, Manslayers, Peace-breakers, Theevs, Robbers, Burglarers and other Capital offenders, where no magistrate is near hand, also to apprehend without Warrant, such as one overtaken with drink, swearing, Sabboth-breaking, lying, vagrant persons, night-walkers, or any other that shall offend in any of these. Provided they be taken in the manner, either by right of the Constable, or by present information from others. As also to make search for all such persons, either on the Sabboth day or other, when there shall be occasion, in all houses licenced to see either beer or wine, or in any other suspected or disordered places, and those to apprehend and keep in safe custodie, till opportunitie serve to bring them before one of the next Magistrates for further examination. M.D. Howe, Readings in American Legal History (1949) (emphasis added). Nightwalkers are distinguished from a variety of other categories of offenders in a more recent Massachusetts statute which read in part: "Rogues and vagabonds, persons who use any juggling or unlawful games or plays, common pipers and fiddlers, stubborn children, runaways, common drunkards, common nightwalkers, both male and female. . . ." Massachusetts Annual Laws Chapter 272 p. 653 (1976) (originally passed in 1921; underlined only portions still in effect). In contemporary American police parlance the term, "nightwalker," refers to prostitutes.

46 Massachusetts Law provides that: "During the night time (police officers) may examine all persons abroad whom they have reason to suspect of unlawful design, and may demand of them their business abroad and wither they are going. . . Persons so suspected who do not give a satisfactory account of themselves. . . may be arrested. . . . " Massachusetts Annual Laws Chapter 41 Section 98 (1976) (underlined portion repealed in 1967). New Hampshire Law provides that: "Every watchman may arrest any person whom he shall find committing any disorder, disturbance, crime or offense, or such as are strolling about the streets at unreasonable hours, who refuse to give an account, or are reasonably suspected of giving a false account of their business or design, or who can give no account of the occasion of their being abroad. N.H. Rev. Stat. Ann. Chapter 363, Section 12.

47 People v. Macklin, 186 N.E. 531 (1934)

48 A. Bruce and S. Rosmarin, op. cit., 521, 523. The first part of this question is something of a restatement of the court's question in another case, Miles v. Weston 60 Ill. 361 (1871), which they cite approvingly. That case involved an action of trespass and false imprisonment. The court had referred to Lawrence v. Hedger, supra, and Tooley's case, 2 Lord Raym. 1296, and then went on to say:

> "What family, in a large city like Chicago, so frequently infested with burglars and other desperate criminals, could retire to their beds and enjoy the quiet and respose due to them, when they were conscious that suspiciously acting

> persons were lurking about their premises? And will it be said that the law gives no right to have such persons arrested and removed, until a burglary is actually committed or attempted?"

The court answered its own question negatively, citing the common law doctrine of the nighwalker. However, this was merely dicta. Idem.

49 Warner, The Uniform Arrest Act, loc. cit., p. 316.

50 Warner, Investigating the Law of Arrest, 26 A.B.A.J. 151 (1940). [Hereinafter cited as Investigating the Law of Arrest.]

51 Warner, The Uniform Arrest Act, loc. cit., p. 315.

52 Idem.

53 Warner, Investigating the Law of Arrest, loc. cit., p. 151 and 155. (Emphasis added.)

54 Warner, The Uniform Arrest Act, loc. cit. p. 320.

55 Ibid., 344.

56 Ibid., 324. He cites Rule 470 of the Rules and Regulations of the Police Department of the City of Chicago (1933) which provides in part: "When making an arrest, or stopping and questioning a suspicious character he [the police officer] shall be on guard against the use of any concealed or deadly weapon by such person. He shall be justified at such times in passing his hands over the clothing for the purpose of finding any deadly weapons at any place where the arrest may be made." Ibid., 324 n. 21.

57 Ibid., 325-326.

58 Ibid., 327 n. 23. See also Inbau, Firearms and Legal Doctrine, Tulane Law Review, Vol. 7, p. 529 (1933).

59 Professor Hall cites a 1922 study that reported a long list of the behavior brought under the disorderly conduct charge in Chicago. It included many such things as: "2012, no home discharged"; "pool room raid, discharged"; 2012, sleeping in wagon, discharged"; "2012, sleeping in alley, drunk, discharged"; "2012, out of work, 1 month, probation 6 months; F.W. for sleeping in the prairie because he had just got a job and had no other place to go that night." Op. cit. p. 368 n. 88. See also Note, Philadelphia Police Practices and the Law of Arrest, University of Pennsylvania Law Review. Vol. 100, p. 1182 (1952). [Hereinafter cited as Philadelphia Police Practices]; and Foote, Vagrancy - Type Law and Its Administration, University of Pennsylvania Law Review, Vol. 104, p. 603 (1956).

60 The Chicago City Council Committee on Crime in 1915 pointed out the special value of the vagrancy statutes in this regard. Ordinarily the charge of "disorderly conduct" was used which resulted in a small fine or complete discharge. Under the vagrancy law, sentence of six months imrisonment was possible. Hall, op. cit. at 369. Hall reports that after that Committee's report many cities resorted to these laws to arrest repeatedly, to punish, and thereby get rid of criminals. For example, "Mayor Hogue yesterday gave the formula that he said had been effective in frustrating racketeers" 'Don't wait for a complaint against him. Jail him and keep jailing him until he leaves town. . . . In Jersey City, the police don't wait to see a crime committed. They don't wait for a complaint. When a gangster

or racketeer shows up, we lock him up under the Disorderly Persons Act. There's no bail. He gets out in ninety days. When he gets out and persists in hanging around, we give him another jail dose. We keep that up until he departs.' Ibid., 369 n. 90. See also Eimbeck, Some Recent Methods of Harassing the Habitual Criminal, Saint Louis Law Review, Vol. 16 p. 148, 151-158; Kooker, Ethics in Police Service, J. Crim. L.C. & P.S. Vol. 38, pp. 61, 169. (1947); Hopkins, Our Lawless Police 96 (1931).

61 During the labor disputes in the Imperial Valley in 1933, an employee of the International Labor Defense was arrested for "roam[ing] about from place to place without any lawful business," California Penal Code Section 467 (3) (1949), when she drove into Imperial Valley to obtain legal assistance for some of the hundreds of farm strikers arrested on similar charges. Note, Use of Vagrancy-Type Laws for Arrest and Detention of Suspicious Persons, Yale Law Journal, Vol. 59, pp. 1351, 1363 n. 35 [hereinafter cited as Note, Use of Vagrancy-Type Laws].

Four union organizers who went to Jersey City to address a meeting of workers involved in a strike were convicted under New Jersey Laws c. 133 Section 1 (1934) (similar to Disorderly Persons Act, New Jersey Stat. Ann. Section 2:202-16 [1939]). Idem.

Instances have been reported where mixed groups of whites and Negroes have been arrested simply because of their fraternization. A Negro girl with a white boyfriend stated that she was told to pay a certain member of the vice squad $100 if she wished to avoid arrest every time he saw her. She refused to comply and was picked up twice, once being formally booked for disorderly conduct. Disorderly conduct charges have been made against members of the Progressive Party, allegedly for no other reason than their party affiliation or that they met in mixed groups. Philadelphia Police Practices at 1203. See also Grossman, Who Is A Vagrant in California? California Law Review, Vol. 33, p. 306 (1935). For numerous cases documenting police use of these laws to break strikes, prevent meetings, or intimidate citizens, see Report of the New Jersey Civil Liberties Union to the Attorney General of the United States on Interference with Labor and Civil Rights in Hudson County, New Jersey (1938) (typewritten), 2 Int'l Jurisprudence Ass'n Bull. No. 6, at 2 (1933); 3 Int'l Jurisprudence Ass'n Bull. No. 10, at 2 (1935); 5 Int'l Jurisprudence Ass'n Bull. No. 5, at 54 (1936); Hopkins, Our Lawless Police 179-80 (1931).

62 The Wickersham Commission reported that arrests on suspicion were widespread in the cities visited. In cities where "suspicion" arrests were illegal, the vagrancy charge was used as a subterfuge. Many police officials regarded such arrests as especially helpful to police work by allowing ample time to investigate. See, generally, Wickersham Commission, Lawlessness in Law Enforcement. See also, Hall, op. cit.; Foote, op. cit.; Note, The Use of Vagrancy-Type Law, loc. cit. The dragnet or "round-up" was a widely used police method of arresting numerous persons at once and detaining them while the police investigated their alibis. This practice was illegal under the law in most states unless vagrancy-type statutes were used.

63 Note, The Use of Vagrancy-Type Laws, loc. cit. p. 1358-1360.

64 Idem.

65 It had been in existence since 1942 but by 1957 it had been adopted in only three states, in slightly modified form, see Del. Code Ann. tit.

11, Sections 1901-22 (1953); New Hampsire Rev. Stat. Ann. Sections 594: 1-25 (1955); Rhode Island General Laws Ann. Sections 12-7-1 to 13 (1956).

66 See, e.g., Foote, op. cit.

67 Douglas, Vagrancy and Arrest on Suspicion, Yale Law Journal, Vol. 70, pp. 1, 12 (1960).

68 Mapp v. Ohio, 367 U.S. 643 (1961).

69 Miranda v. Arizona, 384 U.S. 436 (1966).

70 For an extensive bibliography of articles on this subject which appeared in the mid-sixties see LaFave, Street Encounters and the Constitution: Terry, Sibron, Peters and Beyond, Michigan Law Review. Vol. 67, p. 40, n. 4 (1968).

71 New York Code Crim. Proc. Section 180a (McKinney Supp. 1967).

72 A.L.I. Model Code of Pre-Arraignment Procedure Section 2.20 (Tent. Draft No. 1, 1966). The members of the ALI were in general not opposed to allowing the police to frisk for weapons in order to protect themselves. However, some members feared that the police would abuse this power and conduct a general search for narcotics and other contraband. E.g., 43 ALI Proceedings at 114-7 (1966).

73 President's Commission on Law Enforcement and Criminal Justice, Task Force Report: The Police (1967) at 184 (hereinafter cited respectively as President's Crime Commission and The Police).

74 Idem.

75 Idem.

76 Ibid., 185.

77 See also P. Valentine, "silence Supported in Wrongful Arrest," The Washington Post, 12/25/74, B1. The D.C. Chief of Police signed a new order barring officers from requiring wrongly arrested persons to sign official documents or give identifying information as a condition of release from custody. Under the new procedure the names of the mistakenly or incorrectly arrested persons shall be placed in the so-called "detention journal," a confidential record locked up in all station houses.

78 Personal communication to the author.

79 Boydston, San Diego Field Interrogation: Final Report (1975).

80 Ibid., 3. The study notes that "reasonable suspicion" is not susceptible to precise definition. The lack of precision in definition probably accounts for much of the difference between the two studies in the rate of incidents per unit of observation.

81 There is no certain measure of the amount of police time actually spent on patrol. The Metropolitan Police Department Annual Report for 1973 (p.5) gives the distribution of police personnel by assignment in terms of a daily average. Adding the figures given for all patrol assignments in which stops and frisks are possible (and counting two-man scout cars as "one man") one gets a total of 998 police personnel on patrol per day. Assuming, conservatively, that only half of the 8 hour shift of these patrol personnel is actually spent on patrol (i.e. excluding time spent on administrative, mechanical, and other matters), there were 3,992 hours of real patrol time per day.

82 A.J. Reiss, The Police and the Public (1971) p. 92. It is noteworthy that the 25,230 frisks yielded only 113 weapons, creating a weapons-productivity rate of less than half of one percent.

83 National Commission on Marihuana and Drug Abuse, Marihuana: A Signal of Misunderstanding Appendix Vol. 2. (hereinafter, Marihuana Report).

84 Dispositions "between apprehension and formal trial with the effect that no further processing is undertaken by participants in the system." Ibid., 644.

85 Ibid., 648.

86 However, this conclusion cannot be firmly drawn on logical grounds from the data. It is only a suggested conclusion. A different conclusion may in fact be in order. It may be that while there were many Terry-type arrests in these two categories, it was not them but other cases which accounted for the high termination rates. For further discussion of the dangers in reaching our suggested conclusion see discussion of the "ecological fallacy" in E. Bobbie, The Practice of Social Research p. 56 (1973).

87 National Commission on Marihuana and Drug Abuse, Drug Use in America: Problem in Perspective, Appendix Vol. 3 (1973) pp. 495-650.

88 A "prior drug-related investigation" is any form of pre-arrest police involvement in detecting possible drug offenses. Ibid., 518.

89 Ibid., 518-542. The reasons for the nonpublic and nonvehicle related arrests did not involve "suspicious behavior" in those cases where the reasons were known.

CRIME CONTROL: A THEORETICAL VIEW

Robert M. Rich

Introduction

Crime control is a type of social control, mainly coercive but also containing persuasive elements. The component parts of the criminal justice system utilize the concept of crime control to suppress crime through the use of the methods of surveillance, apprehension, and punishment.[1]

Crime control methods have adopted the social reform technique, i.e., policies and actions deliberately intended to alter selected aspects of a segment of society so as to bring it into clear harmony with particular value-attitudes.[2] Crime control overlaps with crime prevention at many points yet according to Newman the objectives are distinct enough in purpose and implementation to be analyzed separately.[3]

The basic objective of crime control is present oriented and deals with the discovery of past criminal behavior (i.e., the criminal justice system functions in a relative world set by charging criminal statutes which vary from jurisdiction to jurisdiction).

The function of crime control according to Quinney is the preservation of the existing social order with all its social, economic, and racial inequalities. The legal order that formulates crime control policy is controlled by the ruling class which is the power behind the existence of the state (i.e., the state and its legal system reflect and maintain the status quo which keeps the ruling class in power). The function of crime control is to coerce the population through the criminal law process so that the ruling class will not be threatened and will be able to continue to rule society.[4]

Reasons states that Quinney has not been able to find a society that does not create law apart from private interests. Therefore crime control mechanisms for all societies are based on the inherent inequalities between those who hold power and privilege and those who want to become the holders of power and privilege.[5] Since society is not static, differentials in power and privilege are continuously changing as will be seen from the following overview of theory and practice of crime control. This struggle will be demonstrated by the comparative examination of the crime-control and due process models which are prominant components in any analysis of crime control theory.

Crime Control Theory - General

Based on the writings of Herbert L. Packer,[6] one can examine the operations of the criminal justice system (see Table I). The crime-control model stresses rapid, efficient processing of clients while the due process model places the individuality of clients above the standardization process of the crime-control model, thus being less efficient, more time consuming, and costly.

Because of this basic difference between the two, the crime-control model is bureaucratic in orientation stressing administrative and managerial practices while the due-process model is judicial in orientation stressing a fact finding process. Lastly both models emphasize the repression of criminal behavior but utilize different means to that end. The crime-control model assumes guilt of the person processed while the due-process model assumes innocence until proven otherwise by legal rules not administrative procedures.

Crime Control Objectives

According to Newman,[7] there are three major objectives of the criminal justice system (see Table II). These goals can be achieved by following either the crime-control model which posits the punitive ideal or the due-process model which posits the rehabilitative ideal.

The first goal (crime-control objective) is to detect, apprehend, convict, and incarcerate offenders. As stated, the crime-control model is oriented toward implementation of the punitive ideal. Thus high arrest, conviction, and punishment rates fulfill the goal. The due-process model is oriented toward implementation of the rehabilitative ideal. Thus diversion of as many suspects as possible from the punitive goal as possible is the aim of this model. To this end, community based treatment methods (i.e., probation, halfway house, etc.) are resorted to as much as possible as the ideal way to reform the offender.

The second goal is to deter potential offenders from perpetrating crimes. Two approaches have been utilized by the criminal justice system, the overt deterrence model and the covert deterrence model. The former attempts to achieve its end openly showing that crime does not pay while the latter model tries to get across the idea of omnipresence and omnipotence which pervades society and controls criminality on a confidential basis.

The third goal is to create an ordered and stable society (i.e., as Quinney would say, maintain the status quo). The traditional model which represents both the punitive and rehabilitative ideals is an instrument of the capitalist state.

According to this model, the traditional

elements of efficiency and vengeance of the criminal justice system solidify social solidarity. These elements are reinforced by such symbolic and ceremonial forces as criminal court ritual, severity and solemnity of court architecture and court personnel, and the traditional uniform of law enforcement personnel.

More important, the criminal justice system is the agent of the ruling elite. Thus criminal justice personnel, knowingly or unwittingly, act as agents of the status quo and periodic attempts at change or reform are fought as proof of their inefficiency and inability to deal with social problems. Tradition and ceremony therefore tend to retard social reform.

The need for an orderly and stable society implies more than lip service to the concept of law and order. There is a desire that the criminal justice system (i.e., police, court, and corrections personnel) effectively protect the property and activities of the elite from criminals (i.e., any non-elite which demands a radical change).[8]

On the other hand, the radical model is an instrument of the socialist state. This model states that the legal system serves only the elite and their subordinates. The preservation of domestic order is for the maintenance and promotion of elitist economic interests. The state operates the legal order and must defend the interests of the elite. Thus crime control becomes a way of defending special interests. Therefore the criminal justice system is not a neutral agency which mediates disputes in a pluralistic society but is a coercive force benefitting the ruling class. This is basically the argument of Quinney who states, "when there is no longer a need for a legal system to secure the interests of the capitalist ruling class, then there will no longer be the need for crime."[9]

Crime Control Policies

Crime control policies can be placed into two categories, one based on an impact model which is crime-control oriented and the other based on a compliance model which is due-process oriented.[10] Both models can be used to evaluate crime control measures as well as criminal justice statutes (see Table III).

The impact model accepts the crime control measure as an absolute regardless of the type of social system in which it is expected to exert control. Thus it is the ideal type to which policy makers are oriented rather than to the behavior (i.e., obedience or nonobedience) of the offender.

The compliance model accepts the crime control measure as relative, that is a concern for the type of social system in which the measure is expected to exert control is manifested. The compliance model thus is oriented toward specific system behaviors rather than with an absolute concern with ideal typologies.

Therefore the compliance model must deal with subcultural contexts, reference groups, and socialization processes rather than administrative commands applied bureaucratically in a Gesellschaft like oriented atmosphere. Formal social controls are replaced by informal social control mechanisms applied from within the group and/or community structure so that persuasive social controls can be used by the societal legal structure rather than coercive social controls applied from without the group and/or community structure as in the case of the impact model. The compliance model implies the existence of a neutral legal structure which mediates disputes for all segments of society while the impact model implies the existence of a special interest oriented legal structure dedicated to the maintenance of the status quo (i.e., rule of the elite.)

Crime Control Trends

Crime control trends can be analyzed according to the crime-control -- due-process model dichotomy.[11] The former model is committed to formal processing of offenders which envisions the individual rapidly processed through the criminal justice system until his final resting place in an institutional setting while the latter model is equally committed to diverting the offender from official processing to treatment in a community setting (see Table IV).

Secondly the crime-control model values uniformity in criminal justice processing so that all offenders ideally receive the same uniform treatment while the due-process model values individualization which requires an appropriate examination of all the social-psychological circumstances surrounding the illegal behavior of the offender. Criminal justice personnel have more discretion under the individualization concept than under the uniformity concept which could ultimately bring about social change in the criminal justice system.

Third local autonomy in criminal justice decision making typifies the crime-control model whereas most adherents to the due-process model adhere to the central control concept. Local autonomy in decision making helps maintain the status quo and perpetuate the power structure while central control of the criminal justice system can make it more professional and efficient through standardization of programs as well as facilitate top to bottom changes in policy (i.e., the centrally controlled bureaucracy can direct and control change on a large scale with little disruption of day to day efficiency).

Last there is a great amount of secrecy generated by those adhering to the crime-control model. The basic issue is the preservation of privacy so that the criminal justice system will be one step ahead of the offender and also be able to protect the system if it has to investigate those who might cover up if they knew of such a pending investigation (i.e., Watergate).

The proponents of openness (due-process model) feel that the adversary system of justice cannot function properly under a cloak of secrecy. Increased efficiency of the criminal justice system demands sharing of data at all levels in order to facilitate discretionary actions on the part of all system personnel. Ideally only openness can eliminate graft, corruption, and special interest manipulation of the criminal justice system according to adherents of the due-process model.

V. Crime Control Practices

Under this heading, let us examine diversionary (due-process) alternatives to the traditional formal processing methods of the crime-control model. Diversionary alternatives have increased rapidly in all areas of the criminal justice system from police to corrections. There are three types of programs: community based facilities, which are new concepts put into practice; old concepts which represent little more than articulation and justification of existing practices (i.e., family crisis intervention units of police departments); and programs that eminate from legislative changes (i.e., those which redefine certain criminal behaviors as forms of mental illness).[12]

There are a great number of contemporary crime control practices which utilize diversionary alternatives. Halfway houses, community treatment centers, and work-release programs comprise the majority of programs in both public and private sectors. In addition there are other programs such as alcoholic rehabilitation centers, drug rehabilitation centers, youth counselling and opportunity centers, family crisis intervention centers, and suicide intervention centers.

Halfway Houses

Halfway houses are temporary residences for those under supervision of parole departments, those who have completed their sentences, and those on probation who serve in lieu of confinement in prison. The houses are usually located in the community in which the offender resided before incarceration or as near to that community as possible. The typical halfway house is under the supervision of a correctional authority and houses a small number of individuals, usually no more than fifty persons. Halfway house residents can look for a job, work on a job, meet with family and friends, and begin to assume normal community roles.[13]

Community Treatment Centers

Community treatment centers today are used mainly as halfway houses for individuals leaving prison. The basic purpose of the community treatment center is to carry out a total correctional plan to reintegrate the offender into the community by serving as a transitional step back to the community for those completing an institutional sentence; a diagnostic resource to the federal courts; and a supplemental resource for those under probation supervision.[14]

Treatment centers function to provide some continuity with education and training programs begun in the correctional institution; assist the offender in obtaining adequate employment; increase utilization of community resources; and provide needed support during the initial adjustment period.[15]

A number of programs exist which combine characteristics of both halfway houses and community treatment centers. The Highfields (New Jersey) program is a type of treatment-oriented short term small residential group center. Residents usually work outside the institution and participate in regular group therapy.[16] The Pinehills (Provo, Utah) program was a variation of the Highfields program where the offenders lived at home.[17]

Synanon is a community treatment center where former criminals and drug addicts help themselves and live like a "family" together. They are all voluntary participants, and staff members are successful Synanon "graduates" who help new participants help themselves. Through the vehicle of group psychotherapy and active participation with members of the community, participants are gradually resocialized into the functioning community of the outside world. Thus the Synanon experience is a total environmental one where all participants learn and grow from each other's experiences within the institution and out in the community. Synanon residents are expected to live in the institution indefinitely and if residing outside of Synanon to stay in permanent contact with the organization.[18]

The Delancy Street Foundation (San Francisco) in general is similar to Synanon but differs in a number of aspects. The Foundation tries to prepare residents to live as nonaddicts in the community and to acquire occupational skills so they can be successful in the community. A resident is allowed up to two years in this program which is family-oriented. The Foundation operates its own business enterprises which include a restaurant, a moving company, and a florist shop. There is also a work-training program and maintenance work within the residence as well as in the community at large. Formal education is encouraged. Group therapy provides a continuous therapeutic environment to help the ex-addict continue to reject drugs and overcome personal problems.[19]

Daytop Lodge (Staten Island, New York) is a small residential treatment center for drug addicts on probation and is also similar to Synanon. Leadership is provided by a former addict and a therapeutic environment with group sessions are provided to all residents.

The addicts remain in residence for one year where he is treated under close supervision. Only during the last two months can he work outside in the community but must sleep at the center. After satisfactorily completing this program, the probationer is allowed to live at home in his community but must maintain contact with the Daytop Lodge administration.[20]

Diagnostic Parole & Parole Clinics

Diagnostic parole pertains to the process where all commitments from a court jurisdiction are referred to a diagnostic center to be screened for eligibility for parole either immediately after sentencing or after serving a short time in prison. These quick release from prison programs enable the offender to reintegrate into the community under supervision of parole and treatment personnel.[21]

Parole clinics are operated for offenders who are deemed still in need of psychiatric care after serving their sentence and for those offenders who may benefit from concentrated outpatient services rather than serving a sentence in prison or commitment to a mental institution.[22]

Work Release Programs

Work release is a program where offenders go from prison into the community for work and return to the institution or a halfway house at night to stay. Work release serves as an alternative to total confinement for inmates with only a short time left to serve (usually six months) in prison. Work release programs usually allow vocational training as well as actual employment. In some jurisdictions, it is also used as an alternative to imprisonment by providing an opportunity for offenders to maintain normal employment while serving sentence.

Inmates must meet certain eligibility requirements to enter the program such as not be a high security risk, not be likely to commit violent crimes, be trustworthy, and have the potential to be rehabilitated. In other words, the best candidates for work release programs are those least likely to recidivate.

The objectives of work release programs are the upgrading of job skills, accumulating savings for after release from prison, making restitution or paying of legitimate debts, strengthening family ties through contributions to family support, and reducing the risks to the community and fears of the offender concerning his ability to adjust after imprisonment.[23]

Similar and parallel to work release programs are work study, new careers, employment and manpower projects, Youth Opportunity Centers, and Job Corp.

Work study programs are similar to work release programs except that instead of going to work inmates go to school (i.e., secondary, vocational, community college, or state university).[24]

The New Careers program is a type of self-help enterprise which uses inmates and ex-offenders to train other inmates and serve as staff assistants in the field of corrections research and innovation, work in parole projects such as helfway houses, and serve as resource personnel in community action projects.[25]

Employment and manpower projects, youth opportunity centers, and the former Job Corps are all programs that try to teach vocational skills to unemployed and undereducated youth who are or might become juvenile delinquents as well as young adult offenders. In a way these are both crime prevention and crime control programs simultaneously. These programs have for the most part been funded by the federal government although some states have funded a portion of these projects. Success has been limited in reaching youth with delinquent and criminal records since both agency personnel and their prospective clients have been cautious about each other. Since 1973, the federal government has reduced funding and potential employers have declined due to economic and political conditions and orientations.[26]

Conclusion

This paper is a survey of the various theories and practices concerning crime control. A theoretical dichotomy was created so as to compare and analyze the crime-control model with the due-process model which are typical of the American criminal justice system. The therapeutic and institutional models were not considered in this study.[27]

Crime control theory was divided into theory proper, objectives, policies, and trends. One conclusion is that the crime-control model shows that important decisions about offenders processed through the criminal justice system are made by personnel without a clear cut ideology about how to deal with these individuals. Since very broad discretionary powers are delegated to system personnel by legislation, the Anglo-American legal tradition, or simply assumed as a function of the office (i.e., police), some criminal justice functionaries utilize the crime-control model, some the due-process model, others the therapeutic model, or even the institutional model.

According to Newman, crime control efforts have traditionally been tested against two general standards. The first is the effect of intervention procedures on the offender. In the past effectiveness of techniques have often been given high priority by criminal justice administrators. Under this standard past research was strongly oriented toward the evaluation of criminal justice programs in terms of increase in arrests, decrease in recidivism, and so forth.

The second standard is the suitability of intervention procedures in terms of societal politico-legal ideology. At present emphasis has been placed on methods of decision making and control rather than on their results. This has been felt to be quite proper and suitable and in line with the due process ideology (i.e., stressing the civil rights of offenders processed with priority placed on means, not ends).[28]

A number of crime control programs were examined to illustrate typical contemporary crime control practices. Most programs today are alternatives to traditional institutional programs. There are of course a number of problems to be solved concerning these crime control alternatives to incarceration practices. There is initially the need to convince legislators and criminal justice administrators that these programs are worthwhile and necessary (i.e., the premature demise of Job Corps and the Pinehills program).

Next there is the lack of trained manpower to staff these community based programs. Ex-offenders, para-professionals, and volunteers from the community, especially college students would be quite useful if training programs could be developed. Correctional staff at traditional institutions should be involved in such programs along with the training institutions that prepare one for a correctional career. Social work and mental health agencies should also be involved in these alternative programs.

Lastly the involvement and participation of the community in which a program is to be establised is absolutely essential for the success of such a program. Various grass roots organizations and professional planning associations such as criminal justice, urban affairs, mental health, and educational planners should be involved to insure public awareness and financial support for such crime control practices.[29] If this is not done these alternative programs might end up the same way as most War Poverty community programs.

TABLE I

Crime Control Theory*

Crime-Control Model	Due-Process Model
(1) Sees the efficient, expeditious and reliable screening and disposition of persons suspected of crime as the central value to be served by the criminal justice process.	(1) Sees the efficient, expeditious, and reliable screening and disposition of persons suspected of crime as subordinate to the maintenance of the dignity and autonomy of the individual involved in the criminal justice process.
(2) This model is administrative and managerial. It can be likened to an assembly line. Speedy processing is sought through informal and standardized procedures. The assembly line process represents investigation, arrest, postarrest investigation, preparation for trial, trial or entry of plea, conviction or acquittal, and disposition of the convicted offender. A high rate of apprehension and conviction defines success which necessitates the utilization of routine procedures for most efficient handling of client.	(2) This model is adversary and judicial. It can be likened to an obstacle course. This means that impediments are set up against the further progress of the defendant through criminal justice processing. Reliability of fact finding is continuously challenged by witness errors, coerced confessions and other possible distortions. Legal rules must be satisfied apart from the question whether the defendant was guilty or not. Processing is slow and individualized. Routine procedures are utilized only up to a certain point since success is not determined by a high rate of conviction but by seeing that justice is done. Thus a heavier work load is placed on the administrative apparatus.
(3) Emphasis is on repression of criminal behavior. A presumption of guilt enables the overall criminal justice system to operate more efficiently. This procedure can prejudice the rights and guarantees of the individual under the state and federal constitutions.	(3) Emphasis is on the repression of criminal behavior coupled with the prevention of criminal behavior. A presumption of innocence until proof of guilt is determined in procedurally regular fashion according to legal rules.

*Adapted from Herbert L. Packer, Two Models of the Criminal Process, University of Pennsylvania Law Review, 118 (1964); 1-68; ___________. The Courts, the Police, and the Rest of Us, Journal of Criminal Law, Criminology, and Police Science, 57 (September, 1966), 238-243; _______________. The Limits of the Criminal Sanction, Stanford University Press, Stanford, California, 1968, 154-173.

TABLE II

Objective I: To detect, apprehend, convict, and incarcerate offenders

Crime-Control Model (punitive ideal)	Due-Process Model (rehabilitative ideal)
(1) The criminal justice process should be involved often, vigorously, and fully against offenders in society.	(1) A better and more effective criminal justice system could be achieved when it acts reluctantly and when its purpose is the diversion of as many suspects as possible from criminal justice processing. If arrest and conviction must occur then it is better to remove offenders from the system as quickly as possible.
(2) Measures of effectiveness include high arrest rates, the charging of the highest crimes possible with available evidence, the convicting of offenders as charged, and the sentencing of violators to maximum terms.	(2) Measures of effectiveness include arresting only under extreme conditions, diversion of violators to other available community agencies and to process defendants to charges only according to what seems best for the offender. Only after conviction is the individual to be put in a community correctional facility or on probation and then for as short a time period as is necessary to rehabilitate him.
(3) Use of the punitive ideal whereby punishment is the best way to reform the offender (a modified form of this ideal involves the use of the justice system much like a process of hospitalization with goals of treatment, rehabilitation, and return of offenders eventually to the community when deemed that their behavior patterns will conform to those of the community.) Physical control of the individual is maintained while treatment proceeds, i.e., individual and group counselling, educational programs, self-help groups, etc. while in prison.	(3) Use of the rehabilitative ideal whereby social work techniques and/or other forms of rehabilitation in the community is the best way to reform the offender.

TABLE II Cont.,

Objective II: To deter potential law violators

Overt Deterrence Model	Covert Deterrence Model
(1) Belief in the certainty of criminal justice processing and a hope that the severity of official reactions when offenders are caught will deter people from initiating criminal activities. Thus there is a desire to make the criminal justice system omnipresent, visible, certain, and swift through overt actions.	(1) Belief that criminal justice system should operate efficiently but at low visibility. Thus enforcement efforts should be kept confidential but give an impression of omnipotence through use of covert actions that imply certain apprehension and stern punishment of offenders.

Objective III: To create an orderly and stable society

Traditional Model	Radical Model
(1) The criminal justice agency is an agent of the ruling class which uses the legal system through the state mechanism to maintain the status quo in society.	(1) The criminal justice agency must become an agent of the people, not of the elite. Thus the state must act as an agent of social change.
(2) Law is the means by which the state secures the interests of the elite. Crime control is the coercive means of checking threats to the status quo and maintaining domestic order.	(2) Law must become an instrument of the people and destroy ruling class interests. Crime control must be equitably applied to all classes and not be an instrument of special interests.

*Adapted from Donald J. Newman, Introduction to Criminal Justice, J. B. Lippincott Company, Philadelphia, 1975, 39-44.

TABLE III

Crime Control Policies*

Impact Model (Crime-Control Oriented)	Compliance Model (Due-Process Oriented)
(1) This model evaluates crime-control measures including the criminal law in terms of narrowly defined relationships between the causes of deviance and the outcome of measures taken against it.	(1) This model is concerned with the process of acceptance of a given crime control measure largely prior to its point of impact.
(2) The analysis of the effects of a crime control measure regards the measure itself as the crucial variable in determining either obedience or non-obedience, rather than the overall sociocultural context within which the deviant evaluates the sanctions threatening him.	(2) This model broadens the sphere of concern to include predispositioning processes and the feedback effects of the obedience or non-obedience outcomes of the measure taken against deviance. Upon entering the event, individuals to which the control measure apply have varying predispositions to conform to the norms that have been legalized.
(3) Some sets of events cause policy makers to take certain actions which are evaluated in terms of their effects in reducing the incidence of the deviant events.	(3) These predispositions have been shaped by socialization of the individuals' personality (i.e., learning effecting the determination whether a given control policy will serve as positive or negative reinforcement) and the relevance of the norms of the individuals' reference groups to the achievement of the policy's goals.
	(4) Control measure acceptance must be self-generating to some degree if coercive social control is to be meaningful.
	(5) Through feedback mechanisms, control measure acceptance should influence the predispositioning processes to favor the insertion of new norms into the socialization process causing resocialization of both the individual and his reference group. In this predispositioning process, formal social controls become a means of introducing informal control mechanisms to promote future compliance to the criminal statutes.

TABLE III Cont.,

	(6) This model provides an opportunity to remedy defects caused by an arbitrary imposition of punishment based upon the tolerance levels of policy makers of various forms of deviance over time and space. This is accomplished by proposing that policy makers fit their measures to the socio-psychological forces which either reinforce or oppose conformity. Feedback effects can be applied to avoid counterproductive use of coercion and substituting more promising methods of control.
	(7) By emphasizing the place of criminal law within the total community control system, this model sees the exercise of power in terms of mutual social interactions between groups possessing varying degrees of power and ability in the decision making process. This model implies the study of feedback effects of crime control measures and thus identifies the self-interests of the political power structure in a community with the development of at least partial common interests among all groups in the community.

*Adapted from Jerry N. Clark et al., Compliance, Obedience, and Revolt: An Overview, In Samuel Krislove et al., (eds.), Compliance and the Law, Sage Publications, Beverly Hills, California, 1972, 11-12; Elmer H. Johnson, Crime, Correction, and Society, The Dorsey Press, Homewood, Illinois, 1974, 636-638.

TABLE IV

Crime Control Trends*

Crime-Control Model	Due-Process Model
(1) Formal processing - Full scale criminal justice processing which is formal, adversary, and results in placing the offender in an institutional setting (i.e., prison or mental hospital).	(1) Diversion - A decision or program designed to divert offenders from official processing to less formal, less adversary and noninstitutionalized community based settings.
Formal processing has the long-range effect of producing persons who are more dangerous or more psychologically damaged than they were upon entry into the criminal justice system. This results in part from the degrading and physically harsh nature of the criminal justice process and part from the results of the labelling process which makes the individual think as a criminal and continue in this role after release from prison. Thus this program is counter-productive to rehabilitation and deterrence.	Diversion involves keeping otherwise eligible persons totally out of criminal justice processing by settling whatever issues are involved without arrest or charging or by moving the offender into a different treatment process (i.e., halfway house). A second form of diversion is exemplified by practices and techniques designed to ameliorate the crime problem or treat the offender without invoking the complete criminal justice process. If criminal processing cannot be completely avoided, steps are taken as early as possible to keep the person from moving further into the criminal justice system. This is accomplished by postarrest, middle-stage diversion, or by seeking alternatives to incarceration.
(2) Uniformity - Uniformity in criminal justice processing was a basic political ideal typifying the classical school of criminology.	(2) Individualization - Individualization became popular with the rise of the psychological and sociological school of criminology.
Uniformity demands the automatic implementation of the laws (i.e., full law enforcement for all equally).	Individualization requires the exercise of discretion in proper fashion to achieve sensible and just distinctions in law implementation (i.e., selective law enforcement).
A result of this practice may be arbitrary and capricious intervention, discriminatory enforcement, and sentence disparity due to the double standard in crime control (i.e., wealthy vs. poor which denies the equal protection test of the Constitution in practice).	A result of this practice is a desire to achieve justice by fitting the consequences of criminal intervention to the actual harm done by the person.

TABLE IV Cont.,

This process is in favor of nondiscretionary criminal justice processing, the abolition of plea bargaining, and legislatively fixed mandatory sentences.	This process of individualization utilizes the concepts of plea bargaining, increased discretion of those who operate the criminal justice agencies, and use of the indeterminate sentence (i.e., length of jail term set by corrections and parole personnel).
This practice relies on automatic implementation of all procedures which does not easily lead to increased professionalization of staff personnel.	This practice relies on expertise of criminal justice personnel which increases professionalization of staff.
(3) <u>Local autonomy</u> - The criminal justice system is geared toward emphasis on local control and life-style variation. Variation and relevance are emphasized over efficiency and uniformity. A variety of local programs and projects designed to increase local autonomy, highlight and capitalize on regional differences, and varying standards and procedures are emphasized. Efficiency and uniformity are viewed as dull and ineffective in both enforcement and in reintegration of offenders.	(3) <u>Central control</u> - The criminal justice system is viewed as more efficient and professional if controlled by the state or federal government. Central control enables standardization of programs, utilization of staff in more varied roles, and an end to proliferation and duplication of criminal justice functions and services. The bureaucratic structure can provide for increased professionalization of staff.
(4) <u>Secrecy</u> - The rationale for secrecy in the criminal justice system ranges from necessity to preventing the escape of lawbreakers to a desire to protect individuals from reputational damage of premature disclosure of possibly damaging information.	(4) <u>Openness</u> - The rationale for openness has developed as the criminal justice system has become more judicialized and more adversary. Data is needed for decision-making as well as matter of fairness to offenders and accuracy to increase efficiency of operation.

TABLE IV Cont.,

The basic issue in secrecy is the extent to which operational details and raw records are shared with the public and persons processed by the criminal justice system. Generally the police, court, and correctional files have been closed to the public but even resistance has been demonstrated toward sharing information with other criminal justice agencies within the same system (i.e., the system has been relatively closed both internally and to outsiders including suspects, defendants, and the public).	The basic issue in openness is the increased need to improve decision making in the system, to increase professionalism at all levels, to expose improper actions, and to justify increased discretionary powers of criminal justice personnel. Openness will prevent the misuse of police and court files, eliminate graft and corruption, and allow the poor and the criminally processed the right of equal protection since data will be available to all not just to those in the criminal justice system (i.e., staff personnel).

*Adapted from Donald J. Newman, Introduction to Criminal Justice, J. B. Lippincott Company, Philadelphia, 1975, 389-400.

Notes

1 Elmer H. Johnson, Crime, Corrections, and Society, Homewood, Illinois: The Dorsey Press, 1974, p. 268.

2 Thomas F. Hoult, Dictionary of Modern Sociology, Totawa, New Jersey: Littlefield, Adams & Co., 1969, p. 302.

3 Donald J. Newman, Introduction to Criminal Justice, Philadelphia: J.B. Lippincott Company, 1975, p. 38.

4 Richard Quinney, Criminal Justice in America, Boston: Little, Brown & Company, 1974, pp. 8-25.

5 Charles E. Reasons, The Criminologist: Crime and the Criminal, Pacific Palisades, California: 1974, pp. 99-104.

6 Herbert L. Packer, Two Models of the Criminal Process, University of Pennsylvania Law Review, 118 (1964), pp. 1-68; H.L. Packer, The Courts, the Police, and the Rest of Us, Journal of Criminal Law, Criminology, and Police Science, 57 (September, 1966), pp. 238-243; H.L. Packer, The Limits of the Criminal Sanction, Stanford, California: Stanford University Press, 1968, pp. 154-173.

7 Donald J. Newman, Introduction to Criminal Justice, Philadelphia: J.B. Lippincott Company, 1975, pp. 39-44.

8 Donald J. Newman, Introduction to Criminal Justice, Philadelphia, J.B. Lippincott Company, 1975, pp. 42-43.

9 Richard Quinney, Criminal Justice in America, Boston: Little, Brown & Company, 1974, pp. 21-25.

10 Jerry N. Clark et al., Compliance, Obedience, and Revolt: An Overview, In Samuel Krislov et al., (eds.), Compliance and the Law, Beverly Hills, California: Sage Publications, 1972, pp. 11-12.

11 Donald J. Newman, Introduction to Criminal Justice, Philadelphia: J.B. Lippincott Company, 1975, pp. 389-392.

12 Donald J. Newman, Introduction to Criminal Justice, Philadelphia: J.B. Lippincott Company, 1975, p. 390.

13 Oliver J. Keller & Benedict S. Alper, Halfway House, Lexington, Massachusetts: Heath, 1970; Richard L. Rachin, So You Want to Open a Halfway House, Federal Probation, XXXVI, no. 1 (March, 1972) pp. 30-31; Martin R. Haskell & Lewis Yablonsky, Criminology: Crime and Criminality, Chicago: Rand McNally, 1974, p. 562; National Institute of Mental Health, Halfway Houses: Graduated Release, Washington, D.C.: U.S. Government Printing Office, 1971, pp. 15-22.

14 George T. Felkenes, The Criminal Justice System: Its Functions and Personnel, Englewood Cliffs, New Jersey: Prentice-Hall, 1973, p. 296; Elmer K. Nelson, Community-Based Correctional Treatment: Rationale and Problems, Annals of the American Academy of Political and Social Science, 374 (November, 1967), pp. 82-91; Elmer H. Johnson, Crime, Correction, and Society, Homewood, Illinois: The Dorsey Press, 1974, pp. 515-536.

15 LaMar T. Empey, Alternatives to Incarceration, Office of Juvenile Delinquency and Youth Development Studies in Delinquency, Washington, D.C.: U.S. Government Printing Office, 1967, pp. 37-40; Bertram S. Griggs & Gary R. McCune, Community Based Correctional Programs: A Survey and Analysis, Federal Probation, XXXVI (June, 1972)

pp. 7-13; Martin R. Haskell & Lewis Yablonsky, Criminology: Crime and Criminality, Chicago: Rand McNally, 1974, p. 563.

16 H. Ashley Weeks, Youthfull Offenders at Highfields, Ann Arbor, Michigan: University of Michigan Press, 1958, xvii-xviii; L.W. McCorkle, A. Elias, & F.L. Bixby, The Highfields Story: An Experimental Treatment Project for Youthful Offenders, New York: Henry Holt & Company, 1958; Martin R. Haskell & Lewis Yablonsky, Criminology: Crime and Criminality, Chicago: Rand McNally, 1974, p. 561.

17 LaMar T. Empey & Jerome Rabow, The Provo Experiment in Delinquency Rehabilitation, American Sociological Review, XXVI, (October, 1961), pp. 679-696; LaMar T. Empey, Alternatives to Incarceration, Office of Juvenile Delinquency and Youth Development Studies in Delinquency, Washington, D.C.: U.S. Government Printing Office, 1967, pp. 37-40; Task Force on Corrections, Corrections, The President's Commission on Law Enforcement and Administration of Justice, Washington, D.C.: U.S. Government Printing Office, 1967, pp. 38-39.

18 Lewis Yablonsky, The Tunnel Back: Synanon, Baltimore: Penguin Books, 1967; Martin R. Haskell & Lewis Yablonsky, Criminology: Crime and Criminality, Chicago: Rand McNally, 1974, pp. 580 & 590.

19 Martin R. Haskell & Lewis Yablonsky, Criminology: Crime and Criminality, Chicago: Rand McNally, 1974, pp. 590-591.

20 Joseph A. Shelley & Alexander Bassin, Daytop Lodge: Halfway House for Drug Addicts, Federal Probation, XXVIII (December, 1964), pp. 46-54; Martin R. Haskell & Lewis Yablonsky, Criminology, Crime and Criminality, Chicago: Rand McNally, 1974, p. 590.

21 George T. Felkenes, _The Criminal Justice System: Its Functions and Personnel_, Englewood Cliffs, New Jersey: Prentice-Hall, 1973, pp. 300-301.

22 Vernon Fox, _Introduction to Corrections_, Englewood Cliffs, New Jersey: Prentice-Hall, 1972, p. 218.

23 Elmer H. Johnson, Work Release: Conflicting Goals Within A Promising Innovation, The Canadian Journal of Corrections, 12, no 1 (January, 1970), pp. 67-77; Elmer H. Johnson, Report on Innovation - State Work Release Programs, _Crime and Delinquency_, XVI (October, 1970), pp. 417-426; Stanley E. Grupp, Work Release and the Misdemeanant, _Federal Probation_, XXIX (June, 1967), p. 7; Stanley E. Grupp, Work Furlough and Punishment Theory, _Criminology_, VIII (May, 1970), pp. 63-79; Vernon Fox, _Introduction to Corrections_, Englewood Cliffs, New Jersey: Prentice-Hall, 1972, pp. 218-219; George T. Felkenes, The Criminal Justice System: Its Functions and Personnel, Englewood Cliffs, New Jersey: Prentice-Hall, 1973, pp. 297-298; Martin R. Haskell & Lewis Yablonsky, _Criminology: Crime and Criminality_, Chicago: Rand McNally, 1974, pp. 565-566.

24 Vernon Fox, _Introduction to Corrections_, Englewood Cliffs, New Jersey: Prentice-Hall, 1972, p. 219.

25 LaMar T. Empey, _Alternatives to Incarceration_, Office of Juvenile Delinquency and Youth Development Studies in Delinquency, Washington, D.C.: U.S. Government Printing Office, 1967, pp. 37-40; J. Douglas Grant, The Offender As Participant, Not Recipient, In the Correctional Process, Canadian Journal of Corrections, IX (July, 1967), pp. 236-237; Vernon Fox, _Introduction to Corrections_, Englewood Cliffs, New Jersey: Prentice-Hall, 1972, pp. 223-224.

26 Frank H. Cassell, New Dimensions in Employment Services for Youth, Employment Service Review, (May, 1966), pp. 1-6; Bureau of Employment Security, U.S. Department of Labor, Guidelines for Youth Development Centers, Washington, D.C.: U.S. Government Printing Office, 1965, pp. 1-9; Martin R. Haskell & Lewis Yablonsky, Juvenile Delinquency Chicago: Rand McNally, 1974, pp. 448-451; Bertram S. Griggs & Gary S. McCune, Community-Based Correctional Programs: A Survey and Analysis, Federal Probation XXXVI (June, 1972), pp. 7-13.

27 Conversations and correspondence with Dr. Michael Kelly, Dean of the University of Maryland Law School, who worked on developing four models to describe the American criminal justice system under a LEAA Fellowship.

28 Donald J. Newman, Introduction to Criminal Justice, Philadelphia: J.B. Lippincott Company, 1975, pp. 381 & 384.

29 Task Force on Correction, Corrections, The President's Commission on Law Enforcement and Administration of Justice, Washington, D.C.: U.S. Government Printing Office, 1967, p. 44.

Ideology and Gun Control Legislation

Matthew R. DeZee

Introduction

Man's frequent attempts to comprehend and presumably rectify the perplexities enveloping our social structure oftentimes leads to the creation of opposing camps divided as to whether or not the phenomenon of concern should continue existence in society. This is obviously oversimplified in that many of the more prominent issues throughout history were in reality less concerned with such absolutes as existence or nonexistence of a phenomenon as they were with the degree of existence. Similarly, both opposition and support groups became internally divided and unpredictably shifted allegiance. Yet, a few of these concerns so excited the passions of man that the final resolutions were decided by civil and international war.

To understand why such occurrences have emerged and to provide viable (and hopefully less violent) alternatives, we as social scientists posit causal explanations ranging from personality anomalies to territorial rights. A common concern tangentially related to the manifestations of social upheavals and offered as a common denominator to social conflict is the influence of ideology. Obviously, it is exceedingly important to account for the role of ideology -- its influences and ramifications -- vis-a-vis events that have directed the course of history. However, just as important is accounting for how certain ideological convictions affect contributions to academic research, which in turn may influence social policy.

This latter interest becomes increasingly paramount in the realization that for the past several years many social scientists have directed their energies towards supplying the appropriate government agencies with information designed to guide the direction of public policy. In the broad arena of social problems, these informational inputs are ideally used to assist the government officials in making decisions for initiating one or several mechanisms specifically constructed to alleviate the societal detriment. Although this method does not always produce the elusive panacea sought (witness busing to achieve racial equality in schools) it is undoubtedly a viable method destined for future use in our efforts to rectify the problems permeating our social structure. The danger that exists from this approach is that the personal convictions of the academician/researcher could possibly bias the conclusions of his report which subsequently may result in the enactment of faulty or socially destructive policy.

Presently, there exist several unsettled social affairs which are receiving special attention by official sources and academicians. An issue which particularly lends itself to the mode of analysis described above, as well as being deeply rooted in ideological controversy, is that of gun control. Virtually every level of government is allocating resources to academicians for assistance in determining whether or not gun control legislation is effective in the prevention or reduction of the problem. The following analysis will attempt to synthesize the ideological assumptions behind the arguments of both the proponents and opponents of legal gun controls, analyze the strength of the primary issues pertaining to the controversy and provide some insight into the influence of ideology in reference to the topic.

Ideology and Research

Ideology is a rather evasive term subject to differential debate concerning its most appropriate and accurate meaning. For our purposes, the term will refer to an individual's preconceived notions of the most desirable arrangements of the various facets of his social structure.

That is, we can think of ideology as a personal prescription of reality -- how our social structure should be ordered. Contiguous to this definition is the recognition that such beliefs are, for the most part, categorically endorsed without evaluative examination, tenaciously defended against conflicting perspectives and frequently used as reference points to mold an individual's views on specific issues (Miller, 1972:142). Thus, one may suspect an individual (to include the academician) to consciously or unconsciously protect any attacks upon existing social phenomenon which corresponds to his belief despite overwhelming evidence to the contrary.

One can readily find material verifying the influence of ideology in scholarly endeavors. Gouldner (1970:55) for instance, posits the notion that social scientists (sociologists), notwithstanding their fervent claims of objectivity, are subject to the same social forces which help shape the beliefs of the social beings they study. Their background assumptions about the nature of man and the order of society will influence the scientists' endorsement or rejection of specific theories. Similarly, Myrdal (1944:1038), in his discussion on racial prejudices indicates that the scientists' ideological convictions exert a "strong influence on both the selection of research problems and the conclusions drawn from research. In a sense, it is the master scale of bias in social science." Consequently, even research methodologies, adopted by sociologists to technically factor out the effects of personal convictions "is commonly infused with ideologically resonant assumptions about what the social world is, who the sociologist is, and what the nature of the relation between them is" (Gouldner, 1970:51). Parenthetically, the consequences of these notions have become a great concern in some of the more recent works in the field of 'critical criminology (See Reasons, 1975; Taylor, Walton and Young, 1975; Wuinney, 1974).

Ideological Assumptions and Gun Control

To get a better understanding of some of the basic assumptions underlying the gun control controversy, a rather extensive amount of both academic and popular writings were reviewed.[1] Although, the majority of these writings would be labeled "popular" or quasiacademic at best, it was felt that these writings represented the interest and concerns of the "gun culture." From the review, it soon became apparent that both opponents and proponents of gun control legislation make some straight forward assumptions about the nature of man and his environment. Those who resist legal restraints to the access and use of firearms appear to assume that man is a rational being with the capabilities of freely determining the course of his actions. While the majority of gun owners engage in legal and proper shooting activities, there are minority elements (criminal types and subversives) who use guns for illegal and violent purposes. Thus, it is not always the volume or presence of firearms in society that present problems, rather it is the type of people (criminals) and their behaviors that generates conflict. (This can be easily gleamed from the pro gun slogan "GUNS DON'T KILL PEOPLE, PEOPLE DO.")

Secondly, the works of the opponents suggest that man has an inalienable right to the security of his domain which is partially articulated in the Second Constitutional Amendment. Given the inefficiency of the Criminal Justice System, compounded by the escalating rate of crimes and violent attacks on government establishment, the citizenry urgently needs to arm itself for self-protection. And, even the most innocent appearing attempt by official sources to regulate firearms, represents only the first step in leaving citizens hopelessly vulnerable to total political domination.

In regards to the amount and scope of the works of opponents, the writings of the proponents of restrictive legislation are comparably limited and narrow. Their primary attention is given to the high incidences of firearms violence in society. However, a notion which consistently permeates the tone of their works is the assumption that certain powerful groups with vested economic interest guide the direction of public policy. That is, agents of the gun industry greatly influence the outcome of political elections and/or hold sufficient power to insure that political representatives vote against key gun control bills. Thus for those favoring controls, ideological convictions enter the realm of economic and political influence.

While the various rationales can be clearly identified, and while it would be admittably desirable to neatly divide opposing camps into easily distinguishable groups, the highly emotional nature of the controversy tends to generate confusion and contradictions. For example, both opponents and proponents may support restrictive legislation (over the concern for the increasing rate of firearms accidents); oppose legislation for the same reason (the possible misuse of informational files by government officials that could arise from licensing requirements); support controls for different reasons (opponents may deceptively support relatively weak 'waiting period' laws to exemplify their concern with the misuse of firearms, while proponents will support more restrictive measures to undermine the concentration of power in the hands of the lobbyist); or, oppose controls for different reasons (opponents may visualize the restraints as an attempt to undermine their constitutional rights, while proponents may interpret such laws -- e.g., Sullivan Law -- as being politically motivated to increase the arrest powers of political opposition groups in their attempts for control). These, obviously, are only some of the contradictions which have arisen and are only a hint at the potential difficulty in analyzing issues. So, to better comprehend the role of ideology in defining the parameters of the controversy, the substance of the most prominent issues ((1) Second Amendment; (2) self protection; (3) power of the gun lobby; (4) firearm violence; and (5) efficacy of restrictive laws) will be analyzed in order to determine whether or not the positions taken on the issues can be verified by existing data.

Second Amendment Guarantees

The judiciary has been consistently pellucid in determining that the second amendment does not allow for unrestricted individual armament -- as suggested by both extreme groups and unaware citizens (see Newton and Zimring, 1970:195-197). Through a series of decisions, the courts have adamantly held that private ownership is subject to the legal confines set forth by the state and federal government and that the right of "people to keep and bear arms" primarily refers to state militias in protection from aggressive military actions by the federal forces. These legal interpretations were set forth long ago in the 19th Century (United States v. Tot, (1842) 131 F. 2d 261; United States v. Cruikshank, (1876) 92 U.S. 542; Presser v. Illinois, (1886) 166 U.S. 264; Miller v. Texas, (1894) 153 U.S. 535; Robertson v. Baldwin, (1897) 165 U.S. 275), strongly reinforced in 1939 (United States v. Miller, 307 U.S. 174) and reconfirmed recently in 1972 (Cody v. United States, 460 F. 2d 34). Although the court actions strongly indicate that there is no real evidence to substantiate this area as a viable issue, opponents still rely on the Second Amendment as strengthening their position or suggest that the composition of the judiciary is composed of individuals with competing ideological interests (Jennings, 1976:77). However, this approach is sufficiently weakened given the lengthy time period over which the decisions were reached and consequently the change in judicial personnel. In consideration that the federal courts have not (at least to the best of our knowledge) interpreted the amendment as suggested by the opponents, then it seems unlikely if this area is legitimately disputable.

Gun Possession For Self Protection

According to Newton and Zimring (1970:6), over two-thirds of hand gun owners surveyed purchase their weapons for the purpose of self-protection. Undoubtedly, many people seriously believe that the presence of a firearm in their abode will protect their families from harm or at the least, deny an intruder the opportunity of completing his criminal intents. Overwhelming data suggests however, that very few individuals get the opportunity to use their gun to prevent a felony and the mere presence of a gun in the household drastically increases the probability of a family member being seriously injured or killed. McKay's (1974) study of all known felonies committed in Honolulu between 1970-1974 reports that not a single offender was apprehended by a citizen with his weapon. Spiegler and Sweeney (1975:19) found similar results in that only one intruder was killed by an armed homeowner over a one year period. The most convincing evidence indicating the futility of gun ownership for self-protection is presented by Yeager, Alviani and Loving (1976:14) using data from "Crime in Eight American Cities", (1974):

> "... from a total of 66,151 robberies, only 3.5 percent of the victims had the opportunity to use a weapon for self-protection... These data strongly support the belief that in the vast majority of cases, the victim is taken by surprise and has little time to use a weapon... In addition, when compared to using a weapon, running away or reasoning with the offender are almost as effective in thwarting an offender, and, less likely to result in the injury to the victim."

Although these examples focus on robbery and burglary, the purchase of firearms for protection against other type of felonious acts (rape and assault) is comparably ineffective. Since the large majority of assaults are committed by strangers and outside the victims home, there are very few times when the victim will even have his weapon. And, being that surprise is a vital ingredient in most crimes of rape, victims like the robbery or burglary victim has very few chances to use her handgun (Yeager et al., 1976:22-33).

There are also two other considerations which of themselves do not directly question the efficacy of gun ownership vis-a-vis self-protection, but nonetheless do raise serious doubts about the usefulness of private ownership in the reduction of crime. The Uniform Crime Report gives annual testimony to the high incidence of residential burglaries. According to at least one study, in over 90% of all burglaries the victim is not at home. Further, burglary victims were somewhat more likely to have firearms in their home than non-victims (Reppetto, 1974:150). Thus there appears to be a reasonable probability that the weapon purchased for self protection will be stolen by the illegal intruder. This is partially substantiated in Davis's (Director of the Bureau of Alcohol, Tobacco, and Firearms) report to Congress that over 100,000 guns are stolen annually from private residents which represents more than twice the number of guns taken from interstate carriers, manufacturers' and dealers' premises combined (Yeager et. al., 1976:7).

Secondly, the presence of a firearm in the house is of danger to the young and inexperienced. Heins, Kahn and Bjordnal (1975:326-330) study of children admitted to the hospital for gunshot wounds concluded that guns bought for self protection were responsible for the majority of accidental shootings. Likewise, research done over a fifteen year period indicated that there were six times as many accidental firearms deaths in the home as opposed to purposeful killings of illegal residential intruders (Hirsh, Rushforth, Ford, and Adleson, 1975:504).

It appears then that owning a gun for self protection is not effective, may be supplying intruders with firearms and unnecessarily endangering the lives of family members. Thus, concern over self protection seems to emanate more from untested ideological convictions than empirical examination. If there is data to refute the information presented, it is inaccessible.

Power of the Gun Lobby

The gun lobby, comprised of representatives of the firearms and ammunitions industries and sporting organizations (e.g., National Rifle Association -- NRA) is usually visualized as the omnipotent nemisis of gun control legislation. Proponents of restrictive legislation are quick to point out the enormous amount of money spent on firearms and ammunition annually (in access of $600 million) and the amount of money (around $500,000) one organization allocates towards promoting their anti-gun control position (Philadelphia Inquirer, 1975). Due to the economic power and obvious self-interest generated from an industry of this monetary scale, proponents therefore assume that the lobbyists are able to manipulate the direction of gun control legislation. The viability of this assumption is also questionable.

If the lobby has as much power as they are given credit for, and since they do publicly admit to actively taking part in political campaigns, then one would suspect at least a moderate degree of success on the part of the lobby. Yet by their own admission in the 1974 Congressional elections: "Not a single Congressman who sponsored restrictive firearms legislation, lost his seat in November. Twenty-seven Congressmen who either introduced or supported measures favorable to firearms owners went down to defeat" (American Rifleman, 1975:56). On a similar note the strength of the lobby is questioned in Ralph Nader's recent project. Operating under the premise that the gun control issue is not necessarily a 'single issue vote' for all voters, it probably is for NRA members. Thus NRA members would most likely cast their votes based on the candidates position on restrictive legislation.

> "Yet even if all NRA members in a state had cast their vote for the winner in 1970, the switch of the entire membership to the loser would have effected the outcome of only Senate race (Schuck, 1975: 325-326).

This information does not suggest that the lobby does not exert some political influence -- especially in light of national surveys indicating that over 70% of the American public support some type of controls, over 60% would support politicians who supported restrictive legislation and over 60% of gunowners would support legal restraints (Erskine, 1972:455-473). Rather it possibly suggests that while the lobbyists do not carry the immense power they are intuitively assigned, they may be politically wise enough to influence only key individuals (like committee chairpersons) who can single-handedly determine the life or death of proposed legislation. However, a direct linkage between the lobby and these certain congress people has not been established yet.

Firearms Violence

The high incidence of firearms violence seldomly leads to disagreement between the opposing camps; the main point of departure (which will be discussed shortly) involves the assignment of blame for the violence. Both sides will utilize the Uniform Crime Reports to establish, at least on a superficial level, the high volume of gun use for purposes of criminal violence. Firearms are used in over 65% of all murders, 45% of all robberies and 26% of all known aggravated assaults (Uniform Crime Reports, 1974). More rigorous studies (from both camps) which have taken the time to analyze the relationship between the existence of firearms and the total incidence of violent crimes, have found an extremely strong relationship. Seitz (1972:596) using information collected in 1967, found "an astonishing .98 correlation between the firearm homicide rate and the total homicide rate based on aggregate data for the 50 states". An unpublished study by the gun industry (Olin Mathieson Company) found the exact same correlation (.98) using state data in comparing the "murder rate per 100,000" and the "gun murder rate" (Newton and Zimring, 1970:182). Even in recognition that these zero-order correlations do not account for the influence of other variables the almost perfect linear relationship over time does suggest that the mere presence of firearms can be considered problematic.

The opponents, while admitting to the misuse of firearms, will attempt to lessen the significance of these findings by focusing their attention only on "criminals" via recidivism rate among violent offenders. This approach is of course more in line with their basic assumption of the nature of man, yet it brings contradictions and deceptions in reference to the proposed effectiveness of the laws. This can be seen in Dyer's (1976: 6-7) article which says that firearms violence constitutes only 4% of the 10 million "serious crimes" reported to the FBI. This is accurate, but the author fails to inform the reader that approximately 9 million of those crimes (auto theft, larceny, and burglary) are not crimes of personal violence or that guns are used in well over 40% of reported violent crimes (Uniform Crime Report, 1974). He continues his argument that restrictive laws would not lower crime rates and only leave a large group of well armed "career criminals" by relying on Wolfgang's (1958) substitution thesis that applies specifically to crimes of passion and not in the killing of police officers (Dyer, 1976: 6). Yet, in the next paragraph Dyer tries to strengthen his point by showing that 77% of all known police killers had prior records. He concludes by indicating that restrictive gun laws would be counterproductive in that they would deny good intentioned citizens the ability of forming vigilante groups to fight corrupt laws and law enforcement practices when the need occurs. The illogic of this position has been succinctly and eloquently stated by Holfstadter:

> "In all societies, the presence of small groups of uncontrolled and unauthorized men in unregulated possession of arms is recognized to be dangerous. A query therefore must ring in our heads: Why is it

> that in all other modern democratic societies those endangered ask to have those men disarmed, while in the United States alone they insist on arming themselves?" (1970: 84)

Groups in favor of gun controls strongly emphasize the volume of firearm violence, but depart from the opponents' analysis by concerning themselves with the enormous amount of lives lost to firearms in accidents, suicides and crimes of passion (see for example, Riley, 1974; Curtis, 1974). Although such groups admit that it would take some time for the laws to be effective against the criminal population, restrictive legislation will drastically reduce the killings resulting from arguments between loved ones and acquaintances. To bolster their contentions, they will rely on the Uniform Crime Report data which suggests that over 70% of all murders are classified as crimes of passion and that firearms were used in 67% percent of the murders. Thus, they speculate, if firearms are prohibited or restricted, these types of killings will undoubtedly be reduced.

Efficacy of Gun Laws

Using the information supplied by both opponents and proponents, it is more than reasonable to assume that sufficiently valid relationship exists beteen the presence of firearms and the incidence of criminal violence (especially homicide). Yet from this data it still remains unclear as to whether gun control laws will reduce gun violence. In this instance, one needs to ascertain whether restrictive legislation will inhibit access to firearms which will in turn precipitate a decline in criminal violence. This indeed is the crux of the issue towards which the opposing camps direct their attacks. Regretfully, and as one may suspect, the existing research is marred by ideological rhetoric and visable methodological errors.

In this area however, ideologically laced assumptions are not only present in the analytic "popular" works but may also be found in the works of academicians. Although a direct linkage cannot be drawn between the assumptions of the scholars and the results of their findings, the obvious violations of the canons of research and statistics raises serious doubts concerning their judgement.

Due to possible ideological bias, one should be automatically skeptical of three works (Krug, 1967; Snyder, 1969; and the Olin Mathieson Company study) claiming that laws exert little if any influence on rates of criminal violence, as well as one (Clark, 1970) claiming the opposite. Krug was at the time the Director of Research for the National Shooting Sports Foundation, Snyder was an editor for "The American Rifleman", Olin Mathieson is part of the gun industry while Clark is simply stating opinions without figures or references.

Research conducted by academicians appears less overtly bias, but their serious methodological limitations renders their conclusions suspect. Zimring, a published proponent of gun control (1968a; 1968b; 1975) accurately establishes in his Chicago study that guns are the most deadly (efficient and impersonal) weapons readily available for use in criminal endeavors. However, he goes on to suggest that laws restricting access to guns will lower the rates of homicide (1968a; 721-737). Yet he does not supply the important and necessary linkage between the effect of the laws on lowering the criminal homicide rate -- it is only by implication that the relationship exists. Similarly, Geisel, Roll and Wettick (1969: 647-676) use more advanced statistical techniques to provide evidence suggesting gun control laws do reduce the rates of criminal homicide by effectively making firearms less accessible. While this work is notable for its attempts to apply sophisticated procedures to the area, its theoretical and methodological limitations identified by Bordua and Andes (1974: 2-6) justifiably dubs the conclusions of the article totally invalid.

It would be rather difficult, if not libelous to suggest these works represent only the personal conviction of the authors. However, a recent study appearing in what most sociologists consider a respectable journal[2] adds credence to the lack of objectivity indicated in the beginning of this work. Murray (1975: 81-93) selects fifteen rather standard social factors associated with the rates of criminal behavior (percent black, medium education, age, density, etc; see Harries, 1974) for use in a stepwise regression analysis to explain between 66-81% of the variance in rates of criminal violence (e.g., homicide, aggravated assault, robbery and suicide). The author then codes the restrictiveness of existing gun laws for the 50 states (using Bakal, 1966: 346-352), and while statistically controlling for the influence of the social factors, finds that the severity of these laws do not significantly affect the violent crime rates. Using basically the same methods to measure the effects of laws on possession of handguns (using data from Eskine, 1972) he concludes that the laws do not influence whether or not a person owns a gun. Finally, he adds information on handgun possession from the Harris (1968) and Gallup Polls (1973) to his formula and suggests that since they do not increase the explained variance, the availability of handguns does not effect rates of violence.

Without going into technical problems like multicollinearity, weighting procedures or the logic behind his causal model, there exists enough reason to question the results if not the motives of the study. Why, for instance, does the author use gun laws from 1966, crime rates from 1969, census data from 1970 and ownership data from 1968 and 1972, when all this information is available for the same years? Could be possibly be because that by using crime data, census data and state gun laws from one year (1970) there exists a difference in which variables are significant at the P=.05 level?[3] Or why does Murray take data (ownership) on a regional level and apply the percentages to the individual states or use 75 different regression equations, when he criticizes Geisel, et al., for the same procedures? Finally, why does the author find it necessary to give a detailed critique of works claiming that laws are effective, and then gloss over the limitations of those works which claim the opposite? Finally, why does he conspicuously overlook an article published in a journal well respected by both sociologists and criminologists[4] that has been used in both state and federal congressional committee hearings (Seitz, 1976)? Could it be that Seitz's study (1972: 595-613) which indicates that gun control laws strongly effect firearm accessibility which subsequently reduces criminal homicides rates is the most statistically sophisticated work to date and has not been seriously damaged even in attempts by respectable opponents like Bordua and Andes (1974: 6-7)?

The critique of Murray's work does not in any way suggest that any unethical practices were used. However, it does suggest that since his opening pages hint at an advanced knowledge of research and statistics, yet goes on to violate basic methodological rules, that possibly the author may have been influenced by personal beliefs on the subject matter. This could have serious implications in light of the fact that the study was partially funded by a NCHS Grant and could possibly be used to direct governmental decisions.

Conclusion

From all the information presented, it should be apparent that three of the positions on gun controls (Second Amendment, self-protection and power of the gun lobby) are based more on ideological assumptions than verifiable fact. For obvious reasons, public policy makers would not want to place a great amount of emphasis on these positions in their calculus for determining what actions need to be taken. Clearly some measures need to be employed since both sides tend to agree that firearms are problematic to society. However, there still is not enough evidence to conclude that laws restricting access and use of guns is the solution to the problem. This does not necessarily indicate that "more" research is the answer. Rather, it does suggest that reliable research, not fraught with personal convictions, needs to be conducted.

In noting that ideology has permeated the existing works on gun control, we cannot assume that future research by academicians will be unbiased. And given the government's increasing reliance on works by social scientists, some procedures need to be established to insure reliable research is conducted. If we are really interested in responsibility affecting public policy, then the burden should clearly lie with our profession. Possibly, nonpartisan referee committees, working in liaison with public and private grant awarding agencies, could be instituted to review and monitor proposed works, Obviously, these committees would not be without problems and take a great deal of time, money and coordination to be successfully operated. But, in continuing present practices or by taking no actions at all, the credibility of our profession will surely be undermined. Then one would have to question whether our efforts are done merely for reasons of self-satisfaction or directed towards positively influencing the workings of our social structure.

NOTES

[1]An excellent way to familiarize yourself with the notions and perspectives on the issue is to read the commercial publications of the "gun culture" (e.g., The American Rifleman, Guns and Ammo, etc.) as well as other lengthy reports like Krug (1968a; 1968b; and 1970) and Zimring (1968a; 1968b and 1970). Other sources are Bakal (1966), Davidson (1969), Kenneth and Anderson (1975), Kukla (1973) and Sherrill (1973).

[2]For a ranking of journals used by sociologists see Glenn (1971: 298-303).

[3]Using the same procedures as Murray, the significance level and 'strength' of the relationships for certain variables changes when using data for the same year.

[4]Law and Society Review is recognized by both sociologists and criminologists as consistently publishing articles of respected quality (see DeZee, 1975 and Glenn, 1971).

References

American Rifleman. "New Congress Poses Risk of Anti-Gun Laws." (January) 1975, 55-57.

Bakal, Carl. The Right to Bear Arms. New York: McGraw-Hill, 1966.

Bordua, David and Steven Andes. "Firearms Use and Control." A Proposal submitted to the Innovative Research Program, National Institute of Law Enforcement and Criminal Justice, 1974.

Clark, Ramsey. Crime in America. New York: Simon and Schuster, 1970.

Curtis, Lynn. Criminal Violence. Lexington, Massachusetts: Lexington Books, 1974.

Davidson, Bill. To Keep and Bear Arms. New York: Arlington House, 1969.

Devensor, Charles. Gun Registration Now - Confiscation Later? New York: Vantage Press, 1970.

DeZee, Matthew. "The Sociology of Criminology: A Study of Graduate Schools of Criminology and Criminal Justice." A paper presented to the 1975 Annual Meeting of the American Society of Criminology, 1975.

Dyer, Danzel. "Guns, Crime and the Law: A Case for the Defense." Law Enforcement Journal VI (August) 6-7, 1976.

Erskine, Hazel. "The Polls: Gun Control." Public Opinion Quarterly XXXVI (Fall): 455-469, 1972.

Geisel, Martin; Richard Roll and Stanton Wettick. "The Effectiveness of State and Local Regulations of Handguns: A Statistical Analysis." Duke Law Journal (August) 647-676, 1969.

Glenn, Norval. "American Sociologists' Evaluation of Sixty-Three Journals." American Sociologist (November): 298-303, 1971.

Gouldner, Alvin. The Coming Crisis of Western Sociology. New York: Avon Books, 1970.

Harries, Keith. The Geography of Crime and Justice. New York: McGraw-Hill, 1974.

Heins, Marilyn; Robert Kahn and J. Bjordnal. "Gunshot Wounds in Children." American Journal of Public Health 64 (April) 326-330, 1975.

Hofstadter, Richard. "American as a gunculture." American Heritage 21 (October), 1970.

Jennings, Lester. Letter to the editor. Crime and Delinquency 22 (January) 77, 1976.

Kenneth, Lee and James Anderson. The Gun in America: The Origins of a National Dilemma. Westport, Conn.: Greenwood Press, 1975.

Krug, Alan. The True Facts on Firearms Legislation: Three Statistical Studies. Riverside, Conn.: The National Shooting Sports Foundation, 1968a.

_________. Does Firearms Registration Work? A Statistical Analasis of New York State and the New York City Crime Data. The National Shooting Sports Foundation, 1968b.

_________. Fact pact II on Firearms Ownership. The National Shooting Sports Foundation, 1970.

Kukla, Robert. Gun Control. New York: Stockpole Books, 1973.

McKay, John. "Gun Control: A Report on a County Priority." Honolulu, Hawaii: Law Enforcement Planning Office (January) 1974.

Miller, Walter. "Ideology and Criminal Justice Policy: Some Current Issues." Journal of Criminal Law and Criminology 64 (June) 141-162, 1973.

Myrdal, Gunnar. An American Dilemma: The Negro Problem and Modern Democracy. New York: Harper and Brothers, 1944.

Newton, George and Frank Zimring. Firearms and Violence in American Life. Washington, D.C.: U.S. Government Printing Office, 1970.

Philadelphia Inquirer. "NRA seeks money for the gun lobby." (May, 25), 1975.

Quinney, Richard. Critique of Legal Order; Crime Control in Capitalist Society. Boston: Little, Brown and Company, 1974.

Reasons, Charles. "Social Thought and Social Structure: Competing Paradigms in Criminology." Criminology 13 (November): 332-365, 1973.

Reppetto, Thomas. Residential Crime. Cambridge, Mass.: Ballinger, 1974.

Riley, Robert. "Shooting to Kill the Handgun: Time to Martyr Another American Hero." Journal of Urban Law 51-49, 1974.

Sherrill, Robert. The Saturday Night Special. New York: Charterhouse, 1973.

Spieyler, Jeffrey and John Sweeny. Gun Abuse in Ohio. Cleveland, Ohio: Administration of Justice Committee, 1975.

Seitz, Steven. "Firearms, Homicide and Gun Control Effectiveness." Law and Society Review 6 (Spring) 596-613, 1972.

Schuck, Peter. The Judiciary Committee. New York: Grossman, 1975.

Synder, John. "Crime Rises Under Rigid Gun Control." American Rifleman 117 (October) 54-55, 1969.

Taylor, Ian; Paul Walton and Jack Young. The New Criminology. New York: Harper & Row, 1973.

Uniform Crime Reports. Crime in the United States, 1974. Washington, D.C.: U.S. Government Printing Office, 1974.

Wolfgang, Marvin. Patterns in Criminal Homicides. New York: Wiley, 1966.

Yeager, Matthew; Joseph Alviani and Nancy Loving. How Well Does the Handgun Protect You and Your Family? United States Conference of Mayors, 1976.

Zimring, Franklin. "Games with guns and statistics." Wisconsin Law Review 1968 (No. 4): 1113-1126, 1968a.

______________. "Is Gun Control Likely to Reduce Violent Killings?" The University of Chicago Law Review, 35: 721-737, 1968b.

______________. "Firearms and Federal Law: The Gun Control Act of 1968." Journal of Legal Studies Vol. IV, 2 (January) 133-198, 1975.

Criminological Theory and Ideology: Four Analytical Perspectives in the Study of Crime and The Criminal Justice System

Finn Hornum and Frank Stavish

It has been more than a decade since David Matza launched his attack on criminological positivism in Delinquency and Drift.[1] Since then, much controversy and rhetoric have prevailed in our discipline and charges of ideological bias have been exchanged. A "New Criminology" and/or a "Critical Criminology" has emerged to challenge the assumptions, hypotheses and theories many of us had come to accept. Indeed, it would not be an exaggeration to say that the subject matter of criminology has been transformed or is in the process of transformation. It is interesting to note that this development has occurred at the very same time that so called "establishment criminologists" were receiving fiduciary rewards from a more generous government concerned with crime control.

Walter Miller,[2] Don Gibbons and Peter Garabedian[3] have recently identified the ideologies pervading criminology as well as criminal justice practice. Miller delineates a "left" and a "right" dichotomy and elaborates, through juxtaposition of opposing views on this ideological spectrum in the areas of criminal responsibility, criminal justice policy with respect to offenders, and criminal justice policy with respect to the criminal justice agencies themselves. Defining "ideology" as:

> a set of general and abstract beliefs or assumptions about the correct or proper state of things, particularly with respect to the moral order and political arrangements, which serve to shape one's positions on specific issues.[4]

Miller notes the pre-conscious rather than explicit nature of ideological assumptions and the emotional charge of ideological rhetoric. Gibbons and Garabedian[5] identify "conservative", "liberal-cynical", and "radical" criminologies as their "ideal type" specifications of current criminological thought and describe the reactions of academic (and liberal) criminologists to the "radical" perspective as "emotion-laden metaphors".

In the same article, Miller[5] also points to the dire consequences of ideologies in criminology and criminal justice practice. He points to the danger of "polarization" that may become an obstacle to the accomodation and compromise necessary for criminal justice planning. He describes the process of "reverse projection" which tends to appear in ideological controversies resulting in a perception of the middle-of-the-road position as being untenable. He further points to the danger of "ideologized selectivity" in both the choice of research problems, in policy-making and in resource allocation. "Informational constriction" resulting in an anti-research stance; a tendency toward "catastrophism" in viewing the consequences of opposing policies; a magnification of the empirical prevalence of phenomena related to areas of ideological concern; and a tendency to distort the views of the opposition are additional dangerous consequences which need to concern us.[6]

We find ourselves in general agreement with Miller regarding the possible consequences of ideology in criminology and also accept the three authors' version of contemporary ideologies in both criminology and criminal justice practice. However, in this paper we suggest that the criminological enterprise not only may have to accept the continued existence of competing ideologies but, further, accept the proposition that these ideologies actually mask sound sociological and theoretical perspectives which can and should be applied systematically to our subject matter.

Our first contention, that ideological polemics are likely to be a continuous and ubiquitous feature of criminological thought, is based upon the well-documented explosion[7] of the myth of a value-free sociology held so dearly by empiricists. We shall not elaborate further on this view here but simply state that if all thought is of necessity ideologically based, surely the study of crime and criminal justice, involving strong moral and ethical imperatives, cannot be untouched.

In this paper we want to focus on the contention that criminology, rather than dwelling upon the ideological bias of its varied schools of thought, might well view these divergent perspectives as complementary versions of reality which lead to different questions about our subject matter and thus enhance, rather than hinder, the development of criminological theory. In the course of our own thinking and teaching we have identified four analytical perspectives developed in sociological and social-psychological theory which may be productively applied to the three-fold task identified by Sutherland, so many years ago, as the proper subject matter of criminology: the making of laws, the breaking of laws, and the social reaction to the breaking of laws. These four perspectives, <u>functionalism</u>, <u>conflict theory</u>, <u>interactionist theory</u>, and <u>learning theory</u>, have an ideological base but also serve to delineate different facets of the reality of crime and criminal justice practice.

Functionalism

The macro-theoretical perspective in sociological thought, variously referred to as "functionalism" or "structure-functionalism", has dominated sociological and criminological research for many years. Based upon the writing of Durkheim and elaborated upon, in modern times, by Talcott Parsons and Robert K. Merton, functionalism contains many of the same assumptions about the nature of social reality as one finds in the "conservative" and "liberal-cynical" ideologies delineated by Gibbons and Garabedian. Chambliss' summary[8] of the functionalist assumptions most relevant to criminological thought suggests four basic characteristics:

1. society is a reality unconnected with a a particular historical period, i.e., all societies have certain social needs (functional prerequisites in Parsonian terminology) which must be met irrespective of time and place

2. the social needs are given for a particular society and must be met to maintain the social system in a state of equilibrium

3. The social scientist must be "value-free" in his assessment of societal conditions and must not engage in the implementation of social change.

4. Society is characterized by value-consensus, the law represents this value consensus and mediates between conflicting interest groups by upholding those values which are fundamental to the maintenance of the social order and protection of the public interest.

These views are clearly allied with both conservative ideology emphasizing "crime control" as well as liberal-cynical ideology emphasizing "due process" and reform and their validity is the very source of debate between the functionalist and conflict-theoretical frameworks. Nevertheless, is it not conceivable that the acceptance of these assumptions for analytical purposes, have generated and can generate significant questions for criminological theory and research?

Chambliss has provided a set of hypotheses derived from the functionalist assumptions. We cannot reproduce all of these here but an example from his analysis should illustrate the usefulness of the functionalist approach. In the area of crime causation he lists the following hypothesis:

> Criminal acts are more frequent among lower classes because the agencies of socialization (especially the family, but also the neighborhood, schools, other adults and peer groups) are less likely to work effectively, i.e., in ways that lead to the internalization of noncriminal norms of behaviors.[10]

Surely, the proliferation of research and theoretical studies dealing with the role of the family, the peer groups, the school and the neighborhood in relation to crime and delinquency cannot be dismissed as useless flights of fancy that have contributed nothing to the advancement of criminological knowledge.

In our work with courses in criminology and criminal justice we have found it useful to direct students to analyze term project topics within the framework of functionalist theories, not only in the Durkheimian tradition, but also from the writings of Parsons and Merton. The Parsonian "pattern variables of action orientation",[11] for example, have proved an indispensable tool in role-status analyses of criminal justice personnel.

The now classical Mertonian[12] paradigm of deviant behavior has been indispensable in the formulation of "opportunity theory" and "anomie theory". In short, the questions generated by (possibly invalid) assumptions of the functionalist school have been especially productive in the study of the etiology of criminal behavior and in organizational analyses of the criminal justice system. It appears to have minimal utility, on the other hand, in the sociology of criminal law and in the analysis of the power relationships determining criminal justice policy.

Conflict Theory

The macro-theoretical perspective labelled as "conflict theory" has recently gained considerable prominence in criminology. Based largely on the Marxian version of social theory Ralph Dahrendorf,[13] several years ago, critically examined functionalist paradigms and suggested a conflict-oriented alternative which has had considerable impact upon sociological theory. More recently the conflict perspective has been introduced into criminology, notably by William Chambliss,[14] Richard Quinney[15] and the triumvirate of Ian Taylor, Paul Walton and Jock Young.[16] Much of the material produced by so called "radical" criminologists seem solidly grounded in conflict theory. In Richard Quinney's writings, for example, one can trace the development of concern with a conflict perspective and a social constructionist mode of inquiry in his textbook, The Social Reality of Crime, toward an increasingly more "radical" perspective (referred to as "critical criminology") in his later works (Critique of Legal Order and Criminology).[17]

Relying again on Chambliss' comparison of functional and conflict perspectives, the basic assumptions of conflict theory can be summarized as follows:

1. the needs, characteristics, ideologies and institutions of a particular society are a reflection of what society's historical condition - especially the material conditions at that particular historical moment.

2. since the social needs are specific to time and place and may contribute to the oppression of the members of that society, a critical analysis of the social order is necessary and requires a specification of what life could be like if the material conditions were changed.

3. the social scientist, through his critical analysis of the existing order and through his participation in the process of change itself, is a necessary instrument for change.

4. society is viewed as a plurality of interest groups with differing value systems and the dominant value system, if there is one, serves the interests of the ruling class rather than representing a value consensus.

The hypotheses derived by Chambliss from these assumptions illustrates the utility of the conflict perspective for criminological research and theory. This is particularly apparent in the shift in emphasis from a preoccupation with etiology toward a greater concern with the sociology of criminal law, almost ignored by the criminologist working in the positivist-functionalist tradition. Since, in this perspective, acts are not defined as criminal because they offend a moral consensus among members of society by "because it is in the interests of the ruling class to so define them", there is little interest in studying the supposed biological, psychological or social conditions distinguishing criminals from non-criminals or deviants from normals.[19] Instead the focus of criminological theory and research becomes the defining process, the application of the criminal definitions, and the consequences for the actor and his environment to their application. Since the exercise of power by the ruling elite is seen as the main source of social order it becomes a crucial concern for the criminologist to expose the locus of such power, the ways in which power is utilized and the extent to which power fails to meet social needs.

We have already begun to see in the literature how the application of this perspective has thrown new light on the drug problem,[20] on white-collar or corporate crime,[21] on political trials,[22] on prison reform[23] efforts and, of course, on the origin and development of criminal laws.[24] In our work with students the conflict perspective has proven especially useful in directing their attention to the historical development of both criminal law and criminal justice policy as well as focusing their analysis on interest group influences. Thus, the conflict-theoretical perspective offers a complementary analytical mode to the functionalist perspective arising rather obviously when you ask, as we have frequently asked our students, "functional for Whom?"

Social Learning Theory and Interactionist Theory

Unlike the functionalist and conflict perspectives discussed above, interactionist theory and social learning theory are less general and more microanalytic in their respective positions. More specifically, conflict perspectives and functionalist perspectives are metatheoretical distinctions which provide, unlike interactionist and learning theory, a comprehensive view of society from different ideological vantage points. Both interactionist theory and social learning theory have attempted to provide a variety of narrow range and middle range theories of social deviance.

Recent contributions of social learning theorists to problems of crime and deviance have shown renewed commitments to a tradition which goes back at least as far as Thorndike.[25] Social learning theorists view social psychological studies in deviance as having attended excessively to intervening processes while oversighting, to a considerable degree, considerations of potentially manipulable features of the social environment. All behavior is in their view a function of such environmental features. Accordingly, social learning theorists have viewed human behavior in its social dimension as being functionally related to the stimuli from past and present environments. While some, such as Sutherland,[26] Burgess and Akers,[27] would ascribe theoretical and heuristic importance to intervening processes such as motivation, consistency, information processing and the like, most would take, as a basic position of departure, an inquiry into stimulus events of human behavior, an understanding of which is an inviolable prerequisite to any attainable and comprehensive account of human performance.

For sociologists generally and criminologists specifically Sutherland's differential association hypothesis has been a major contribution within social learning theory. The learning aspect of deviant careers as Sutherland saw it fits clearly into what Paulo Freire calls a "banking Model" of learning and experience.[28] The human actor in Sutherland's work seems by implication to be a passive and rather highly absorbent recipient of experiences, motivations and definitions. While early learning theory, distinquishing between classical and operant perspectives, grants essentially different roles to making choices or discriminations based upon the consequences of previous behavior, differential association falls readily within the limits of an "actor-as-determined" assumption.

While a variety of ideological textures might develop we would argue that the biases of both functionalism and the social behaviorism of the Chicago tradition are powerfully evident. In common, not only as the work of Sutherland exemplifies but also as interactionist and labeling theorists such as Blumer and Becker suggest, the Chicago tradition is rooted in a positivistic and somewhat pedestrian view of man in society. Sutherland's attempt to reconcile the external constraint of the social environment with his assumption of man as a free moral agent never succeeded in any meaningful or consistent sense.

We contend that the ideological implications of any social learning theory on crime, and of Sutherland's as a case in point, may not be readily obvious until the point at which the intellectual audience or consuming public raises questions about appropriate or desirable remedial actions. The questions emerge from the same set of functionalist or consensual assumptions about the relationships between the society and its deviants. The answers, variously developed and presented, may involve fundamentally either an appeal to the stick which has wide popularity among conservative political movements, emphasizes the need for more police, more guns and the need for greater risks, and hedonically defined, greater deterrence for the potential deviant. The appeal to the carrot, having wide appeal among liberal political movements, typically emphasizes the preservation of individual civil liberties and procedural due process in the administration of criminal justice, the creation of equal opportunities in education, employment, etc., and the increased efficiency of the formal and ancillary agencies of social control.

The tendentially functionalist texture and the system-centered tack which social learning theory has taken within sociology[29] is powerfully reminiscent of the Chicago tradition. For Chicago, the sociological imperative consisted in the discovery of the principles and practices compatible with the achievement and maintenance of society's, particularly urban society's "biotic balance". The separate directions taken in the growth of interactionist theory on the one hand and of social learning theory on the other, both owe their growth and development to a common origin: The Chicago Ecological Tradition.[30]

The social interaction theory of Mead and Thomas as well as those of contemporary writers such as Blumer and Becker share, now as then, both the strengths and the weaknesses of the Chicago tradition. This genus of deviance research had eschewed the manicheanism and condescension of previous studies, that is to say, were able to deal with the realm of deviance as real, authentic and important in its own right. But they did not in any meaningful sense acknowledge or even explore the position of the deviant in society within a comprehensive theory of power and interests. More importantly, and compatible with their position of liberal functionalism, they never examined or evaluated their own work within a larger frame of power brokerage and interest advancement, anesthetized as they may have been by their commitment to positivism's dream of objectivity and American sociology's myth of value neutrality.

Labeling theorists, as architects of the most highly visible variety of interactionist theory, have been responsible for shifting traditional sociological foci in the study of crime and deviance. Whereas American functionalism preoccupied itself with the problems which the deviant or criminal posed for the social order, labeling theorists took issue with the problem which the social order created for the deviant. An underdog sociology at first sight to be sure is one which has over time invited attention to the liabilities which secondary deviation creates for the ordered society as well as for the "disordered deviant". Labeling theory served to call considerable attention to the likelihood that the putative solutions and remedies to crime were in fact part of the problem. The tendential liberal ideology of this particular variety of interaction theory is evident in its reformist rather than revolutionary prescriptions.

In spite of these considerations and nevertheless we contend that both of these two microanalytic perspectives have enormous value in the development of criminological inquiry. Social learning theory, on the one hand, raises the many questions and tap the underlying realities spoken to by functionalism, and, on the other hand, repeatedly invites the inquirer's attention to the methodological demands and perspectives of the behaviorist and reinforcement traditions. Labeling theory generates propositions of either an implicity functional or explicity conflict variety and importantly underscores the pervasive reflexivity of human interaction generally and criminological inquiry specifically.

We have found with our own students, that social learning theory readily invites consideration of the more or less consistently predictable products of the human environments. Specifically, social learning theory preserves the emphasis of sociology as an environmental discipline at the individual and small group levels in instances where conditions and characteristics of social structure, culture, and history alone are not sufficient to the needs of explanation and prediction. Interactionist theory, focusing on a comparably restricted frame of micro-process, has served to heighten for our students an understanding of subjectivity and inter-subjectivity in human behavior. Specifically, interactionist theory helps to reveal the highly problematic and negotiable qualities of human interaction generally and of order and meaning specifically.

Notes

1 David Matza, Delinquency and Drift, New York: John Wiley, 1964.

2 Walter B. Miller, "Ideology and Criminal Justice Policy: Some Current Issues", The Journal of Criminal Law and Criminology, 64, June, 1973 pp. 141-162. Reprinted in Charles E. Reasons, The Criminologist: Crime and the Criminal, Pacific Palisades, California: Goodyear Publishing, 1974 pp. 19-50.

3 Don C. Gibbons and Peter Garabedian, "Conservative, Liberal and Radical Criminology: Some Trends and Observations" in Charles E. Reasons, Op cit., pp. 51-65.

4 Miller, Op. cit., p. 20.

5 Gibbons and Garabedian, Op. cit., pp. 52-59.

6 Miller, Op. cit., pp. 30-33.

7 Alvin W. Gouldner, "Anti-Minotaur: The Myth of the Value-Free Sociology", Social Problems, 9, No. 3 Winter, 1962. Reprinted in Irving Louis Horowitz (ed.), The New Sociology, New York: Oxford University Press, 1965.

8 William J. Chambliss, "Functional and Conflict Theories of Crime", Module 17: pp. 1-23 New York: MSS Modular Publications, 1973.

9 Ibid., p. 4.

10 Ibid., p. 9.

11 Talcott Parsons, The Social System, Glencoe, Ill.: The Free Press, 1951.

12 Robert K. Merton, Social Theory and Social Structures, Glencoe, Ill.: The Free Press, Revised and Enlarged Edition, 1957, pp. 131-160.

13 Ralph Dahrendorf, "Out of Utopia: Towards a Re-Orientation of Sociological Analysis," American Journal of Sociology, 64, No. 2 September, 1958.

14 Chambliss, Op. cit. pp. 17-23. See also William J. Chambliss and Robert D. Seidman, Law, Order, and Power, Reading, Mass: Addison-Wesley, 1971.

15 Richard Quinney, The Social Reality of Crime, Boston: Little, Brown, 1970; Critique of Legal Order, Boston: Little, Brown, 1974; Criminology, Boston: Little, Brown, 1975.

16 Ian Taylor, Paul Walton and Jock Young. The New Criminology, London: Routledge and Kegan Paul, 1973, and (eds.) Critical Criminology, London: Routledge and Kegan Paul, 1975.

17 Comapre Quinney, The Social Reality of Crime, Chapter 1 to Critique of Legal Order and Criminology, Chapters 1, 3 and 6.

18 Chambliss, Op cit., p. 4.

19 Note here, however, the utilization of traditional etiological theories in Quinney, The Social Reality of Crime, Chapters 7 and 8 and in his Criminology Chapter 6 when he posits the existence of age, sex, and race and class structures in American society which place its members "at risk" in the criminal labeling and defining process.

20 See e.g. Charles Reasons, "The 'Dope' on the Bureau of Narcotics in Maintaining the Criminal Approach to the Drug Problem" in Charles

Reasons, Op. cit., pp. 144-155, Howard S. Becker, Outsiders, New York; The Free Press, 1963; and Alfred R. Lindesmith, The Addict and the Law, Bloomington: Indiana University Press, 1965.

21 See e.g. Edwin M. Schur, "A Society of Frauds" and Gilbert Geis, "Deterring Corporate Crime" in Charles Reasons, Op.cit., pp. 239-259.

22 See e.g. David Sternberg, "The New Radical-Criminal Trials: A Step Toward A Class-For-Itself in American Proletariat" in Richard Quinney (ed.), Criminal Justice in America, Boston: Little, Brown, 1974, pp. 274-294.

23 See e.g. Vernon Fox, "Prisons: Reform or Rebellion?" and Lloyd Allen Weeks, "The Prison of Tomorrow" in Charles Reasons, Op. cit., pp. 388-413 and Robert Martinson, "The Age of Treatment: Some Implications of the Custody-Treatment Dimension" and Anthony Platt "The Triumph of Benevolence: The Origins of the Juvenile Justice System in the United States" in Richard Quinney (ed.) Criminal Justice in America, Boston: Little, Brown, 1974, pp. 322-339 and 356-389.

24 See e.g. William J. Chambliss, "A Sociological Analysis of the Law of Vagrancy", Edwin H. Sutherland, "The Diffusion of Sexual Psychopath Laws" and Howard S. Becker, "The Marihuana Tax Act" in Richard Quinney (ed.) Crime and Justice in Society, Boston: Little, Brown, 1969, pp. 56-68; 88-97 and 98-105 respectively.

25 Edward L. Thorndike, Animal Intelligence: Experimental Studies, New York: Macmillan, 1911. A parallel tradition of attack and criticism against Thorndike from field and cognitively oriented theorists goes back just as far (1898).

26 For Sutherland this was most evident in his early subscription to "Multiple Factor Theory" and showed rapid erosion in the 1930's as his commitment to systematic theory increased. His latter contributions in the 'Sutherland Papers' series show an evident influence of such theorists as Cooley, Thomas and Mead and also show a repudiation of biological and psychodynamic, especially psychoanalytic, theory along with a strong commitment to the position that criminal behavior, in common with other forms of behavior is learned.

27 Robert L. Burgess and Ronald L. Akers, "A Differential Association-Reinforcement Theory of Criminal Behavior", Social Problems, 14, No. 2 Fall, 1966, pp. 128-147.

28 Paulo Freire, Pedagogy of the Oppressed New York: Seabury Press, 1974.

29 Among behavioristically oriented theorists such as Burgess and Akers (in common with the earlier theorists, such as Thorndike) the learning process was approximately viewed as an intervening variable between experience in one instance and changes in behavior in another. While Sutherland did not stress symbolic social interaction and inter-subjectivity as a main context for learning to the extent that others have, he did seemingly view as equally important both the psychological mechanisms of learning and the social processes involved in learning.

30 In one sense the emergences of interactionist theory and social learning theory may be called an antecological trend within the larger synecological trend which has been synonymous with the Chicago school. In another sense, the distinction suggested by Park between social and sub-social types of ecological concerns serves

within the rubric of human ecology, to suggest a boundary between the subjectivism of interactionist theory and the anti-subjectivism of social learning theory. See in this regard Robert E. Park, "Human Ecology" American Journal of Sociology, 42 1936, pp. 1-5.

Prevention of Delinquency by Antistigmatization

F. X. Ribordy

Introduction

In spite of the combined efforts of thousands of experts over the last hundred years, no definitive treatment of the problem of criminality has been evolved. Such efforts have, generally speaking, tended rather to increase the problem than to diminish it. Must we therefore conclude that criminality is an uncontrollable social problem?

Criminologists, like other social scientists, go to enourmous pains to treat this illness in the social body; but the illness is one that cen be defined only in imprecise and relative terms and the resulting definition is closer to a value judgment than to a description of symptoms. In order to fight crime, therefore, we should ponder the definition rather than the offense or the offender, and this is the only way forward for this science that stagnates within the narrow framework of the traditional definition of crime. Criminology should, instead, move on towards a new definition, in which crime would no longer derive from the State for the purpose of Social control. Such a fresh definition can only be reached by a dialectical process that will end up by toppling the (present) system of justice. This will come about by means of a process of demonopolization, and by a universal and cumulative education in law beginning right from the first year of school.

Criminology is at present caught between two theoretical poles: positivism or functionalism on the one hand conflict theory on the other. Table #1 (Chambliss 1975) shows the basic differences between these two viewpoints. According to the conflict hypothesis, forming the good citizen means delivering him into the hands of the ruling class and instilling in him the feeling of guilt so dear to the professional clinism whose duty it is to control the deviant, to the priest as he tries to induce repentance, and to the judge who has to inflict punishment. Clearly then, what is required is to educate the common people to take an oppositional stance.

Table I

On the content and operation of the criminal law

	Functionalist Hypotheses	Conflict Hypotheses
1.	Acts are defined as criminal because they offend the moral beliefs of the members of the society.	Acts are defined as criminal because it is in the interests of the ruling class to so define them.
2.	Those who violate the criminal law will be punished according to the prevailing customs of the society.	Members of the ruling class will be able to violate the laws with impunity while members of the subject classes will be punished.
3.	Persons are labeled criminal because their behavior goes beyond the tolerance limits of the community.	Persons are labeled criminal because it is in the interests of the ruling class to so lable them, whether or not the behavior would be tolerated by "the society" at large.
4.	The low classes are more likely to be arrested for an convicted of crime because they commit more crimes.	The lower classes are more likely to be labeled criminal because the bourgeoisie's control of the state protects them from such stigmatization.
5.	As societies become more specialized in the division of labor, more and more laws will become restitutive rather than repressive (penal).	As capitalist societies industrialize and the gap between the bourgeoisie and the proletariat widens, penal law will expand in an effort to coerce the proletariat into submission.

Until now, law as taught in the schools has formed part of a general education in citizenship, the intention being to train the young to become citizens obedient to the rules.[1] Rather than forming citizens who are either submissive to, or opposed to the ruling class, such instruction could give each of them the chance to use the law as an instrument, just as the propertied class does. By knowing the law, the propertied class can commit crimes and evade punishment as research on white-collar crime and self-reported delinquence prove. In the same way, the stigmatic approach to delinquence prove. In the same way, the stigmatic approach to delinquency brings to light the differential selection that occurs at the point of entry into the criminal justice process.

If the general public were aware of its rights and of the laws, crime (i.e. the crime rate as measured statistically) would most certainly go up while at the same time the number of arrests and charges (i.e. the process of labelling and stigmatization) would go down, the reason being that individuals would be much more able to get around the monopolization that has taken place of the entire legal apparatus: they would make use of the existing system, as the big corporations, business men, and members of the crime syndicates do at present.

A widespread knowledge of the judicial process, along with an increase in the incidence of crime would doubtless lead to the congestion of the judicial system, for even if arrests were to decline, there would still be a sharp drop in the admission of guilt (the positivist criterion), and thus a lengthening of the proceedings.

Once the system was completely clogged up and was unable to exert its authority -- having lost all of its credibility in the eyes of the public -- it would retain only certain kinds of crimes that it could still manage to control, while declassifying the others. This would lead to a sharp drop in the incidence of crime and to a new definition of crime.

For this reason, after looking at the stigmatic approach to delinquency, we will take up the question of awareness and knowledge of the law amongst the general public and finally set out a program of decriminalization based on the teaching of law to all children attending primary school.

The Stigmatizational approach to delinquency

The labeling approach to juvenile delinquency may be contrasted with the epidemiological. In 1866 Tarde gave a warning to criminologists when he said that an individual becomes a criminal not only because he commits an act forbidden by law, but just as much by reason of society's reaction to the act. There is, indeed, a distinct difference between the causes of crime and the reasons for being taken into custody.

Studies done in America on this point in the last thirty years bring out the diversity of treatment undergone by individuals guilty of the same offense. At the present time, criminology places much more emphasis on the study of the process of choice and the differential selection that is practiced by the public and by the criminal justice system (police, courts, probation, and parole, etc.) than on the factors contributing to the commission of the act. But briefly, it is concerned with the status of criminals, rather than with their behavior. (Turk, 1969; MacNaughton Smith, 1968). Leblanc (1969, 1971) in his study of labeling and juvenile delinquency in Montreal set out to discover which young people are selected to go through the judicial process and what the criteria of selection are; for labeling is a selective process based on certain criteria, of which the most frequently referred to are race, social class, sex, attitude to authority, and previous criminal record.

The criminal justice system selects at all levels, sending out individuals into sub-systems with a regularity that has been studied by a great number of investigators whose results we partially review in what follows.

Police Labeling

Differential labeling as a function of socio-economic status was the subject of several studies prior to the sixties (Mitchell, 1957; Porterfield, 1946; Robinson, 1936; Schwartz, 1945; etc.). Such studies led experts to posit the hypothesis that the higher the person's economic status, the less likely he is to go through the criminal justice process, and the easier it is for him to make his way out of it rapidly. Such hypotheses have been confirmed by the work of Goldman (1963), Bodine (1964), McEachern and Bauzer (1967), Terry (1962, 1967), Cicourel (1968), Chapman (1968), Hardt (1968), Monahan (1968), Shannon (1963), Stephenson and Scarpitti (1968), and Leblanc (1971), Thus, there are two kinds of criteria that are mostly associated with labeling: social status (age, sex, socio-economic standing) and features of the act, (its nature, whether recidivist). All the same, the nature of the relationship with the police seems to be of prime importance, and as is evident from Bordua and Harris (1966), Guthrie, (1963), Piliavin and Briar (1964), Wattenberg and Buge (1963), and Wertham and Paliavin (1967), the last mentioned criterion appears to outweigh all others in the process of labeling. Others associate this subjective selection -- or this interaction - with the degree of bureaucracy obtained by the particular police force in its internal organization

(Chapman, 1968; Goldman, 1964; Sterling, 1962; Wilson, 1968).

The police system is truly the gate way leading into the criminal justice process: it chooses its clients in response to politically determined criteria, and is nothing more than an arm of the political system (Tardif, 1974). The choices the police make are merely tied in with other subsystems. A special case is represented by the example of the lower-class individual who joins the police as a means of acquiring status and, in order to avoid the risk of returning to his former status, adopts an attitude toward his former peer group that is even more rigid than that called for by his superiors. This situation tends to bring about an endless campaign of oppression directed at the disadvantaged class of society: it seems that those policemen who were once the victims of stigmatization, now stigmatize those whom they believe to be negatively marked. This hypothesis stems from the work of Reiss (1968, Despatis, 1972):

> All their victims were delinquents and all were members of the lower social stratum ... not one member of the middle or upper classes, white or black, was ever the target of the excessive use of force. It turns out that it is the members of the lower class who bear the brunt of police victimization... At least half the cases involve defiance of police authority (39%) or resisting arrest (%). Open defiance of police authority is what the policeman defines as his own authority and not necessarily his authority qua official (p. 1).

Thus according to this finding, members of the lower class are kept under by those of their own class who have gained superior status.

Judicial labeling

Studies dealing with judicial labeling are not so numerous as those dealing with police labeling; yet they reach the conclusion that here too there is a differential selection in operation, based on the socio-economic environment (Reiss and Rhodes, 1968; Cohen, 1963; Terry, 1967; Stephenson and Scarpitti, 1967; Cicourel, 1968; Lahman, 1965; Chapman, 1968; Naese, 1966; Gold, 1966).

There is a systematic bias stemming from a subjective notion of a delinquency - prone class. Such bias is easily explained in North America by the fact that the judge is chosen politically. According to Marchand (1973);

> Judges are not specially chosen on account of their ability but rather by reason of their political allegiance and as a reward for servicing rendered to the party in power. If it does happen that they are chosen from amongst the opposition, it is to get rid of an embarrassing opponent, or to open up a territory for a friend of authority (p. 79).

The research on sentencing (Hogarth, 1971; Hood, 1974; Smith and Blumberg, 1967) proves that judges come from rather wealthy middle class families. Being political appointees, they work under certain pressures and gear their decisions to their own needs (Nguyen, 1972). The decisions made by a judge reflect to a certain extent his socio-economic status, but differences in the severity of sentences handed out appear to be due mainly to the pressures of the moment, or their absence.

Judicial psychology and theories of symbolic interaction show that the court is the scene of a role play in which certain individuals have an advantage, and in which verbal intelligence, ease of expression, and even pedantry have an important place. (See the works of Libman and Emmanuel, 1974; Floriot, 1973; Laplante, 1973; Enzenberger, 1967; Tomeo, 1973).

All things considered then, the administration of justice is nothing but the expression of a class justice, giving maximal advantage to persons defined as members of the establishment, to those closest to the dominant or ruling class, which sets the rules in accordance with its own needs and interests.

It is a proven fact that the judiciary is a system, a machine, but one which does not simply survive by means of the cases regularly submitted to it; rather its livelihood depends on its sub-systems: a policeman will use his discretion and send home a young delinquent, knowing as he does that the youngster has a pretty good chance of being let off by the court. He will use his discretion in the same way to gun down a criminal out on parole (an index card on every prisoner about to be set free on parole is sent to the police services by the parole board), knowing that this is the one way to prevent recidivation. A judge will sentence a convicted person to a longer term of imprisonment, knowing that the sentence is always subject to remission, whether statutory or conditional. A report drawn up before sentencing by a probation officer, or a decision to discharge a convict submitted by an officer of the parole board, will depend on the ability of the members of the sub-system to deal with the case, far more than on the question of rehabilitation for the person under consideration.

Criminal statistics

It is generally recognized that a small number of crime categories account for the greater part of the crime statistics. In the United States, ten crime categories account for 51% of the crimes known by the police to have been committed, and these are without exception crimes against public order,[1] which can be considered as crimes without victims (Schur, 1965; Schur and Bedau, 1975). The majority of the crimes of this nature, are habitually committed by the class which is subject to control, i.e. the lower class. In the second place, the figures only reflect known or reported crimes but do not include what is commonly referred to as the dark figure. Now it is quite certain that for the major offences such as bank robbery and robbery with violence involving large sums of money, the figures show the true picture. For most of the others, however, including serious crimes, surveys carried out in the United States in which the victims of crimes have been questioned (see Hood and Sparks, 1970) reveal that only from one third to one half of the offences are reported, for this category.

The visibility of crimes seems to depend wholly on the extent to which they are recorded statistically, and the hidden economic crimes of the business or white collar world are those which have the least chances of appearing in statistics. (Sutherland, 1940; Kellens, 1968). The same applies to crimes committed by large bodies such as trusts, organizations, groups, and politicians (Barnett, 1975).

Statistics on crime are of no use in measuring its actual incidence; they form the image which it is considered desirable to convey to the public. Criminal activity is centered largely within the lower social strata, because the elite considers that only acts committed by members of the lower orders can be defined as criminal. In this way, crime directs the attention of the working class towards certain of its members and away from the exploitation to which it is subjected at the hands of capitalism and the economic system.

There can be no doubt but that the statistics reflect a certain picture of criminality sketched by the ruling class for the benefit of the general public in order to maintain their control and to create a feeling of guilt. All of which is easy to prove in the light of comparative studies that have been carried out in a number of countries: the clearest evidence comes from predictability studies (Robert, 1974; LeBlanc, 1974).

Congestion of the criminal justice system

In the report of the Katzenbach Commission (1968), the system of criminal justice is compared to an enourmous funnel ending up in a thin tube, in which many are called and few are chosen. The gap between the number of reported crimes and the number of arrests is considerable; it shows that the police are unable to deal effectively with infringements; moreover, it differs from one police force to another due to factors such as the numbers on the force, the tightness of their inner power structure, their degree of corruption, their technical equipment, their scientific knowledge, etc.

2,780,000 index crimes reported
727,000 arrests
177,000 formal
felony
complaints
160,000
sentences
63,000
to prison

Of the 727,000 arrests made by the police, only 177,000 formal charges ever reach the courts; these in turn give rise to 130,000 pleas of guilty and only 38,000 trials. Even with this selection process the courts are saturated and some have waiting lists as long as two years. To remedy this situation, more expeditious courts have been set up (small claims courts) the number of judges has been increased, law clinics have been instituted, and certain judges are able to handle 200 to 300 cases a day.

The criminal justice system relies essentially on the plea of guilty which in turn is based on the rule of the reasonable man (Ferracuti and Newman, 1971). As for mens rea it is based on criteria normally used by clinicians; it has no connection with actus reus (Guttman and Ravah, 1970): these criteria are the rules of moderation and adaptation, sociability, rationality, and reality.

Although essentially subjective, this rule remains in use, for it acts as a brake to prevent the saturation of the judicial apparatus. If those charged with an offence for the most part plead guilty (130,000 as opposed to 38,000), it is because their experience with the system teaches them that this is the easy way out. The practice of plea bargaining tends in the same direction, for arrangements and deals between the defence and the judge were brought in to avoid delays in reaching adjudication by means of a trial.

Cost analyses of the criminal justice system (Canada, Department of the Solicitor-General, 1971; Robert and Bombert, 1970; Robert and Godefroy, 1973) emphasize not only the enormous costs of the administration of justice but also the impossibility of getting rid of the plea of guilty within an anglo-saxon system.

Decriminalization

One way of lowering the incidence of crime is to limit the indexed felonies: if crime is nothing but a definition, then the ideal way to eradicate it is through decriminalization. Intermediate forms such as legitimation, or depenalization, can only be substitutes that keep a crime in existence a little while longer.

As we have seen, the definition of crime is purely relative, both from the social and the judicial points of view. In support of this, Szabo and Fattah (1969) cite as an example the ten crimes punished by stoning in hebraic law: idolatry, incitement to idolatry, making an offering to Moloch, magic calling up spirits, stubborn disobedience to parents, breaking the sabbath, blashphemy, ravishing the betrothed of another, misconduct of a girl as shown by the absence of evidence of virginity at the time of marriage. Of these ten crimes, nine are no longer considered as such, and the tenth, the ravishing of another's betrothed, though still valid, has a completely different meaning in the modern context. On the other hand, certain acts that are now considered to be criminal, such as infanticide, at one time were not. The relativity we find in time also applies to space: e.g. the frontier between two nations, states or even provinces, such as the one between Canada and the state of New York in the matter of abortion. Certain criminal acts can be committed only by certain groups (e.g. rape); other acts are committed universally, but the punishment is reserved for certain individuals.

If one accepts the rules of normal behaviour, a criminal act that is committed by the majority of the population must be considered as normal but the judicial apparatus pursues only some individuals, so as to inhibit the idea of a consensus in the minds of the population at large, and to provide them with a positive view of the effectiveness of the judicial system. An example of this was brought to my attention on the occasion of a visit to Brussels: the traffic is so heavy there and parking places so rare, that traffic flow is held up by excessive double parking, cars parked on sidewalks and in no-parking zones, etc. In doing this sort of thing most drivers don't feel any guilt, knowing that there are not enough policemen or auxiliaries to ticket all the offenders, and even if they could, they would be unable to track down those who did not pay their fines - for want of the necessary personnel. Such an operation would not, then, be worth while. The result is that with a limited force, and relying on 10% voluntary payment and catching a few odd offenders here and there, it is always possible to demonstrate that the authorities have the situation well in hand. The decriminalization of such violation of the highway code would certainly not solve the problem, but what would happen if the whole population found out how small were the risks involved in breaking the law?

Another example of the criminalization - decriminalization process is discussed in the research work of Ross, Campbell and Glass (1968/1970) on the introduction of the breathalyser in Connecticut and in England. At first when the appartus was introduced, the judicial authorities claimed complete success. They backed up their claim with traffic accident graphs that gave every indication of a crackdown, and yet, a few weeks later, an examination of the graph in which accidents were plotted against time showed that the curve was back to normal. According to similar research in Ontario it was found that the introduction of the breathalyser in December of 1969 had no effect at all on the graph. The biggest change came later when the amount of material damage requiring police notification was raised from \$100 to \$200. So that it can be said that criminalization, or the use of better detection methods for certain crimes, has no influence on the crime rate, while decriminalization produces more encouraging results.

Ideally, decriminalization should be resorted to when public opinion reaches a consensus on the relative innocuousness of a type of behaviour for society in general. What appears to happen in actual fact, however, is quite different: decriminalization does not come about until such times as those in power are confronted with the fact that the behaviour in question is common amongst the ruling class. Take for example the decriminalization of homosexuality in Canada, which took exactly the same course here as everywhere else, a course which conforms entirely to the one we have just outlined (Stravers, 1973); and it was the same for abortion - when wives of government ministers said they were for it, and stated openly that they had undergone such an operation themselves.

However, it is when a crime becomes general throughout the ruling class that decriminalization most frequently occurs: for when it does, the rulers can no longer make use of such behaviour as an instrument of class domination. Decriminalization may also follow when the subjugated class becomes aware of crimes being committed by members of the privileged class, or if the latter commit certain crimes but manage to avoid arrest and prosecution, or even deliberately allow themselves to be arrested with a view of congesting the judicial system.

<u>Popular awareness of and familiarity with the law</u>

Aubert, Eckoff and Sveri (1952), as well as Kutschinsky (1971), set up a distinction between <u>consciousness of the norm</u>, that is to say awareness of the fact that there exists a law governing behavior in a particular context, and knowledge of the norm, that is to say familiarity with the rule, or in other words, the quantity of information a person possesses with respect to the content of a given normative regulation. Consciousness of the norm must logically precede the knowledge of it, for it is impossible to imagine knowing something without knowing of its existence. In the learning process -- whether practical or academic -- one must first know that a fact exists before one can find out something about it. In his scheme for bringing jurisprudence to the people, Friedland (1974 a - b) would have them use as sources of information such legal "instruments" as advocate, legal clinic, information centre, library, computer, etc. But, how can ordinary people go and look for information about a rule if they are not aware that the rule exists?

To illustrate this point, let us consider the income tax law: since taxes are automatically deducted at source from wages, an individual who is unaware of the existence of the tax laws will accept such routine deductions without argument. If, through some source, he finds out that income tax claim forms exist, that the Department of National Revenue puts its staff at the disposal of taxpayers in order to help them to fill out their claim forms, that there are agencies where he can have them filled out for a fee, then the taxpayer will have gained both a consciousness and a knowledge of the tax laws. At the upper end of the scale we find the individual who has thoroughly mastered the law in question: having internalized it, he makes good use of its every loop hole. This example is a good illustration of the importance to the average citizen, of consciousness of the law, followed by knowledge of a particular provision. It is clear that someone who, unsuspectingly, and unaware, allows himself to be taxed automatically by officialdom, is going to pay a much higher amount of taxes, proportionately, than someone else who goes to a specialized agency, and more still than a person who himself knows the income tax law inside out. Consciousness is here seen simply as a precautionary measure, to guard against the inequities of a system where a minority in power decrees laws, rules, and norms in order to protect its own class interests.

Aubert et. al. (1952), Innstilling (1960), Aubert (1966), Shuyt and Ruys (1971), and Kutschinsky (1972) have done research on consciousness of the law and conclude that inter-personal communication has more influence on consciousness than on knowledge of the particular law itself. In the case of moral judgments Berkowitz and Walker (1967) show there is a slight tendency for certain people to be influenced in their opinions by a consciousness of the law. This investigation also showed, however, that simply knowing that the laws exist does not play as large a part in modifying the moral judgments a person makes, as the awareness of a consensus of opinion among his peers.

From a different standpoint, Kutschinksy's study of knowledge of the law highlights the ignorance of the law among the underprivileged social classes, and particularly among delinquents and criminals in prison. This serves to support the thesis that individuals labeled as criminal are not knowledgeable about the law.

By making the people at large consciously aware of the law, it will be possible to create a consensus, and, as a result, to instill a knowledge of the law. Moral behavior has been proved to be associated not so much with knowledge of the law as with "fear of the policeman", so that by providing instruction and information our aim should be to prevent arrest, labeling, and stigmatization, rather than to prevent the impulse to act.

Prevention of crime by antistigmatization

It has been accepted almost universally among criminologists that deviance

> is not a quality of the act the person commits, but rather a consequence of the application by others of rules and sanctions to an offender. The deviant is one to whom that label has successfully been applied; deviant behavior is people so labeled (Becker, 1963, p.9)

For a number of writers, including LeBlanc (1971) delinquency is not a particular phenomenon, but rather an epiphenomenon of adolescence: it is normal in the young of whatever social class or background. In spite of this, the label delinquent is more likely to be applied to youth from a lower class social background and, as we have seen from the stimatic approach to delinquency, middle class youths are much less likely to enter into the criminal justice process than those belonging to the working class. This is due not only to the values of the judges who apply the law in accordance with the criteria prevalent in the upper middle class of society to which they belong, but also to the differential labeling practised by the police, the creature of the bourgeois establishment. Another reason for this differential selection is to be found in the fact that, on the one hand, those who administer justice are provided with an instrument, the law, which they use, and abuse; while on the other hand, though we say that ignorance of the law is no excuse, yet it is beyond the capability of an accused person to conduct his own defence. Jurisprudence has become such a specialized instrument that it can be manipulated only by a few experts.

We believe that, in order to remedy this situation, there is a pressing need to make this instrument available to the people at large, by imbuing them with a consciousness of the law. Rather than try to teach them the formal aspect of legal norms, emphasis would be placed on general principles of justice and good sense. Thus, the law would come alive instead of being shrouded in dry-as-dust formality. Quite a large number of conflicts would be resolved more appropriately at the level of consciousness than that of knowledge, on the human plane, rather than on that of the experts. Indeed, at the level of consciousness, the law has no need of experts: the parties to the dispute can discuss the matter in front of an impartial third party and an amicable settlement is arrived at. That is all that is needed. The tribunal would thus become more human than our hierarchic, bureaucratic, and solemn law-courts. Such a tribunal would not be above the level of the layman, it would be accessible, using a language devoid of all specialized jargon, and protocol would be reduced to the uttermost limit. In such a system of adjudication there would be a tendency by reason of its rather loose structure, for punishment to be replaced by compromise.

The teaching of law in the schools was already started in the city of Winchester in 1961, and after that in several American cities. Later it was taken up and developed by the Canadian Society of Criminology (McGrath, 1964, 1973). Such teaching is recommended by the Commission on Law Reform in Canada (1974-75) and also by the Canadian Police Chiefs' association (Winnipeg Congress, 1974). All such measures are aimed at producing the traditional good citizen, who conforms to established rules of conduct, and submits to the laws as he is portrayed by McGrath (see the criticism in Trepanier, 1974) and in the report of the Canadian Commission on law reform:

> If shared morality is part of what holds society together, as many argue, then law reform must take into account, articulate, and help to shape those common values underlying the law. Upholding them, expressing them, developing them -- this in the ultimate analysis is what the law reforms are all about (p.8)

These points of view, based on positivist theories, are rejected by modern theorists in the fields of sociology of law and criminology (Chamblis, 1973; Quinney, 1974; Taylor et. al., 1973; de Sousa Santos, 1973). Similarly, while positivists assume a model of society in which law constitutes a shield of defence for the moral values of its members, such hypotheses are strenuously opposed by models of conflict, in which law is regarded as mirroring the values, customs and beliefs of the dominating class, the object being to oppress the working class. The positivist teaching referred to aims at only one thing, to submit the young to the values, rules, and norms of authority, and this is why all the experiments tried so far have been failures. These young people are no fools! They want to have no part in a programme designed to make them into creatures of the central power, submissive, and under control.

From the point of view of conflict theory, the teaching of law in the schools has a quite different purpose, namely to make the instruments of authority available to the student, that is, to enable him to engage in equal combat with those who up to now monopolized the field. There is nothing really revolutionary about this; the idea is simply to give back into the hands of the common people an instrument which belongs to them, but which jurists and legislators have made so specialized that they have made it into an instrument for the use of experts only. It is true that a movement is afoot to demystify the law: an every growing number of books are appearing in the bookstores on getting to know the law, as well as some do-it-yourself type of literature. Yet these books are still too specialized, they are written by jurists for the benefit of those who already have some training, but with no thought for what previous knowledge the common man brings to the task of understanding.

That is why it seems necessary to teach the science of law right from the first year of primary school. Thereby a major portion of juvenile delinquency could be prevented by giving the young person a legitimate means of defense against labeling: after all, it shouldn't be difficult to teach him what the average policeman knows. It is to be hoped that in the not too distant future every citizen will be educated in the law, at least so as to enable him to read and understand legal texts, and so to guard himself against any infringement of his rights.

Research Proposal

Piaget's researches on child development (1932, 1969) have shown that the child acquires a moral sense at an early age, around eight years, after which comes a sensitivity to law; as early as age ten, he is capable of acquiring specific legal knowledge. On the other hand, research done in Europe by the K.O.L. team (Knowledge and Opinion about Law) has shown that the general public is almost totally ignorant about law and judicial matters. Behind this lack of specific knowledge, however, one does catch from time to time a glimpse of a moral and a legal consciousness, both of which do exist, though they may vary from one sector to another of the population.

We propose, therefore, to calculate the degree to which a knowledge and a consciousness of the law exists within a sample of the school population of Sudbury, a small mining city of 100,000 inhabitants in mid-northern Ontario. Because of its cultural diversity, Sudbury can be viewed as a sort of microcosm of Canada: indeed, ethnically, one third of the population is of French origin, another third is English, and the rest is a melting pot of 35 different ethnic groups. The sample will cover the whole school population from age ten (grade five) to adults attending continuing education classes at Laurentian University. The questionnaire to be used in the survey will be based on the K.O.L. research, as well as on the on going study by Tomeo (1975) of a secondary school student population in Italy.

The purpose of our proposed survey is to measure first the moral consciousness, then the legal consciousness and knowledge of the school population, and to relate these findings to the customary objective variables as well as to a number of criteria for which numerical scales have been devised by Adorno (1950; submissiveness, conventionality, agressivity), Leonardi (1968; opinion of the laws), and Tomeo (1975; sanctions), for attitudes toward the law can not really be understood by means of the usual factural variables such as age, sex, ethnicity, religion etc. (Podgorecki, 1974).

Consequent upon the proposed investigation, the teaching of law can be introduced into the schools beginning in Grade I (and not, as for civics, at the secondary level). The programme will be concerned mainly with consciousness of law, and will be strictly positive; it is rights, and not prohibitions that must be taught, for a negative approach would simply magnify the barrier of shyness that separates the child from the adult in authority. The programme of instruction will start at Grade I, and will be implemented in each succeeding grade. It will therefore have to be cumulative, dynamic, and flexible, so as to conform to the numerous transformations to which the law is subject. Right from the first grade, an important task for the educator will be to have the young student internalize this aspect of temporal relativity, for what was true of the law yesterday is no longer true today. Books, pamphlets, documents, films, all will have to be constructed in such a manner that they can be altered as required when used in school workshops in the various localities.

In view of the need to demonopolize and deprofessionalize the law, the actual instruction will be given by regular school teachers, rather than by policemen or lawyers as tends to be the practice. In the first place, the latter have no pedagogical training; moreover, the training a policeman does receive is based primarily on repression, and if programmes of instruction in law implemented by policemen have repeatedly fallen through, this is due first and foremost to the inquisitorial compulsion that is part of the policeman's personality.

This school programme, as has been said repeatedly should not aim at producing the good law-abiding citizen, but first of all, at developing both a consciousness and a knowledge of the law that will enable the individual to defend himself against any usurpation of his rights by those who have the monopoly of the law. Secondly, it should provide the individual with the basic knowledge he needs in order to understand formal texts and reports, so that, when it come to litigation, or signing a contract, he may be capable of examining the contents of documents without help.

Popularization of the law, then, is designed to counteract narrow professionalism, jargon, obscurantism, and esoterism. There must be a retooling of the law, and it must be put at the disposal of all, for it belongs to the population at large and not to the experts. Finally one may ask how commissions of enquiry, ministries, organizations for law reform, the laws, justice, how can they all count on the support of the citizenry, if the latter show evidence of an utter and complete ignorance of the very foundations of juridical science? Even with the best will in the world, there can be no reform in the future, as long as the people are persistently kept in ignorance.

References

Adorno, T.S. et al. The Authoritarian Personality. New York, Harper & Row., 1950.

Aubert, V., Some social Functions of Legislation, Acta Sociologica, Vol. 10, 1966, pp. 98-120.

Aubert, V., Eckhoff, T., Sverick, En lov i søkelyset. Sosialpsykologisk underskelse av den norske hushjelplov. Akademisk Forlag, 1952.

Barnett, A.N., On the Unsuitability of Crime Statistics for Sociological Explanations of Crime. Criminology made in Canada, Vol. 2, no 2, 1975, pp. 3-11.

Berkowitz, L., Walker, N., Laws and moral Judgments, 30, 1967, pp. 410-422.

Bodine, G.E., Factors related to Police Disposition of Juvenile Offenders. 59th Annual Meeting of the American Sociological Association, Montréal, 1964.

Bordua, D.L., Harris, J.W., Police Decision Making with Juveniles. Madison, Midwest Sociological Society, 1966.

Chambliss, W.J., Functional and Conflict Theories of Crime, New York, MSS Modular Publications, Module 17, 1973, pp. 1-23.

Chapman, D., Sociology and the Stereotype of the Criminal, Toronto, Tavistock, 1968.

Ciale, J., Témognages. Le comité sénatorial permanent des affaires juridiques et constitutionnelles, Ottawa, Information Canada, 1972.

Cicourel, A., The Organization of Juvenile Justice, New York, Wiley, 1968.

Cohen, Y., Criteria for the Probation Officer's Recommendations to the Juvenile Court Judge, Crime and Delinquency, Vol. 7, no 2, 1963, pp. 269-280.

Commission de réforme du droit du Canada, Un reflet fidèle, 1973-1974, Ottawa, Information Canada.

Canada, Ministère du Solliciteur Général, Le coût de l'administration de la justice et de la criminalité, Ottawa, Information Canada, 1971.

De Sousa Santos, B., La loi contre la loi, Esprit, No 708, 1973, pp. 67-84.

Despatis, M.A., La stigmatisation; Rapport inédit présenté au Département de Criminologie, Université de'Ottawa, 1972.

Enzenberger, H.M., Politique et crime, Paris, Gallimard, 1967.

Ferracuti, F., Newman, G., Perceptions clinique et psychologique de la déviance, Strasbourg, Conseil de l'Europe, 11 novembre 1971.

Floriot R., Préface: Vous et la loi, Paris, Laffont/Centurion, 1973.

Friedland, M.L., Access to the Law, Gazette, Vol. VIII, No 2, June 1974.

Friedland, M.L., Making Law available to the people, The Globe and Mail, Monday, February 11, 1974, p. 7.

Gold, M., Undetected Delinquent Behavior, Journal of Research in Crime and Delinquency, Vol. 3, No 1, 1966, pp. 27-47.

Goldman, N., The differential Selection of Juvenile Offenders for Appearance in Court, New York, N.C.C.D., 1963.

Goldman, N., The Disposition of Juvenile Arrests by Urban Police, in E.W. Burgess and D.J. Bogue (eds.) Contributions to Urban Sociology, Chicago, University of Chicago Press, 1964, pp. 577-591.

Guthrie, C.A., Law Enforcement and the Juvenile: A Study of Police Interaction with Juveniles. Los Angeles (Cal.), Université of Southern California, thèse de doctorat inédite, 1963.

Guttman, L., Ravah, G., Offense Classification in two Dimensional Space, Israel Studies in Criminology, Vol. 1, 1970, pp. 35-76.

Hardt, R.H., Delinquency and Social Class: Bad Kids or Good Cops, in I. Deutscher and E. Thompson (ed.) Among the People: Encounters with the Poor, New York, Basic Books, 1968, pp. 132-146.

Hogarth, J., Sentencing as a Human Process, Toronto, Press, 1971.

Hood, R.G., Sentencing in Magistrates' Courts, London, Stevens, 1974.

Hood, R., Sparks, R., La délinquance, Paris, Hachette, Coll. L'Univers des Connaissances, 1970.

Illich, I., La convivialité, Paris, Seuil, 1973.

Innstilling, Til lov om arbeidsvilkar for hushjelp m. fl. fra. Hushjelplov-Komiteen oppnevnt ved kgl. res. av. 8 Oktober, 1954, Oslo, Kommunal-og arbeidsdepartmentet, 1960.

Katzenback, N. de B., The Challenge of Crime in a Free Society, New York, Avon Books, 1968.

Kellens, G., Du crime en col blanc au délit de chevalier. Annales de la Faculté de Droit de Liège, 1968, pp. 106-107.

Krisberg, B., Crime and Privilege: Toward a New Criminology, Englewood Cliffs, Prentice-Hall, Coll. Spectrum Books, 1975.

Kutschinsky B., La perceptionde la déviance: Apercu des recherches empiriques. 9e Conference des directeurs d'Instituts de recherches criminologiques, Strasbourg, 12 novembre 1971.

Laplante, L., Recherchée justice, Montréal, Ferron,

LeBlanc, M., Délinquance juvénile: perspective épidémiologique et stigmatique. Universite de Montréal, Thèse de doctorat inédite, 1969.

LeBlanc, M., La réaction sociale à la déviance juvénile: une analyse stigmatique, Acta Criminologica, Vol. IV, 1971, pp. 114-191.

Leonardi, F., Il cittadino e la giustizia, Padova, Marsilio, 1968.

Libman, C., Emmanuel, H., Justice impossible, Paris, Laffont, 1974.

Lohman, J.D., et al., The Handling of Juveniles from offences to Disposition, Berkeley, (Cal.), University of California Press, 1965.

MacNaughton-Smith, P., Toward (or away from) an Empiric Theory of Crime and Delinquency, Vol. 5, No 2, 1968, pp. 189-198.

McEachern, A.W., Bauzer, R., Factors related to Dispositions of Juvenile Police Contacts, in W.W. Klein and B.G. Myerhoff (eds.) Juvenile Gangs in Context: Theory, Research and Action, New York, Prentice-Hall, 1967, pp. 148-161.

McGrath, W.T., Youth and the Law, Toronto, Gage Educational Publishing, 1964, 1973.

Marchand, P.E., La loi et vos droits, Montréal, Editions de l'Homme, 1973.

Mitchell, G.W., The Youth Bureau: A Sociological Study, Detroit (Mich.), Wayne State University Thèse de maîtrise inédite, 1957.

Naese, B., Measuring Juvenile Delinquency in Hamilton, Revue Canadienne de Criminologie, Vol. 8, No 2, 1966, pp. 133-146.

Nguyen, H., La réaction sociale a la déviance: les définisseurs de déviance, Montréal, Centre International de Criminologie Comparée, 1972.

Piaget, J., Le judgement moral chez l'enfant, Paris, P.U.F., 1969.

Piliavin, I., Briar, S., Police Encounters with Juveniles, American Journal of Sociology, Vol. 70, no 2, 1964, pp. 206-214.

Podgorecki, A., Law and Justice: Central Concepts and Issues. World Congress VIII, Monday August 19, 1974.

Prus, R.C., Revocation related Decision-Making by the Parole Agent: A Labelling Approach, The University of Iowa, Thèse inédite.

Quinney, R., (ed.), Criminal Justice in America, Boston, Little Brown, 1974.

Reiss, A.J., Police Brutality - Answer to Key Wuestions, Trans-Action Magazine, St. Louis, Missouri, July-August 1968.

Reiss, A.J., Rhodes, A.L., A Socio-psychological Study of Conforming and Deviating Behaviour among Adolescents, Washington, D.C., U.S. Government Printing Office, 1958. Office of Education.

Robert, P., L'impact économique et social du phénomène criminel, Paris, S.E.P.C., 1974.

Robert, P., Bombert, J.P., Le coût du crime en France, Paris, S.E.P.C. ronéo, 1970.

Robert, P., Godefroy, T., Le coût du crime en France pendant les années 1970-1971, Paris, S.E.P.C., roneo, 1973.

Robinson, S.M., Can Delinquency by Measured? New York, Columbia University Press, 1936.

Ross, H.C., Campbell, D.T., Glass, C.V., Determining the Social Effects of a Legal Reform, in S.S. Nagel (ed.) Law and Social Change, Beverly Hills, Sage, 1970, pp. 15-31.

Schur, E.M., Crime Without Victims, Englewood Cliffs, Prentice-Hall, 1965.

Schur, E.M., Bedau, H.A., Victimless Crimes: Two sides of a Controversy, Englewood-Cliffs, Prentice-Hall, Coll. Spectrum Books, 1975.

Shuyt, L.J.M., Ruys, J.C.M., Attitudes toward New Socio-economic Legislation. A before-after Study of the Normative Effects of the Introduction of Tax Added Value (TVA), Leiden, Holland, Faculty of Law, State University of Leiden, 1971.

Schwartz, E.E., A Community Experiment in the Measurement in Juvenile Delinquency, Yearbook of the National Probation Association, 1945, pp. 156-181.

Smith, A.B., Blumberg, A., The Problem of Objectivity in Judicial Decision-Making, Social Forces, No 46, 1967, pp. 96-105.

Stephenson, R.M., Scarpitti, F.R., Negro-White Differentials and Delinquency, Journal of Research in Crime and Delinquency, Vol. 5, No 2, 1968, pp. 122-134.

Sterling, J.W., The Juvenile Offender from Community to Court: Two Stages of Decision, Chicago, Ill. Illinois Academy of Criminology, 1962.

Straver, C., Les homosexuels aux Pays-Bas, in De Batselier S. et Ross H.L., Les minorités homosexuelles, Gembloux, Duculot, 1973, pp. 151-208.

Sutherland, E.H., White Collar Criminality, American Sociological Review, 1940, p. 1.

Szabo, D., (ed.), La criminalité urbaine et la crise de l'administration de la justice, Montréal, Les Presses of l'Université de Montréal, 1973.

Szabo, D., Fattah, E.A., Criminologie, Encyclopédie médico-chirurgicale, 37906, 1969.

Tarde, G., La criminalité comparée, Paris, Alcan, 1886.

Tardif, G., Police et politique au Québec, Montéal, L'Aurore, 1974.

Taylor, I., et al., The New Criminology, London Routledge and Kegan, 1973.

Terry, R.M., Criteria Utilized by the Police in the Screening of Juvenile Offenders, Milwaukee, Wisconsin, University of Wisconsin, Thèse de maîtrise inédite, 1962.

Terry, R.M., Discrimination in the Handling of Juvenile Offenders by Social Control Agencies, Journal of Research in Crime and Delinquency, Vol. 4, no 2, 1967, pp. 218-231.

Tomeo, V., Il guidice sullo schermo, Roma, Laterza, 1973.

Tomo, V., Cerutti, P.G., Biancardi, R., Giustizia, norma e sanzione nell' atteggiamento degli adolescenti, Una ricerca pilota, Sociologia del diritto (sous-presse), 1975.

Trépanier, J., Youth and the Law (second Edition by W.T. McGrath) Revue Canadienne de Criminologie, Vol. 16, no 1, 1974, pp. 99-101.

Turk, A., Criminality and Legal Order, Chicago Rand McNally, 1969.

Wattenberg, W.W., Buge, N., The Effectiveness of the Police Youth Bureau, Journal of Criminal Law, Criminology and Police Sciences, Vol. 54, No. 3, 1963, pp. 470-475.

Werthman, C., Piliavin, I., Gang Mambers and the Police, in D.C. Bordua (ed.), The Police: Six Sociological Studies, New York, Wiley, 1967, pp. 56-99.

Wilson, J.Q., The Police and the Delinquent in Two Cities, in S.W. Wheeler (ed.), Controlling Delinquents, New York, Wiley, 1968, pp. 9-31.

The Relationship Between Lawyers and Their Clients

Ibtihaj Arafat and Kathleen McCahery

The successful administration of justice depends upon, among other things, the quality of legal service and the conditions under which this legal service is available to those who need it. According to Herbert Jacob (1972:60), the availability of legal service is "partly a matter of how lawyers are perceived by the public." Many researchers have pointed out that the general public is not well informed about either the availability of legal services or how to find legal assistance (Blaustein and Porter, 1954; Brownell, 1951; Buckner, 1961; Hunting and Neuwirth, 1962). As a result, many legal problems go unresolved even though the individuals involved may be able to afford legal services (Cheatham, 1963; Christenson, 1970; Fox, Jr., 1965).

The problems facing clients who can pay for legal services are only multiplied for those who cannot afford to pay. Robert Lefcourt (1971:30) estimates that each year approximately 60% of all defendants are financially unable to afford counsel. The major source of legal assistance for the indigent is the Legal Aid Society. According to a Legal Aid Society publication entitled Lawyer For The Poor, the Legal Aid Society "exists to make sure that, as the poor man stands there (before the court), he is represented by the best available legal counsel (1966:13)."

One of the most persistent controversies dealing with the legal profession centers around the question of the effectiveness of a Legal Aid or assigned lawyer versus a privately retained counsel. Some critics of the American system of supplying legal help to the indigent argue that the Legal Aid defense is inadequate when compared to the defense offered by private attorneys (Blumberg, 1973; Casper, 1972; Lefcourt, 1971;

Oaks and Lehman, 1973). The New York Times (1968:38) listed some of the criticisms advanced by the private attorneys against Legal Aid: a) it was deliberately turning away poor people; b) Legal Aid lawyers failed to fulfill the proper role of defense attorney; c) Legal Aid allowed known felons to plea bargain; d) Legal Aid lawyers lacked concern for the rights of the defendant.

On the other hand, the Legal Aid Society claims that its lawyers perform equally as well as the private attorneys. A report presented by the American Bar Foundation, including interviews with district attorneys and judges, showed the following:

> "All the judges and district attorneys interviewed in New York and Queens counties were of the opinion that the representation offered indigent defendants by the Legal Aid Society was equal to that offered by privately retained counsel and that the work and professional performance of the Society's lawyers were on a par with that of the district attorneys. Indeed, in several instances, the work of the Society's lawyers was rated higher than that of usually retained counsel or the district attorney's office, and in no instances did any of the respondents find the work of the society's lawyers below the level of the district attorney or average retained counsel (Silverstein, 1965:533)."

While this controversy has been discussed within the legal profession for many years, there has not been a similar effort to explore this controversy as it is viewed by the general public. The legal profession, in the eyes of the layman, is still surrounded by a mystic of technicalities that is difficult for him to understand. The layman, as a client, must lean heavily on the relationship he has with his lawyer in order to understand his position in the eyes of the law. It becomes necessary, then, to delve more deeply into the nature of the lawyer-client relationship in order to discover the basis for the general public's evaluation of the legal services they are receiving.

The purpose of this study is to ascertain the affect of ethnicity, age, sex, income and type of lawyer (assigned or privately retained) upon the relationship that exists between a lawyer and client. This relationship is defined by such variables as: client satisfaction with the defense presented on his behalf as well as the verdict rendered; degree of confidence the client has in his lawyer; client satisfaction that there has been adequate communication between himself and his lawyer; and, finally, the complaints clients have regarding the way their case was handled by their lawyers.

Methods and Procedures

The objective of the researchers in this study is to explore the relationship between lawyers and their clients. Lawyers were categorized as private (personally chosen and retained by the client) or public (assigned to the respondent, such as Legal Aid). Age, sex, income, race, religion, and type of attorney (private or public) used by the respondent were employed as independent variables. Dependent variables included the respondent's satisfaction with his lawyer's defense and the results of his case; his opinion of the lawyer's fee; whether or not he had confidence in his lawyer; the adequacy of communication between attorney and client; any complaints regarding the manner in which his defense was handled; attitude toward the performance of Legal Aid lawyers; and personal preference for type of lawyer.

800 self-administered questionnaires were distributed at different locations in the New York Metropolitan area, of which 610 usable questionnaires were returned. The minimum age for respondents was 17 years, the rationale being that we wanted to avoid juveniles and their problems with their attorneys.

The questionnaire included 22 questions. The first five questions covered demographic characteristics of the respondents. Question 6 was a key question as it asked whether the respondent had ever been a client of a lawyer. All those who responded negatively to this question were eliminated from the study. This question was followed by one which asked about the reasons for seeking the services of an attorney. 11 options were given and the respondents were asked to indicate the reasons which applied to their case(s) in a numerical order. Question 8 asked whether the respondent's lawyer was public or private. The next question asked whether the lawyer was personally retained by the respondent, assigned by the court, or chosen in some other way, which the respondent was asked to specify. Question 10 inquired into the factors that influenced the choice of a public or private lawyer. The next four questions (11 through 14) dealt with the respondent's degree of satisfaction with his lawyer's defense and with the results of his case. Question 15 asked the respondent whether or not he had confidence in his attorney and asked him to state why or why not. The next three questions (16-18) asked for the respondent's opinion of his lawyer's fee, and for any complaints he had with regard to the way his case was handled by his public or private attorney. Question 19 was designed to discover the respondent's knowledge of of the legal system and asked him where he would go to lodge a complaint against his lawyer. The following two questions (20 and 20B) asked the respondent about the adequacy of communication between himself and his (public or private) attorney. Question 21 asked the respondent to classify a Legal Aid lawyer as good, fair, poor, or other (specify). The last question asked whether the respondent would choose a personally retained lawyer or a Legal Aid attorney if he had a choice, and why.

The computer was used in the tabulations and calculations. In the analysis of the data the chi-square test was used to show the degree of significance of the relationships; the contingency coefficient was used to test the strength of the relationships, and percentages were used by facilitate comparisons.

Analysis and Discussion

Of the 610 respondents used in this study, 34.4 percent stated that they had used a public lawyer, while 65.6 percent had used a privately retained lawyer. The ethnic structure of the sample showed that 48.6 percent were White, 35.7 percent were Black, and 15.7 percent were Hispanic. Religious affiliation of the respondents showed that 30.8 percent were Protestants, 17.4 percent Catholics, 5.6 percent Jewish, and 46.2 percent stated no preference or religious affiliation. Of the 610 respondents, 51.8 percent were between 17-29 years old, 18.7 percent were between 30-39 years old, 14.4 percent were between 40-49 years old, and 15.1 percent were 50 years of age or older. The income distribution showed that 29.8 percent earned less than $5,000, 34.2 percent earned between $5,000-$9,999, 17 percent earned between $10,000-$14,999, 9.2 percent earned between $15,000-$19,999, and 9.8 percent earned $20,000 or more.

Of the respondents, 58 percent of the sample were males and 42 percent were females. In relation to sex, however, no significant differences were found to exist between the sexes except on the following four grounds: females were more satisfied than males with both 1) the results of their case and 2) the efforts put forth in their behalf by their public lawyer (P<.001); 3) three times as many males as females stated that the legal fee was relatively cheap, which can imply one of two things: either a) the male is in a higher income bracket than the female and can better absorb the cost of his defense, or b) the female is more economically oriented than the male in evaluating the cost of legal services (P<.06); 4) almost four times as many males as females felt that a legal aid lawyer would be the worst source for one's legal defense (P<.01).

The respondents were asked to give their reasons for going to a lawyer. The results, in order of frequency of choice, yielded the following distribution in percent of the total cases:

Reasons for Legal Services	Distribution % of Total	% Handled By Public Lawyer	% Handled By Private Lawyer
1. Car and other forms of accidents	26.1	7.5	18.6
2. Marital problems	19.7	2.9	16.8
3. Criminal procedures	16.2	9.9	6.3
4. Wills or inheritance	11.7	1.0	10.7
5. Landlord complaints	10.7	9.0	1.7
6. Immigration procedures	6.9	3.0	3.9
7. Other reasons	4.8	0.6	4.2
8. Lawsuits	3.9	0.6	3.3

As can be seen from the above distribution, most of the legal services sought by clients are the type that do not necessarily entail courtroom appearances. Such legal services as drawing wills, lawsuits, etc. represent, by far, the more numerous type of lawyer-client relationship and yet they

As can be seen from the above distribution, most of the legal services sought by clients are the type that do not necessarily entail courtroom appearances. Such legal services as drawing wills, lawsuits, etc. represent, by far, the more numerous type of lawyer-client relationship and yet they involve, for the layman, the least understood areas of legal technicalities. The general image of the lawyer is based on the stereotype of courtroom performance, while the behind-the-scenes manipulation of legal technicalities remains in the realm of the mystic of law. Except for criminal procedures and landlord complaints, the type of lawyer most often used is a privately retained counsel. The public lawyer or legal aid counsel carries the main burden for criminal defense and landlord complaints. As Lefcourt (1971:134) points out, the increase in the use of public lawyers for civil cases was an outgrowth of the Economic Opportunity Act and the Criminal Justice Act of 1964 which provided federal funding for the establishment of neighborhood legal services for the poor. Of the reasons listed above, one of the more dominant problems of the poor is the tenant-landlord relationship. The arrival of neighborhood legal services offered an outlet for the indigent tenant to find a legal solution to improve his living conditions.

The respondents were also asked to list those factors which had an influence on their choice of lawyer. The results, in percent of the total, indicated that 45.4 percent chose their lawyer primarily on the basis of recommendations by friends and/or other professionals. Brownell's (1951) research found that only a handful of people were aware that a legal referal service exists in many large cities to recommend those lawyers affiliated with the local bar association. This problem is aggravated partly by the fact that the legal profession considers it unethical for any lawyer to advertise his services. Hence the mainstay rests with a "word-of-mouth" type of informal referal. The consideration of the question of legal fees was the next main factor for 30.9 percent of the respondents. This question is of paramount importance to the legal consumer who has no way to estimate what the possible cost of any given legal service may be. There is a tendency, as Buckner (1961) reports, for the prospective client to expect that legal fees will be exorbitant. This, in effect, keeps many people from seeking legal advice under the erroneous idea that they may not be able to afford it. As for the remaining factors that influenced an individual's choice of lawyer, ethnicity of the lawyer accounted for 9.7 percent, sex accounted for 6.9 percent, age accounted for 4.7 percent, and religion had the weakest influence since only 2.4 percent were influenced by this factor.

Table I shows the results of the correlation between the independent variables of age, ethnicity, religion, and income with the major questions the researchers have used as dependent variables. Items 1 and 2 indicate the degree of satisfaction the respondents had with the results of their case depending upon the type of lawyer - public lawyer versus private attorney. For those respondents who were represented by a public lawyer such as a legal aid counsel, no significant difference was found to exist by age (Contingency Coefficient "CC" value .122). Ethnicity showed a very high significant difference ($P<.001$, CC .245), religion showed the next highest significance ($P<.05$, CC .195), and income showed the least significance ($P<.06$, CC .212). When the respondents were asked to specify the reasons for the satisfaction or dissatisfaction with the results of their case, age, ethnicity and religion showed a similar distribution, while income showed a different distribution.

Almost 52 percent of the respondents by age, ethnicity, and religion indicated that the main source of satisfaction was due to receiving a verdict in their favor. The income group does not differ radically on this point - 50.8 percent were satisfied because of a favorable verdict. The main reasons given for the dissatisfaction with the results of their case by age, ethnicity and religion showed that 22.1 percent were dissatisfied primarily because they received an unfavorable verdict, 13 percent were dissatisfied because they felt that their lawyer was inadequate, while another 13 percent gave reasons that were too individualized and numerous to report. In comparison, the income group showed a slightly higher level of dissatisfaction based on receiving an unfavorable verdict (27.9 percent). By income, only 4.9 percent showed their dissatisfaction by evaluating their lawyer as inadequate, while a higher percentage, 16.4 percent, had individualized reasons for their dissatisfaction.

For those respondents who were represented by a privately retained counsel, income showed the highest significant difference ($P<.001$, CC .244) wherein the higher the income level, the greater the satisfaction with the results of their case. Age, ethnicity, and religion, however, had a similar affect upon the degree of satisfaction ($P<.06$). The reasons given to explain the degree of satisfaction with the outcome of their case showed a similar distribution on all the variables. Only two reasons were given: a) approximately 81 percent were satisfied because they received a favorable verdict, while b) approximately 19 percent were dissatisfied because the verdict was unfavorable.

The above results point out the importance of the end product in the client's degree of satisfaction or dissatisfaction with his lawyer. Those respondents with private attorneys were concerned only with their lawyer's ability to perform on their behalf. It is only in the realm of the public attorney that the reasons for the degree of satisfaction go beyond the verdict to consider the lawyer per se. As was previously noted, the public lawyer was involved primarily in criminal proceedings and tenant-landlord complaints and this, in comparison to the basically civil nature of the cases handled by private lawyers, places the client more in the traditional role of defendant. In this regard, the client of a public lawyer has more at stake and less control over the situation. Many researchers, such as Carlin (1962), Handler (1967), and Smigel (1964) have pointed out that the practice of civil law entails basically a business office type of operation wherein the lawyer is trying to effect the best possible outcome for his client. This outcome often takes the form of a compromise followed by an out-of-court settlement. In criminal proceedings, this is not the case. According to Casper's (1972:109) research, those defendants represented by a public counsel tend to feel that their lawyer is not working with their best interests at heart. The clients identify their public lawyer as being one of "them" meaning that they see their lawyer as siding with the courts and prosecutor. This idea is reinforced by Blumberg's (1973:81) research wherein he tried to ascertain at what stage in the lawyer-client relationship the question of the type of plea and/or plea bargaining was raised. It was found that almost 50 percent of the legal aid lawyers suggested how his client should plea at the initial stage or at the first meeting, even before the particulars of the case were known. This is compared to only 34 percent of the private attorneys who raised any discussion of the possible plea at the first meeting. The results of this present research can be interpreted as lending support to Blumberg's findings. Only those respondents who were represented by a public attorney felt the need to blame their lawyer for the outcome of their case. Although only 4.9 percent of the income group found their public lawyer inadequate, by introspection it can be seen that 100 percent of this group fell in the income bracket of $5,000 or less.

Items 3 and 4 show the results of the respondents' degree of satisfaction with the type of defense rendered by their public and private lawyers. For those defended by a public or legal aid lawyer, a very high significant relationship was found to exist between the ethnic background of the respondent and his degree of satisfaction ($P<.001$, CC .289). The Hispanic respondents showed a very high degree of satisfaction, while the Black respondents stated a very high degree of dissatisfaction and the White respondents were almost evenly distributed between the two options. Age group differences were found to exist ($P<.06$, CC .199), but they were not highly significant. As for the remaining factors of religion and income, they were found not to be significant as factors affecting the degree of satisfaction with the defense rendered by one's public lawyer. When the respondents were asked to specify the reasons for their satisfaction or dissatisfaction with the defense given by their public lawyers, all the factors showed a similar distribution with regard to the level of dissatisfaction. Almost 13 percent of the respondents felt that the cost was too much, 80 percent said that their lawyer was inadequate, and 7 percent gave a variety of other reasons.

As far as the satisfaction with the defense by a private lawyer is concerned, it was found that age, ethnicity, and income were significantly related to the degree of satisfaction ($P<.01$), but, religion did not have any affect upon the responses. The greatest degree of satisfaction was expressed by the 50 or over age group, White, and in the income level of %15,000 or over, while the greatest degree of dissatisfaction was expressed by those 30 years of age or less, Black, and in the $5,000-$10,000 income level. In specifying the reasons for their satisfaction or dissatisfaction, all the factors again showed a similar distribution with the exception of the income factor. 38.1 percent of the respondents indicated their satisfaction with their lawyer's defense based on the fact that they received a favorable verdict. The income group does not differ very much on this point - 37.5 percent were satisfied because of a favorable verdict. The level of dissatisfaction based on age, ethnicity and religion showed that 38.1 percent were dissatisfied because of an unfavorable verdict, while 23.8 percent felt that their lawyer spent too little time on preparing the defense. The income group showed that 31.3 percent were dissatisfied due to an unfavorable verdict, while 31.3 percent felt that their lawyer did not spend enough time in the preparation of their case - this feeling of being slighted was heavily concentrated in the $5,000-$10,000 income level.

Many studies comparing the public lawyer to the private lawyer have shown that the lawyers for the lower income levels tend to advise their clients to plead guilty somewhat more often than a privately retained counsel (Lefcourt, 1971:30). Haywood Burns (1971:50) states that "there is a structural inequality built into our law which works to the detriment of the poor and the non-white (often they are the same persons, but not always). . . . A similar structural inequality exists in the civil law." The data of this research affirm the continuing estrangement of the Black and lower economic levels. This feeling of dissatisfaction is not aimed at an abstract principle of law or statute, but at the operating mechanics of the legal system, especially as that system is manipulated by the legal profession. The concept of being represented by inadequate legal counsel or by a counsel who is either unable or unwilling to spend enough time to prepare an adequate defense is closely linked to a legal system that gives the facade of equality under law while operating in a contradictory fashion. As this research shows, it is primarily the young, the Black, and the lower income groups who feel the greatest degree of dissatisfaction with the present legal system. As these groups become more aware and vocal regarding their legal rights, they will become less tolerant of the legal system that forces them to play the role of a second rate citizen.

Items 6 and 7 deal with the complaints the respondents may have regarding the way their case was handled by a public or private lawyer. For those respondents represented by a public lawyer, ethnicity is the only factor that showed a highly significant relationship (P<.0001, CC .303) with Blacks having twice as many complaints as Whites and the Hispanic group having the lowest percentage of complaints. The nature of these complaints were similar when considering the factors of age, ethnicity, religion and income. Approximately 58.3 percent stated that the public lawyer spent too little time on the case, 8.3 percent said the case was too expensive, 16.7 percent said that he did not counsel with them and 16.7 percent said that the public lawyer had confused them. Concerning the complaints against a privately retained counsel, ethnicity, religion, and, to a lesser extent, age, were found to have a significant relation (P<.01). Ethnicity, religion and age groupings specified their complaints in that 68.4 percent felt that their private attorney gave them too little time, 26.3 percent stated that he was too expensive and 5.3 percent stated that the lawyer confused them. In this case, the income grouping showed a different distribution since a higher percentage

(78.6) stated that their lawyer spent too little time with them, less stated that he was too expensive (21.4 percent), and none were confused by their lawyer. When the respondents were asked to specify where they would place their complaints against their public or private lawyer, 13.2 percent stated that they would complain to the local bar association, while 86.8 percent would complain elsewhere - elsewhere being unspecified by the respondents.

This aspect of the data confirms what Casper calls the "marketplace ethic." According to Casper (1972:112), "the importance of money and of financial transactions reflects the general socialization into a market economy that the defendants, like all Americans, have experienced. In this sense the defendants . . . were very accepting of the ethic of the marketplace." By paying for the legal services, the defendant is buying not only the loyalty of his lawyer but he is also placing himself in a position of power over his attorney. Money, in this sense, is not equivalent to the concept of buying time but is equivalent to the concept of buying a friend in court. The feeling that your lawyer is on your side and will place his client's needs above that of the court accompanies the payment for legal services. Among those respondents who had a privately retained counsel, none felt that their lawyer was acting independently of their wishes by not consulting with them. On the other hand, those with a public lawyer felt that they were being instructed rather than advised as to the possible alternatives available to them. This leaves the respondent feeling as though he is standing alone without a legal counsel who is on his side. As Brownell (1951) emphasizes, most clients are not knowledgeable of the various associations that govern and review the legal professions. Despite the increasing trend toward the awareness of public rights, almost 87 percent of the sample could not verbalize where they would begin to process a complaint or initiate action against a lawyer. The profession of law is one of the last areas where the general public feels helpless to help themselves.

Items 8 and 9 asked the respondents whether or not there was adequate communication between themselves, as clients, and their lawyers. Adequate communication with a public lawyer was found to be very highly affected by ethnicity (P<.0001,CC.292). Over three-fourths of the White and Black respondents felt the communication they had with their public lawyer was inadequate, while over half of the Hispanic respondents described their communication with their lawyer as adequate. However, ethnicity is not a significant factor when it comes to the communication with a private lawyer and his client, while age and religion are very highly significant (P<.0001). In relation to the age of the respondent, the older the respondent, the more frequent became the evaluation of the adequacy of the communication between lawyer and client.

The question of communication with one's lawyer is intimately linked with Item 5 or the presence of trust or confidence in one's lawyer. A very highly significant relationship was found to exist by ethnicity (P<.0001, CC .216), type of lawyer (P<.0001, CC .356), age (P<.001, CC .196), religion (P<.001, CC .174), and to a lesser extent by income (P<.01, CC .179). The differences among the ethnic groups showed that 88.4 percent of the Whites had confidence in their lawyers compared to 75.6 percent of the Hispanic respondents and only 69.2 percent of the Black respondents. 90.5 percent of the respondents who used a private lawyer had confidence in their lawyers versus the 57.9 percent of those respondents who had a public lawyer. In relation to age, the older the respondent the more trust or confidence he tended to place in his lawyer. As for the income groups, the lower one's income level the less confident they reported to be in their lawyers. When the respondents were asked to specify their reasons for the lack of trust or confidence in their lawyers, the only reason given by the respondents could best be labeled as broken promises.

In order for the lawyer-client relationship to flourish and therefore provide a beneficial experience for the client, the lines of communication must be adequate enough to engender a feeling of trust or confidence between the lawyer and his client. Casper (1972) points out that the clients of public lawyers tend to be suspicious at the start of their relationship primarily due to the presence of the marketplace ethic. For a public lawyer to overcome this suspicion and establish rapport with his client should be an important aspect of the lawyer's role. Instead this suspicion is only hightened by the impersonal and harried nature of the contacts between the public lawyer and his client. The data of this research affirm the negative affect that the involvement with a public counsel has upon the lawyer-client relationship. The main reason stated by the respondents for the lack of trust in their lawyers was broken promises. This is also a result that stems primarily from inadequate communication between the lawyer and his client. In this situation, expectations are raised that the lawyer cannot fulfill - as Blumberg (1973) puts it, the clients are being "conned" by their lawyers. Where communication between lawyer and client was described as being open or adequate, the same categories of respondents also tended to respond that they could trust or have conficence in their attorney and the advice he gave them. Mayers (1964:30) reports that in several cases, after appeals, state prisoners were able to win new trials based on the claim that, although the court provided them with counsel at the trial, the service rendered by such counsel was so incompetent and inadequate that the defendant was, in effect, without benefit of counsel. Casper (1972:116) summarizes the relationship between communication and trust in one's counsel the following way:

> "...Most men represented by the public defender felt that he attempted to tell them what to do rather than discuss the case and simply make suggestions. Most of those represented by private attorneys felt that their attorney had not tried to 'muscle' them, but had merely made suggestions about what they ought to do; moreover, when a lawyer was insistent about a point, the defendant was much more inclined to accept it as an exercise of proper authority rather than as the imposition of will. This acceptance seems to be the product both of the general sense of efficacy that paying a lawyer seems to bring and of the fact that they trusted the advice that the lawyer gave them."

Item 10 indicates the respondents' attitudes toward legal fees. Ethnicity and type of lawyer were very highly significant ($P<.0001$) followed by age and income ($P<.001$) and religion is the least significant factor ($P<.01$). Ethnically, more Whites (39.8 percent) than Hispanics (30 percent) or Blacks (27.7 percent) evaluated the legal fee as being too expensive; whereas, more Blacks (60.2 percent) than White (49.6 percent) or Hispanic (40 percent) evaluated the fee as fair; and lastly, more Hispanic (30 percent) than Black (12 percent) or White (10.5 percent) thought that the legal fee was cheap. In regard to the type of lawyer, 55.1 percent of those respondents with a private attorney versus 43.1 percent with a public lawyer evaluated the legal fee as fair; whereas, more respondents with public lawyers (33 percent) than private lawyers (6.5 percent) evaluated the lawyers' fees as cheap; and lastly, those respondents with private lawyers (38.4 percent) felt the legal fee was too expensive more often than those respondents with public lawyers (23.6 percent). On all income levels, the greatest percentage of responses evaluating the legal fee was centered in the fair category with 44.2 percent of those earning less than $10,000 describing the fee as fair as compared to 62.8 percent of those earning between $10,000-$20,000, and 43.8 percent of those earning $20,000 or more. As the level of income increased, there was a decrease in the percentage of respondents evaluating the legal fee as too expensive; similarly, as the income level decreased, there was an increase in the percentage of respondents evaluating the legal fee as cheap. The age distribution shows that as the ages of the respondents increased, there was an increase in the tendency of the respondents to evaluate the legal fee as fair while there was a decrease in the tendency of the respondents to describe the fee as being either too expensive or cheap.

Blumberg (1973:73) states that "a fee for a felony case which results in a plea, rather than a trial, may range anywhere from $500 to $1,500. Should the case go to trial, the fee will be larger, depending upon the length of the trial. But the larger the fee the lawyer wishes to exact, the more impressive his performance must be." In relation to the concept of the marketplace ethic, defendants tend to be suspicious of what is free since that which is paid for must be better than that which can be obtained for free. The evaluation of legal fees as being fair, cheap, or expensive can be seen as a reflection of the marketplace ethic. Although the respondents are evaluating the monetary cost of a lawyer's services, this evaluation carries with it the overtones of the relationship between the cost, dollar-wise, and the quality of the performance that money was able to buy. Casper (1972:115) points out that "defendants tend to associate the size of the exchange with the efforts of the attorney." The data of this research also support this contention since it is primarily the lower economic levels, the clients of the public lawyers, as well as the Black or Hispanic groups that have evaluated both the quality of the legal services as well as the cost of those services as "cheap".

The respondent's attitude toward the performance of legal aid lawyers (Item 11) varied significantly by ethnicity and type of lawyer (P<.0001). The Hispanic respondents gave the highest rating of good to very good to the legal aid lawyers (70.3 percent) followed by the White respondents with 52.6 percent and the lowest rating came from the Black respondents with only 34.3 percent evaluating their performance as good. Over half of the respondents (52.3 percent) who were represented by a public lawyer rated the legal aid performance as fair or poor with 26.7 percent labeling his performance as poor; 81 percent of those respondents with a private lawyer rated the legal aid counsel as fair to very good. The next significant contribution comes from religion (P<.01, CC .239), then income (P<.02, CC .262), and age has the least significance (P<.05, CC .200) in relation to the evaluation of legal aid lawyers. Religious affiliation shows that the Jewish members were the most positive toward the evaluation of legal aid lawyers with 60 percent rating the performance as good and 40 percent rating the performance as fair; the Protestant respondents were the most negative in attitude with 61.6 percent rating the legal aid performance as fair to poor. Agewise, the most negative attitude toward legal aid performance was located in the under 30 age group (21 percent) while, in relation to income, those respondents earning over $15,000 rated the legal aid performance as poor (87 percent).

Oaks and Lehman's research (1973:165) points out the fact that the negative evaluation given to the quality of the performance of assigned counsels, as compared to a private lawyer, can be substantiated by the use of court statistics: only 8 percent of the cases of the assigned counsel versus 29 percent of the cases of a private lawyer obtain dismissals for their clients; between 70 to 80 percent of the assigned lawyer's clients plead guilty while only 68 percent of the private lawyer's clients plead guilty. Oaks and Lehman note that an appointed counsel may advise his client to plead guilty when there appears to be a lack of resources for an adequate defense; hence, about one-fifth of the assigned counsel's pleas are on reduced charges. The data of this research show that the most negative attitude toward the legal aid performance comes from the Black, the young, and from those who have been exposed to a public lawyer before. It would appear that the negative attitude formed by these respondents goes beyond opinion to an evaluation rooted in fact.

Finally, the respondents answers to Item 12 show their personal preferences for either a legal aid counsel or a privately retained attorney. Age proved to be a highly significant factor ($P<.0001$, CC .232), followed by ethnicity ($P<.001$, CC .187), and to a lesser extent, income ($P<.01$, CC .191). Ethnically, 34.2 percent of the Hispanics would opt for a legal aid lawyer versus the 16.1 percent of the Whites and 12.5 percent of the Black respondents. In terms of age, the 16-29 age bracket showed the highest preference for legal aid counsel (26.6 percent); while, in terms of income, those respondents earning less than $5,000 showed the greatest tendency to choose a legal aid lawyer (27.9 percent). In general, 18 percent of the sample would choose a legal aid attorney over a privately retained counsel, but, when asked to specify why, they gave no explanations for their choice. On the other hand, 87 percent of the respondents would opt for a private attorney and gave the following reasons why: a) He is better paid (52.4 percent); b) He is more competent (34 percent); c) He has more time to devote to his client's interest (13.6 percent). The fact that 87 percent of the respondents would prefer a private attorney highlights the importance of having a lawyer who will represent the best interests of his client in court. The respondent wants a lawyer who will stand with him in court and not a lawyer who functions as a middleman between him and the court. Casper (1972:123) summarizes this concern quite aptly when he states that "there is no system providing counsel to indigents that will convince the poor that they are receiving legal representation equal to that afforded to the rich."

Conclusion

The U.S. Constitution, reinforced by Supreme Court decisions, affirms the right of every citizen to a fair trial and the assistance of a lawyer to prepare his defense. The role of defense lawyer is multifaceted: the lawyer represents his client's only main source of expertise in handling legal affairs; the attorney must also act as an adviser; and, though temporarily, he must also act the role of a loyal and trusted confidant. This states the ideal behavior that should exist between a lawyer and his client; the reality of the legal world, however, is far removed from the ideal.

The data of this research show that the respondents are far from satisfied with the legal counsel that acts as a middleman between the court and the defendant. This type of lawyer, the public lawyer, represents the "worst" possible type of legal assistance in the eyes of the respondents.

The public lawyer may have the legal expertise but he does not use it to the benefit of his client; he does not advise but directs what the client must do; and lastly, he is not the trusted confidant that the client can rely upon to protect his interests. In these areas, the clients of the privately retained attorneys fair better. In general, the most significant factor influencing the respondents' attitudes about the lawyer-client relationship is ethnicity. In particular, the Black respondents showed a greater degree of negative attitude toward the type of legal defense that is prepared by a legal aid counsel; whereas, the White and Hispanic respondents were not as unfavorable.

In summarizing the situation, Casper (1972:125) states that:

> "If, as the Supreme Court so nobly stated in the Gideon opinion, 'the right of one charged with crime to counsel' is deemed 'fundamental and essential to fair trials' in our country, this right must have some real meaning - meaning not only from the viewpoint of legal standards about what constitutes adequate representation, but also in the eyes of defendants themselves. Currently our system does not appear to offer meaningful defense to indigents. It must if we are to convince defendants that they are being treated not as 'files' to be closed but as human beings."

Table I: <u>Table of Significance: Relationship Between Independent and Dependent Variables</u>

I T E M	AGE[1]			ETHNICITY[2]			RELIGION[3]			INCOME[4]		
	X^2 +	P++	CC+++	X^2	P	CC	X^2	P	CC	X^2	P	CC
1. Satisfaction with results of public case.*	3.749	N.S.	.122	15.669	<.001	.245	9.724	<.05	.195	9.112	<.06	.212
2. Satisfaction with results of private case.**	7.389	<.06	.138	5.335	<.06	.117	7.408	<.06	.138	19.108	<.001	.244
3. Satisfaction with defense by public lawyer.	7.582	<.06	.199	16.747	<.001	.289	6.084	N.S.	.179	3.015	N.S.	.147
4. Satisfaction with defense by private lawyer.	15.854	<.01	.208	9.877	<.01	.165	5.811	N.S.	.127	13.832	<.01	.216
5. Presence of trust or confidence in lawyer.	23.038	<.001	.196	27.658	<.0001	.216	17.642	<.001	.174	14.418	<.01	.179
6. Complaints about way case was handled by public lawyer.	3.860	N.S.	.143	18.766	<.0001	.303	1.144	N.S.	.079	4.250	N.S.	.173
7. Complaints about way case was handled by private lawyer.	10.857	<.02	.163	9.999	<.01	.156	14.748	<.01	.189	3.348	N.S.	.102
8. Adequate communication between public lawyer and client.	3.418	N.S.	.118	22.255	<.0001	.292	2.977	N.S.	.112	15.999	<.01	.292
9. Adequate communication between private lawyer and client.	23.758	<.0001	.240	1.415	N.S.	.062	22.196	<.0001	.240	8.696	<.07	.175
10. Attitude toward lawyer's fee.	25.709	<.0001	.219	26.896	<.0001	.223	19.803	<.01	.193	31.548	<.001	.268
11. Attitude toward the performance of legal aid lawyers.	18.508	<.05	.200	32.151	<.0001	.260	26.936	<.01	.239	25.354	<.02	.262
12. Personal preference for type of lawyer (public vs. private)	27.694	<.0001	.232	17.557	<.001	.187	4.353	N.S.	.094	13.989	<.01	.191

N=610 respondents=100 percent of the sample

*Public case=defense by an assigned lawyer such as legal aid
**Private case=a personally chosen lawyer
1Age=16-29 yrs; 30-39; 40-49; 50 or over
2Ethnicity=White; Black; Hispanic
3Religion=Protestant; Catholic; Jewish; Other
4Income=Less than $5,000; $5,000-9,999; $10,000-14,999; $15,000-19,999; $20,000 or over
+X^2=Calculated Chi Square Value
++P=Probability; N.S.=Not Significant (any value <.07)
+++CC=Contingency Coefficient Value

References

Blaustein, Albert and Charles Porter. The American Lawyer. Chicago: University of Chicago Press, 1954.

Blumberg, Abraham. "Lawyers With Convictions," pp. 67-83 in Abraham Blumberg (ed.), The Scales of Justice. New Brunswick, N.J.: Transacgion Books, 1973.

Brownell, Emory. Legal Aid in the U.S., Rochester, N.Y.: Lawyers Co-operative Publishing Co., 1951.

Buckner, George. "What Your Clients Think of You," Journal of the Missouri Bar XVII: 468-469, 1961.

Burns, Haywood. "Racism and American Law," pp. 38-53 in Robert Lefcourt (ed.), Law Against The People. N.Y.: Vintage Books, 1971.

Carlin, Jerome. Lawyers On Their Own. New Brunswick, N.J.: Rutgers University Press, 1962.

Casper, Jonathan. American Criminal Justice. Englewood Cliffs, N.J.: Prentice Hall, Inc., 1972.

Cheatham, Elliott. "A Lawyer When Needed: Legal Services for the MIddle Classes." Columbia Law Review LXIII: 973-986, 1963.

Christenson, Barlow. Lawyers For People of Moderate Means. Chicago: American Bar Foundation, 1970.

Fox, Jr., Cyril. "Providing Legal Services of the Middle Class in Civil Matters." University of Pittsburgh Law Review XXVI: 811-847, 1965.

Handler, Joel. The Lawyer and His Community. Madison, Wisconsin: University of Wisconsin Press, 1967.

Hunting, Roger and Gloria Neuwirth. Who Sues in New York City. N.Y.: Columbia University Press, 1962.

Jacob, Herbert. Justice in America. Boston: Little, Brown and Co., 1972.

Lefcourt, Robert. "Law Against the People," pp. 21-37 in Robert Lefcourt (ed.), Law Against the People. N.Y.: Vintage Books, 1971.

Lefcourt, Robert. "Lawyers For the Poor Can't Win," pp. 123-140 in Robert Lefcourt (ed.), Law Against the People. N.Y.: Vintage Boosk, 1971.

Legal Aid Society. Lawyer For The Poor. N.Y.: J.M. Kaplan Fund, Inc., 1966.

Mayers, Lewis. The American Legal System. N.Y.: Harper and Row, 1964.

New York Times. "Legal Aid Society Criticized on Methods and Quality of Advice to Needy Here." March 18: 38, 1968.

Oaks, Dallin and Warren Lehman. "Lawyers For The Poor," pp. 159-173 in A. Blumberg (ed.), The Scales of Justice. New Brunswick, N.J.: Transaction Books, 1973.

Silverstein, Lee. Defense of the Poor in Criminal Cases in American State Courts. Washington: American Bar Foundation Vol. 3, 1965.

Smigel, Erwin. The Wall Street Lawyer. N.Y.: Free Press of Glencoe, 1964.

The Victims' Role in Crime Prevention

Mary S. Knudten
Richard D. Knudten

Crime prevention efforts frequently focus on increased police patrols and surveillance, environmental design, or other societal actions. The citizen as an individual may also become part of the crime prevention picture through individual and group attempts to eliminate potential opportunities for crime as well as by providing surveillance in neighborhood areas. Innovative efforts such as neighborhood patrols and whistle stop campaigns have emerged as citizens have become more aware and fearful of the potentiality of their own victimization. This paper examines the extent to which persons who have either been victimized or have witnessed a crime take precautions to avoid future victimization.

Project Methodology

The data presented here was gathered by a team from Marquette University from three samples: One of victims and one of witnesses in the criminal justice system, and a third community sample of victims reinterviewed on behalf of the data gatherers by the U.S. Bureau of Census. The in-system groups consist of two saturation samples of citizens actually involved in the criminal justice process in the Milwaukee County (WI) court system. Members of these two samples were contacted as their cases were considered at one of four stages in the criminal justice process: The charging conference in the district attorney's office; the preliminary hearing; the misdeameanor trial; or the felony trial. The questionnaire,

---

The authors acknowledge the assistance of Anthony C. Meade and Willian G. Doerner.

including both fixed answer and open-ended items, was administered to victims and citizen witnesses over four twelve-week periods between December 4, 1974 and November 4, 1975. The average interview time was 15-20 minutes. Of those contacted the overall refusal rate was 17.8 percent.

Part of each sample was interviewed on-site while another portion, composed of those who did not have time or were unwilling to be interviewed while on-site was interviewed by telephone. Of the total in the two samples, 3,000 interviewees, 63 percent were interviewed on site and 37 percent by telephone. A comparison of the responses given on selected items, controlling for the interviewing situation, yielded almost no variation.

The <u>community</u> sample involved the reinterviewing of a sample of victims originally located by the National Crime Survey conducted in Milwaukee by the U.S. Bureau of Census in the early part of 1974. This community sample utilized a double sampling principle. Of a total of approximately 23,700 persons in the initial 1974 sample of citizens, about 5,400 persons age 12 and over were identified as having been victimized by crime. This latter group became eligible for the follow-up survey. Each of the 5,400 persons was placed in a strata on the basis of whether the victimization was of personal or property nature and whether it was classified serious or nonserious. The final randomly selected sample of 2,177 persons included all those who had been victimized of at least one serious personal crime; 1 in 1.009 victims of at least one nonserious personal crime; 1 in 1.009 victims of at least one serious property crime; and 1 in 11.8545 victims of at least one nonserious property crime. The effective remaining sample once eliminations were made for death, institutionalization, underage, or mobility was 1,801. Successful interviews were completed for 89.2

percent of this group, resulting in a final community sample of 1,607.

The characteristics of all three samples are presented in Table 1. With respect to age, both the in-system victim and nonvictim witness samples are very similar to the community group. The in-system samples are slightly better educated than victims in the community but the difference is less than one school year. In-system victims are somewhat likely to be black (31%) than nonvictim witnesses or community victims (20 and 21%). Both in-system sample groups are somewhat more likely to be male, esspecially the nonvictim witnesses.

Comparing the characteristics of the community sample to population characteristics of Milwaukee County yields a finding that males, blacks and young persons are overrepresented among Milwaukee County crime victims. While 10 percent of the Milwaukee County population is black, 21% of the community sample and 31% of the in-system victim sample is black. Similarly, 16% of Milwaukee County population falls between ages 18-24 while 25% of the community and 30% of the in-system victim samples are of this age range. Finally, the percentage of males in the County is 47% while 51% of the community sample and 54% of the in-system victim sample are male.

One other comparison figure is interesting in that it relates to the need for victims to engage in crime prevention efforts. Twenty-eight percent of the in-system victims indicated having been a victim in at least one other crime incident within a twelve month interval. An identical percentage of nonvictim witnesses said they had been a victim of at least one crime in addition to being a witness to the event for which they were in court. Among the community sample 30 percent new incidents were uncovered in the year following the original survey while 68 percent of the individuals indicated having been victimized more than once over a two year period.

In order to monitor the extent to which the respondents in this study generally contributed to the crime prevention effort, the following questions were asked:

a. Do you have a fence for protection?
b. Do you have an alarm system?
c. Do you have a watchdog?
d. Do you have a private patrol service or a security patrol?
e. Do you keep a weapon for protection?
f. Do you have insurance to cover theft, vandalism or injury due to crime?
g. Do you use lights for protection?
h. Do you use locks for protection?
i. Do you watch for strangers or suspicious things in your neighborhood?
j. Do you try to make sure that someone watches your house/apartment while you are away?
k. Do you try to make sure that someone is with you when you go outside?
l. Do you avoid going out at night unless it is necessary?
m. Do you avoid certain areas and places?
n. Do you avoid going outside during certain daylight hours?
o. Have you ever moved from a place of residence to protect yourself from crime?
p. Have you ever changed your job to protect yourself from crime?
q. Have you had your valuables engraved or marked for identification purposes?
r. Have you ever joined a citizen group seeking better protective services?

s. Have you ever requested protective services from the police?

t. Have you ever taken a course in self-defense?

This rather extensive list includes things that people have or do in order to protect themselves from crime. Respondents were asked to note the general frequency with which they do those things listed in g through n. In order to examine the specific behavioral impact of crime upon the individuals involved in this study, the following questions were asked in relation to the <u>specific</u> incident about which they were reporting:

1. Have you obtained, started to use, or increased your use of any of these things because of this crime? (In relation to items a-f).

2. Did you begin doing or increase doing any of these things because of this crime? (In relation to items f-n).

3. Did you do any of these things because of this crime? (In relation to items o-t).

Findings

Summary results for these data are presented in Tables 2 through 5. The values under the Specific Incident heading in each table represent the percentage distribution of types of protective precautions that were obtained or increased as a result of the specific crime incident. Overall, victims (16 percent) were more than twice as likely as nonvictims (7 percent) to have taken as a direct result of the crime at least one of the precautions listed in Table 2. The same 16 percent figure is true for both community victims and those interviewed in the courts.

An interpretive example may be helpful at this point. Twenty-four percent of the in-system victims indicated that they had a weapon for protection. Sixteen percent of this unit indicated that they had obtained or increased using at least one of the things referred to in Table 2 due to the present crime. Thirty-one percent of the group that took a specific incident action indicated that the crime induced precaution was a weapon.

Table 2 shows that other than insurance (61 to 70 percent) none of the precautions were taken by more than 30 percent of the respondents. The most likely precautionary response of all three groups to the present crime was the procurement of a weapon.

Table 3 indicates the association of weapon procurement and type of offense. Higher percentages of victims obtained weapons for assaultive violence offenses. Nonvictim witnesses were more likely to obtain weapons when they were involved with a property crime.

Table 4 presents data on the relative frequency with which people do certain things to protect themselves from crime. Again, the last section entitled "specific incident" refers to the distribution of such precautions among those who have specifically begun or increased doing these things because of the present crime. Respondents were more likely to have taken action regarding the precautions listed in Table 4 as a result of the crime incident than was the case of the precautions in Table 2. Twenty-seven percent of the in-system victims, 28 percent of the community victims, and 12 percent of the in-system nonvictims indicated that they did or increased doing at least one of the things listed in Table 4 in response to the present crime. Again, victims were more than twice as likely as nonvictime witnesses to have taken such action. The most common responses to crime were the use of locks, and the watching for suspicious persons or things within one's immediate environment.

Although the items presented in Table 2 and the use of lights, locks, and the tendency to maintain a watchful orientation are relatively nonrestricting means of decreasing one's vulnerability to crime, this is not as true for all of the precautions listed in Table 4. The fact that fairly large proportions of the respondents in this study avoided certain areas and places in their community, or did not go out at night for fear of crime victimization must not be overlooked. Ecological or night threat amount to an unwarranted deprivation of the freedom of citizens to move about and take part in their community in an unrestrained fashion. At a time when concern with the demise of the rights of the individual under law is a popular position, it is surprising that there is no complimentary emphasis on assuring the rights of the individual to move freely within an ordered society. Restriction of activities, while it may serve to reduce vulnerability to crime, can hardly be considered an appropriate long-term method of crime prevention.

Table 5 extends the time frame of vulnerability precautions by asking respondents about things that they may have ever done to protect themselves from crime. As was the case with items in Table 2, the utilization of such precautions is low. Requesting better police service is the most commonly cited item in Table 5. This vulnerability check was utilized by less than 30 percent of the respondents though it was the most likely precautionary response to the present crime for both in-system samples. On the other hand, community victims were more likely to move. The fact that almost half of the community victims indicating they did something specific because of the incident in question had moved is a significant finding. Even one-fourth of the nonvictim witnesses had also taken this action. In general, however, the behavioral impact of the crime was greater for victims than for nonvictims, with 20 percent of the in-system victims, 17 percent of the community victims, and 11 percent of the in-system nonvictims taking at least one of the precautions listed in Table 5 as a result of the crime. Moving or changing jobs reiterates the tendency noted earlier for crime to infringe upon the rights of the individual in ways beyond the direct harm and/or system-related problems encountered by involvement in the incident.

Direct dollar costs of providing protection were obtained for the in-system samples. Overall, 218 victims indicated that they spent money to secure themselves as a result of the present crime. The mean expense was $215, while the median was $50.86. The mean expense figure for 89 nonvictim respondents was $641, with two respondents making large expenditures. The median cost for these respondents was $46.41.

Association of Use of Precautions and Characteristics of Respondents

A mean precaution score for a composite index was computed for all samples by adding together the twenty specific items included in Tables 2, 4 and 5. On a scale of 0 through 20, the mean precaution scores were: In-system victims, 7.6; In-system nonvictims, 714; Community victims, 5.2 Table 6 shows the extent to which precautionary behavior is related to selected demographic, experiential, and perceptual variables. These variables are:

a. Age of the respondent;

b. Years of education of the respondent;

c. Sex of the respondent;

d. Race of the respondent;

e. Whether respondent has been victimized on another occasion with the past year;

f. Respondent's perceived likelihood of violent crime victimization within coming year; and

g. Respondent's perceived likelihood of property crime victimization within coming year.

Table 6 discloses no between respondent type difference with respect to direction to the observed correlations and very little difference in terms of magnitude. None of the coefficients equal or exceed a value of .20, generally recognized as a minimum to indicate significance. The highest correlation is the .18 value between sex and precautionary behavior. The positive direction of this correlation indicates that females tend to have higher precautionary scores than males. The correlation magnitude, however, indicates that sex explains only 3 percent of the variation in precaution score. While not as high a correlation, the findings presented in Table 6 suggest a positive relationship between perceived likelihood of victimization in the near future and precautionary behavior.

Examination of the correlations of specific precautions and these same sample respondent variables indicates relatively few specific precautions are taken by particular groups. However, it is evident that females decrease their vulnerability by avoidance behavior. Female victims within both the in-system and community samples are significantly more likely than males to say they will not go out alone, will not go out at night and will avoid certain places and areas. On the other hand, males are more likely to take precautions of an active nature (physical defense course) and to have obtained insurance coverage for crime-related losses. For both samples, whites are more likely than nonwhites to have such insurance coverage and the percentage of those having insurance coverage also increases with level of education. Fear of crime among nonwhites is evidenced by the greater tendency of that group to indicate that they avoid going out at night whenever possible. Most interesting is the fact that the only precautionary technique correlated, at least at a .20 level with being victimized more then once during the past year, is the request for better police service. And, this is only for the in-system sample, not the community group. This appears to be a somewhat helpless gesture in the face of multiple victimization.

Perhaps the most significant findings to emerge from these data are the relationships which do not exist. While a great deal of publicity and concern has been expressed about the problems elderly persons have with crime, there is no relationship of significance that shows the elderly taking greater precautions than other age groups. Such findings seem to be counter to those presented elsewhere (Goldsmith, 1975) especially in the popular media. Another relationship which was not evident in the data was one between reporting and not reporting crime and taking precautions. The highest association achieved was .10 (for reporting at least one incident and moving to protect oneself from crime as well as requesting better police service). This indicates that those who report crime are not any more likely than those who do not report crime to engage in more extensive precautionary behavior.

Summary and Implications

Considering the fact that 50 percent of the victimes interviewed expect to be the victim of another crime within the next year, and that over 28 percent had been revictimized during the preceding year, it is reasonable to expect victims to take precautions to reduce their vulnerability. The data here indicate that victims are twice as likely as nonvictims to take at least one precaution because of having been involved in the specific crime incident in question. The most likely responses were to procure a weapon, get insurance or increase insurance, increase use of locks, watch for suspicious persons or things, request better police service, and move. It is also evident that more than half of these groups have insurance for protection, and regularly use lights, locks, watch for strange and suspicious persons, make sure that someone watches their property while they are away, and avoid certain areas and places as a means to protect themselves.

Females are more likely than males to take precautions, particularly to engage in avoidance techniques. Males, on the other hand, are more likely to take a self defense course and to be certain they have insurance. While others have shown that there is a relationship between being victimized and perceiving crime rates as high (Block and Long, 1973; Kleinman and David, 1973), there is no evidence that those who perceive their chances of victimization as high take specific precautions to a greater extent. There is also no evidence that reporters more than non-reporters and the elderly more than others in the population are especially likely to try to protect themselves from crime.

Use of non-restrictive and non-threatening techniques such as lighting systems, locks, alertness, and limited avoidance seem to be reasonable actions for citizens to take. On the other hand, the perceived need and resultant action of citizens, especially females, to restrict their activities to a marked extent by avoiding going out alone and at night seems less reasonable. Similarly, finding that citizens adopt a threatening response, procurement of a weapon, to protect themselves has serious implications. A society already burdened with a high crime rate does not need additional violence.

Victims may take various roles in crime prevention. Passive cooperation roles pose no threat to individuals or to others. Such reactions as limiting activities and procuring weapons do threaten both individuals and society as a whole. Policy makers in a position to affect total crime prevention approaches should be aware that these are actions that citizens are taking.

References

Block, M.K. and G.J. Long. "Subjective Probability of Victimization and Crime Levels: An Econometric Approach," Criminology 11 (May): 87-93, 1973.

Goldsmith, Jack et al. "A Symposium on Crime and the Elderly," Police Chief 43 (February): 18-51, 1976.

Kleinman, Paula H. and Deborah S. David. "Victimization and Perception of Crime in a Ghetto Community," Criminology 11 (November: 307-343, 1973.

TABLE 5

PERCENTAGE OF RESPONDENTS EVER HAVING DONE CERTAIN THINGS TO PROTECT THEMSELVES OR THEIR PROPERTY FROM THE DANGERS OF CRIME

PRECAUTION	GENERAL ACTION			SPECIFIC INCIDENT		
	In-System Victim	In-System Non-Victim	Community Victim	In-System Victim	In-System Non-Victim	Community Victim
N =	1746	1215	1597	138	62	267
Moved	18	16	16	27	25	49
Changed Jobs	5	5	2	10	15	3
Valuables Marked	17	17	14	11	6	19
Joined Citizen Group	3	3	3	5	0	3
Requested Better Police Service	29	25	17	40	48	24
Self-Defense Course	15	18	15	6	6	13
Other	1	1	1	4	1	0

TABLE 6

PEARSON PRODUCT-MOMENT CORRELATIONS BETWEEN COMPOSITE PRECAUTION SCORE AND SELECTED VARIABLES

VARIABLE	TYPE OF RESPONDENT		
	In-System Victim	In-System Nonvictim	Community Victim
Age	.01	.03	.09
Education	-.05	-.04	-.04
Sex[a]	.18	.17	.17
Race[b]	.09	.07	.03
Revictimization	.09	.13	NA
Chances of victimization (violent)	.16	.11	.13
Chances of victimization (property)	.10	.11	.14

[a]Male was coded as 1 and female as 2.

[b]White was coded as 1 and nonwhite as 2.

TABLE 1

A BASIC DESCRIPTION OF THE STUDY SAMPLES

Respondent Characteristic		TYPE OF RESPONDENT: In-System Victim	In-System Non-Victim Witness	Community Victims
Number		1775	1225	1607
Age Range		14-85	14-77	14-88
Mean Age		34	33	33
Education Range		0-24	1-23	0-20
Mean Education		12.3	12.4	11.5
Race	White	69%	80%	79%
	Black	31%	20%	21%
Sex	Male	54%	60%	51%
	Female	46%	40%	49%

TABLE 2

PERCENTAGE OF RESPONDENTS HAVING CERTAIN THINGS TO PROTECT THEMSELVES OR THEIR PROPERTY FROM THE DANGERS OF CRIME

	General Action			Specific Incident		
Precaution	In-System Victims	In-System Nonvictims	Community Victims	In-System Victims	In-System Nonvictims	Community Victims
N =	1763	1215	1597	134	57	248
Fence	25	27	22	3	2	14
Alarm System	12	12	4	21	15	6
Watchdog	25	30	28	11	18	27
Patrol Service	5	7	3	3	12	1
Weapon	24	27	24	31	32	29
Insurance	61	70	63	27	20	31
Other	3	3	4	5	0	6

TABLE 3

RESPONDENTS OBTAINING A WEAPON BECAUSE OF THIS CRIME BY TYPE OF OFFENSE

TYPE OF OFFENSE	TYPE OF RESPONDENT: In-System Victim		In-System Non-victim Witness		Community Victim	
	N	%	N	%	N	%
Assaultive Violence	21	42	6	29	35	49
Person Theft Without Violence	16	32	7	33	10	14
Property Crime	13	26	8	38	26	37

TABLE 4

PERCENTAGE OF RESPONDENTS DOING CERTAIN THINGS TO PROTECT THEMSELVES OR THEIR PROPERTY FROM THE DANGERS OF CRIME

Precaution	GENERAL ACTION									SPECIFIC INCIDENT		
	In-System Victim N=1750			In-System Nonvictim N=1215			Community Victim N=1597			In-System Victim N=251	In-System Non-Victim N=100	Community Victim N=1002
	Regularly	Sometimes	Never	Regularly	Sometimes	Never	Regularly	Sometimes	Never			
Lights	77	11	12	73	14	13	72	16	12	15	13	29
Locks	98	1	1	97	2	1	95	4	1	23	20	50
Watch for Strangers or the Suspicious	71	13	16	67	16	17	51	26	23	18	21	38
Assure that Others Watch Your Property	70	11	19	70	11	19	54	18	28	12	12	19
Avoid Going Out Alone	20	16	64	14	14	72	15	17	68	7	9	11
Avoid Going Out at Night	37	11	51	26	11	63	34	14	52	10	10	17
Avoid Certain Places	59	14	27	55	15	30	55	18	27	12	12	24
Avoid Going Out at Certain Daylight Hours	4	7	89	2	6	93	3	4	94	1	2	2
Other	2	1	0	2	1	0	4	2	94	2	1	5

Evaluation of the Offender Aid and Restoration Program in Northern Virginia

Robert M. Rich

Project Description

The Offender Aid and Restoration program (OAR) was established in Fairfax County, Virginia in 1971 and two evaluations have been made of its programs. The first evaluation covered the period November 1973 through October 1974 and the second the period September 1975 through June 1976. Both evaluations have been primarily descriptive and deal with three areas: characteristics of OAR volunteers, OAR offenders, and services offered by OAR. One hundred and twenty (120) OAR volunteers worked with the three hundred and ninety eight (398) offenders offering them services with seventy one agencies in addition to contacts made on behalf of clients with parole officers, attorneys, judges, public defender's office, division of motor vehicles, and traffic court. Referrals to OAR for assistance came from twenty eight sources, the largest number coming from Fairfax County Jail staff, the office of parole, and the OAR offenders themselves.

Objectives of the Evaluation

The objectives of the Offender Aid and Restoration program became crystallized over a four year period. There are three objectives. The first and paramount objective is the reduction of the criminality of the offender. The second objective is the provision of assistance where ex-offenders and/or their families can receive proven and consistent advice or assistance. The third objective is to provide information and insight to the general community about rehabilitation needs of offenders and ex-offenders.

Evaluation Theories

The Offender Aid and Restoration program's approach to evaluation has been quite pragmatic (i.e., produce some change in the case of offenders and ex-offenders). The focus of the evaluation centers on how successfully OAR reduces the criminality of the individuals it serves (i.e., a reduction in recidivism or a reduction in the number of contact with the criminal justice system).

The theory upon which the program operates is based on symbolic interactionism. According to Ritzer (Sociology: A Multiple Paradigm Science, 1975, Allyn and Bacon, pp 101-105) symbolic interactionism theory consists of the following general assumptions and propositions: "Man lives in a symbolic environment as well as a physical environment and can be stimulated to act by symbols as well as by physical stimuli. Through symbols, man has a capacity to stimulate others in ways other than those in which he is himself stimulated. Through communication of symbols, man can learn huge numbers of meanings and values and hence ways of acting from other men. Through the learning of a culture and its subcultures men are able to predict each others behavior most of the time and gauge their own behavior to the predicted behavior of others. The symbols and other meanings and values to which they refer do not occur only in isolated bits but often in clusters, sometimes large and complex. Man has meaning for himself as well as other objects, actions, and characteristics. Thinking is the process by which possible symbolic solutions and other future courses of action are examined, assessed for their relative advantages and disadvantages in terms of the values of the individual, and one of them chosen for action."

Specifically symbolic interactionism deals with the covert aspects of behavior. Behavior is viewed as a process of interpretation inserted between the environmental stimulus and response of the OAR client. The client is shown that social facts are not viewed as things controlling or coercing him but only as the framework within which symbolic interaction takes place. The OAR client can fit his actions to those of the OAR staff volunteer through the process of interpretation (i.e., the dedicated volunteer will provide a positive personalized role model for the offender eventually allowing the latter to "break criminal career patterns" and become a productive citizen in the community). Through this process OAR clients should form a social group with other clients and staff volunteers, the action of the group serving as a focal point of each group member's behavior. Thus the social psychclogical world of the OAR client should be found in the process of interpretation or orientation of himself vis-a-vis the group.

Evaluation Measures

In order to measure the effectiveness of the program and ascertain whether the objectives are being realized, a model for evaluation of the program was devised called "planned versus actual performance" based on the theory of symbolic interactionism. This model of evaluation consists of first identifying the purpose of each unit of OAR of which there are five.

The outreach unit informs offenders and ex-offenders of OAR services, works with County Jail personnel, and utilizes volunteer resources. Its purpose is to increase the number of clients best suited for OAR services. The program development unit provides data collection through research and record keeping which can be analyzed and coordinated so as to minimize the need for subjectivity when judging project efficiency and effectiveness.

The transitional services unit aids clients during re-entry into the community and directs clients to available community resources. Its purpose is to reduce criminal activity due to poor client adjustment in the community. The volunteer support unit provides liaison between volunteers, their clients, and the professional staff; coordinates volunteer activities; and screens and places volunteers in appropriate activities. Its purpose is to increase the quality and longevity of volunteer relationships. The last unit is economic development which serves as a clearinghouse for information, job bank, training facility, and placement service for OAR clients. Its purpose is to increase economic development opportunities for offenders and ex-offenders.

Second the model identifies eight areas as being crucial for continued success of the OAR program. These areas are: (1) screening of clients, (2) screening and supervising of volunteers, (3) utilization of volunteers with expertise, (4) utilization of community members for OAR support, (5) revision of project objectives, (6) plan for continued volunteer staffing, (7) improvement of data keeping, and (8) matching volunteers with offenders (clients) in order to maximize effectiveness of their relationship.

Each one of the eight areas has been analyzed in terms of procedures implemented in light of past needs as stated by each area's purpose. These have been measured qualitatively so as to aid in predicting the projected future needs and demands of the program.

Area one concerns the screening of clients. Prospective clients are interviewed in jail or community settings in order to obtain a better knowledge of what OAR can offer. More clients are given a one to one relationship with volunteer staff which increases client length of stay in the program due to increased personalization of the relationship. The idea of using former clients in the capacity of helping others developed from this area's analysis.

Area two concerns screening and supervising of volunteers. Staff personnel screen and supervise training. By having a volunteer coordinator present at all times and dividing volunteers into small groups, improved efficiency, morale, and communication develops and continues to grow.

Area three concerns utilization of volunteers with expertise. They are assigned to areas such as housing search, job counseling, academic tutoring, and training new volunteers.

Area four concerns utilization of community members for OAR project support. One should pick target groups within the community such as minority civic associations, church groups, fraternal organizations, and political organizations to inform about the OAR program and from which to recruit new volunteers.

Area five concerns revision of objectives. One should constantly review OAR objectives in light of continuing research findings. An increase or decrease of specific services offered by OAR should be periodically made to meet the needs of the program. The OAR board of directors should include membership from minorities, volunteers, clients, in addition to the professional staff.

Area six concerns the plan for continued volunteer staffing. The OAR board of directors should continuously seek both public and private funding. This can be done by training volunteers with expertise to contact foundations as well as writing grant proposals under staff supervision.

Area <u>seven</u> concerns improvement of data keeping. One should establish a continuous procedure to evaluate all aspects of the program in order to measure progress of program personnel and their clients. This will also enable one to identify problem areas which should insure better administration of the program.

Area <u>eight</u> concerns matching volunteers with offenders. After the training period, staff personnel who have trained volunteers and know their personality types should work with County Jail and parole/probation officers who know their clients' personality types. This will afford more careful matching of volunteers to clients which should result in longer time of volunteer and client involvement in the program. This will also probably result in more expressed satisfaction with the interaction process between volunteer and offender.

Evaluation Outcomes

The evaluation deals with information on volunteers (i.e., age, sex, race, marital status, education, occupation, and length of service as a volunteer). The typical volunteer is a white, married female, in her thirties, with a college degree or more education. She has a current or past job in a professional field and has had some prior volunteer experience. She has been with the OAR program for about one year and has worked with at least two offenders.

The evaluation also deals with information on offender-clients (i.e., age, sex, race, marital status, educational attainment, residence, and legal status of offender). The typical offender dealt with by OAR is a married, white male, in his early twenties, with less than a secondary school diploma who has been an unskilled or semi-skilled worker. He has been assigned an OAR volunteer after six months in county jail. He is usually serving a sentence for committing a felony such as robbery, larceny, or burglary.

An experimental sample of offenders served by OAR volunteers on a one to one relationship was analyzed. Of the forty-six offenders in the three year study, only forty percent remained in the program six months or less, fifty percent stayed two years or less, and the remainder more than two years. Major reasons for project termination are no more help needed, volunteer lost contact with offender, volunteer left program, offender left area, and offender reconfined to jail or became an inpatient in some medical program. Only fifteen percent (7) of the offenders were returned to confinement during the study period. Two of the returned offenders had violated rules of probation-parole while the other five had committed new felonies (i.e., forgery, drug possession, breaking and entering).

The OAR staff has rendered a number of specific services to their clients, mainly in the areas of job counseling and job leads. In addition to these services, the staff has provided assistance in obtaining financial aid, obtaining food, transportation, housing, medical and dental assistance, alcohol and drug treatment, legal assistance, clothing, education, training placement, letter writing, and aid in purchasing tools for a job.

The OAR staff have also contacted a considerable number of community agencies in order to assist their clients such as alcohol or drug treatment centers (i.e., Alcoholics Anonymous, Fairfax Hospital Detoxification Center, Crossroads Drug Treatment Program); education/training (i.e., Department of Vocational Rehabilitation, Northern Virginia Community College, American University,

Veteran's Administration); employment programs (i.e., AFL-CIO Apprentice Program, Fairfax County Personnel Office, Virginia Employment Commission, Offender Employment Programs, Federal Departments of Housing and Urban Development, Social Security Administration, and Veteran's Administration); medical treatment (i.e., Medcap, Medicaid, Northern Virginia Women's Hospital, Fairfax Hospital, Commonwealth Doctor's Hospital); offender programs (i.e., efforts from individual ex-offenders, State Bureau of Rehabilitation, Friends of Women Prisoners, offender employment programs); professional counseling (i.e., Northern Virginia Counseling Center For Women, Northern Virginia Training Center, Northern Virginia Community College Counseling Center, St. Elizabeth's Hospital, Northern Virginia Mental Health Association, Alexandria City and Arlington County Mental Health Centers); referral agencies (i.e., Fairfax County Information and Referral, several hotlines); service and church groups (i.e., United Community Ministries, Catholic Charities, Salvation Army, Y.M.C.A., Fairfax Organization of Christians and Jews United in Service, Red Cross, Lion's Club, Northern Virginia Family Services); and official agency contact (i.e., parole-probation office, bar association, public defender's office, judges chambers, traffic court).

Referrals to the Offender Aid and Restoration program come mainly from the Fairfax County Jail staff, County office of parole-probation, and other OAR clients. In addition calls for help come from such sources as offenders, other OAR programs in other counties, attorneys, State Department of Social Services, State Department of Vocational Rehabilitation, State Prison Camps, County Judges, Families of offenders, information and referral services, Northern Virginia Community College, and OAR volunteers.

Implications For Criminal Justice Evaluation

A major conclusion of the research is that a successful Offender Aid and Restoration program requires the participation of a wide variety of people with varied interests. To this end a clearinghouse should be established in order to facilitate the rapid delivery of services to prospective clients. This means that individuals with a professional or lay interest in Offender Aid and Restoration activities should be screened and subsequently listed for need in delivery of services.

Second there should be strong cooperative liaison patterns established with both criminal justice and community institutions. This will allow OAR personnel and volunteers an opportunity to quickly resolve the maze of problems that an ex-offender goes through during the re-integration process in the community. Further there must be closer ties between OAR staff and County Court and Jail personnel. This will make it easier for research to be conducted on effectiveness of OAR practices and made criminal justice personnel feel at ease with OAR policies.

Next there must be a way to effectively deal with the transiency problem of both offender and staff. This problem of turnover interferes with the long term resocialization efforts of the OAR program. Since county jail inmates serve generally one year or less as do OAR volunteers, there must be a way of keeping in contact with ex-offenders. A resource of community organizations with new potential volunteers to follow up on clients is essential. There is also the problem where clients move from the jurisdiction. A communication network with other OAR programs should be established in order to pick up the ex-offender when he moves to a new jurisdiction so that new problems can be quickly resolved and old criminal patterns do not reappear.

There is also a definite need for minority group and ex-offender participation in the OAR program. A high percentage of problems and concerns come from both these groups, yet both are underutilized in OAR type programs. The special needs and interests of both groups should be incorporated in OAR program planning.

A pressing need for OAR programs is to maintain a small group atmosphere between OAR volunteers and the offender-clients they serve in the community. Only this type of atmosphere provides the opportunity for primary group relationships that furthers the social interaction process. If at all possible a one to one relationship should be maintained between volunteer and client in order to maximize proper resocialization.

Last, continuity in staffing and training of Offender Aid and Restoration volunteers will be a continuous problem for criminal justice planners. This is due in part to the problem of attempting to secure funds from both public and private sources, thus limiting the number of full time professional staff. A core of professionals with proper backup communications staff (i.e., secretarial, telephone, and duplication services) is essential for program stability and success.

The Role of the Patrol Officer in Metropolitan Police Systems*

Robert M. Rich

Introduction

According to Evan, role analysis as applied to the field of criminal justice would concentrate on the various types of personnel functioning in the system (i.e., police, prosecutors, judges, jailers, and administrators of various types).[1] The role analysis concept is defined as the stable aspects of an individual's behavior observed when he interacts with either one other individual or a class of individuals (i.e., a judge in relating to a police officer or a warden relating to a corrections officer). Further if one is to understand the central concept of social role one must utilize a number of concepts relating to it such as role clarity, consensus, and role conflict.

Role clarity refers to the individual's perception of the degree of explicitness provided by other individuals concerning what types of behavior are expected from members of the court/ corrections bureaucracy. This methodological tool may reveal frustrations and strains in playing a

*This research is based on five years work with several police academies and departments in the Washington, D.C. metropolitan area. These consisted of the Metropolitan Police Department (D.C.), Prince Georges Police Department (Md.), Alexandria Police Department (Va.), Arlington County Police Department (Va.), and Fairfax County Police Department (Va.). Informal contacts and interviews were held with approximately 500 officers.

particular role that effects other role play in the entire system. Role consensus refers to the degree to which other role players agree as to the type of behavior expected from a person occupying a certain position. Lastly, role conflict can be defined as the degree to which a role player finds himself confronted by opinions or expectations of others with which he cannot accept or adjust to. One playing a role may resolve the conflict in a manner that may affect the individual, social group, or the social system.

The use of role analysis can be applied to a study of the influences of individual personality on role play and relationships at various status levels in the police and larger criminal justice bureaucracies. In uilizing the role analysis method, one would have to specify the objective forces that impinge on those who occupy specific positions in the bureaucratic police system. These forces are varied and could include not only information received by the police officer from several sources but also the social influences to which one is subjected to within or outside the system (i.e., from the precinct within which one works as well as from special interest groups outside the police bureaucracy such as mass media pressures to reform arrest techniques). Forces can also originate in the total police system from above or below one's level of concern such as court pressures on detention procedures and colleague influences on discretionary actions on the street. Finally one can be overly concerned with the role one plays versus the role relationship one has with others within the police bureaucracy, as well as outside the bureaucratic structure such as in the area of police-community relations.

Second, role analysis is concerned with the socio-psychological pressures operating upon and within the law enforcement officer while role playing in the criminal justice organizational structure. One would assess the perceptions of the police officer concerning his or her professional role, the perceived role of others in the criminal justice system as seen by police, the normative systems (i.e., value-attitudes) that are shaped by the structure of the police institution, and the effect that decisions have upon the law enforcement officer temporarily or at different levels within the police bureaucracy (i.e., administrative decision to use police women in the line function rather than traditional staff functions).

Third, role analysis deals with the objective outcomes of the behavior of those playing key roles within the law enforcement system. Thus, one deals with how one member of the bureaucracy receives information and communicates it to others at subordinate, coordinate, and superordinate status levels within the bureaucratic structure (i.e., juvenile division officer to line officer, patrolman to assistant United States attorney, police officer to probation/parole officer). Thus the norm of reciprocity is utilized to analyze mutual conduct of different members of the criminal justice system in order to comprehend the process of translating role perceptions into role behaviors.

Last, the use of role analysis can be applied to settling issues that are relevant in law enforcement policy. One can study the influences of individual personality on role play and interpersonal relationships upon social policy formation at various stages in the policing process. Resolution to many basic problems can be provided by utilizing the role analysis technique. For example, one can answer the following questions: (1) who in the police system initiates social policy (i.e., police chief, station commander, roll-call commander, or watch officer), (2) who is in charge of staffing and planning, (3) how are data communicated and publicized, (4) who determines institutional sanctions, (5) who determines and organizes intra-elite and inter-elite functions, (6) from whom is project and task force financing obtained and utilized, and (7) how are sanctions and controls applied to each division within the total police bureaucracy.

The Police Role

Police departments in a metropolitan area must function in a number of ways in order to prevent and control crime as well as carry out a variety of civil duties. Through some personal contact but mainly through news and fictional exposures to the police via the mass media, the metropolitan police officer has replaced the romantic cowboy sheriff image (i.e., the officer is viewed as one playing an exciting and dangerous role in the apprehension of inner city criminals of the most deviant types). Thus the urban police are viewed one-dimentionally by both the public they serve and the greater political bureaucracy of which they are part. The takeover of the District Building (D.C.) and B'nai B'rith executive offices by Black Muslims in 1977 is a case in point. The news media covered the event around the clock and were critical of the Metropolitan Police Department for their apparent lack of action. This was despite the fact that the offenders were monitering both radio and television coverage in order to ascertain the movement of the police. Obviously the police were hampered in their rescue attempts of over 100 hostages due to their every movement being shown on television and described over the radio. The American Broadcasting Company (ABC) even had a criminologist appear on local television during the "event" to try to explain the reasons for the taking of hostages and the Public Broadcasting System (PBS) had a special discussing possible solutions that the police could attempt. This type of media coverage could have led to increased tensions between police and the armed gunmen that could have resulted in a tragic conclusion for both police and hostages.

According to the President's Commission on Law Enforcement and Administration of Justice Task Force Report on the Police,[2] there are a number of functions that the typical metropolitan police department must accomplish. These functions are (1) operational, (2) administrative, and (3) executive in nature. Operational functions include a number of roles that the police must perform such as patrol, traffic, detective, juvenile, and vice. Some administrative functions are intelligence and organized crime, training academy, and research-analysis. Executive functions of concern are internal investigation and community relations.

Operational Roles

One of the most significant roles of the police is that of patrol, whether on foot or by motor vehicle. The common conception of police patrol held by the public is that of an officer confronted with a continuous series of exposures to serious offenses in progress in the course of a single tour of duty. The typical tour of duty in reality consists of the performance of a wide range of duties from dealing with serious crimes to keeping order, settling family and other disputes, finding runaway children, and dealing with drunks. In addition, the patrol officer is responsible for the enforcement of traffic regulations and assuring that a veriety of licenses are up to date (i.e., dog, peddler, and business). Lastly the patrol officer must be able to provide emergency services such as dealing with accidents, heart attacks, and even fires (i.e., tasks that are not crime prevention or control oriented).

The main role of the police patrol is crime prevention. The officer attempts to reduce opportunities for the commission of crime. The patrol officer is expected to give protection to individuals who are likely to be victimized such as women, the elderly, children, and businesses. He is also expected to keep an eye on these types of people who often are easy prey to criminals such as alcoholics, mentally ill, or those who are willing consumers of so-called victimless crimes and leave themselves open to the risk of robbery, assault, or worse.[3]

Another important role of the patrol officer is crime control. Thus the officer has the authority to arrest an individual who is in the process of committing a crime. Despite the fact that each officer is responsible for knowledge of specific statutes of the criminal code of his jurisdiction, the arrest process is much more complex than is assumed by the public due to the various circumstances surrounding each incident.[4]

Each officer has discretionary powers that he can exercise in order to determine what conduct is in fact criminal and what conduct is deviant but non-criminal. Even with these powers backed by the standard operating procedures (sop) developed (written or verbal) by his precinct and watch commanders, there is still difficulty for the officer to respond appropriately to the numerous incidents called to his attention during an eight hour shift. Each patrol officer in a metropolitan area whether inner city or suburb is under constant pressure to handle a case load that is beyond his capacity or calls for improvisation that is outside the realm of the written rules and regulations despite roll-call information, inservice training, and criminal justice and sociology courses at the local university.[5]

Whether an arrest is initiated against a person by an officer depends upon his judgment.

Theoretically this judgment is based upon his reading of the statute in the criminal code of the jurisdiction but there are situations where the violator is not arrested by the officer. Among the factors accounting for lack of arrest for certain types of criminal behavior are volume of violations, limited manpower at the scene of the incident, vagueness of the criminal code statute, and community value-attitude concerning specific criminal behavior.[6]

When an officer comes upon highly dangerous conduct on the part of a citizen, he is expected to make an arrest. In reality, however, the patrol officer is selective in making an arrest. For example there is often a failure to make an arrest for serious misconduct of an individual if the parties involved are related, close friends, fellow officers on off-duty status, or politically connected individuals (i.e., politicians, highly ranking military officers, foreign officials, and even major figures of organized crime). Even when the offense is clear cut and there is a desire for police intervention on the part of the victim, the latter may only want the police to temporarily control the offender. Thus the victim will not cooperate with the officer after his intervention so no prosecution can be successfully attempted.[7]

The discretionary powers of an officer also include making the decision not to prosecute an offender who has been arrested after informally reviewing the case. Alcoholics are sometimes taken home or allowed to go home on their own if they appear to be of no real harm to anyone. Juveniles are often taken home and charges dropped after consultation with parents and/or social welfare agency personnel. Even drug addicts and small time pushers are often released from custody especially if they will offer information leading to the arrest and prosecution of major pushers and suppliers. The patrol officer also has authority to issue orders to people regarding their movements, activities, and whereabouts. Thus they respond to citizen's complaints regarding noisy parties, order juveniles or adults congregating on street corners or in shopping centers to disperse, enforce curfew regulations on juveniles, and order suspicious looking individuals from a given residential or commercial area. Finally a substantial proportion of patrol time is devoted to the handling of minor disputes between people (i.e., neighbors, landlord and tenant, merchant and customer, taxi driver and customer, and husband and wife).[8]

The patrol officer normally functions as a traffic coordinator and only calls for assistance from traffic specialists when the need arises. Thus there may or may not be a special traffic division in a given metropolitan area department. Inner city departments usually have a traffic division to respond to rush hour, parking, airport, bus, and rail terminal problems. Suburban departments usually have the patrol officer handle all traffic violations and accidents as they occur with no special division for traffic necessary.[9]

The typical patrol officer on any given tour of duty might have to deal with enforcing traffic regulations, deal with criminal behavior, and perform a number of services for the public. The typical officer spends most of his shift dealing with nonenforcement tasks. Even if an offender is arrested by a patrol officer, the officer does not have the time to conduct a follow up investigation of the offense. Most departments have a small detective division to handle follow up investigations on criminal offenses but they are usually overwhelmed by the caseload. Thus thorough investigations are undertaken only on felony offenses with little time for a thorough search for witnesses or even for finding the perpetrator of the crime.[10]

Thus the detective's role consists in following up where the patrol officer's investigation left off. The detective usually investigates felonies, carries out surveillance on buildings or persons in order to apprehend offenders, and processes and presents evidence in court. Some detectives handle juvenile crimes, some specialize in adult crimes, while others handle property crimes. Lastly the detective is responsible for the continued gathering of information on suspected offenders and their areas of operation within the community.[11]

Because of the high percentage of crimes committed by children and adolescents, patrol officers have frequent contact with the young offender. The patrol officer many times does not have either proper training or experience in dealing with the juvenile. Thus most suburban and inner city departments have a specially trained juvenile division. The role of this officer is oriented toward delinquency prevention through school appearance, recreational activities, as well as dealing with juveniles who are suspected and arrested for violations of either juvenile or criminal codes of the jurisdiction. The juvenile officer must also serve as a link between family and court personnel.[12]

Every patrol officer obtains some limited training in the recognition of vice activities and in the enforcement of laws against so-called "victimless crimes". Most inner city police departments have a separate vice unit but many suburban departments do not have such a unit. Thus a suburban officer may have to handle a problem dealing with gambling, drugs, or prostitution that he is not familiar with and can receive little guidance from colleagues or superiors. This is especially true when attempting to establish and maintain liaison with state and federal agents who have the necessary expertise in the vice area. The department policy on enforcement of statutes dealing with vice is selective even though most forms of vice are illegal in a given community. This is due to the fact that community norms may tolerate some forms of vice and not other forms of vice. Thus an officer must proceed on the basis of both standard operating procedures as well as informal unwritten policy at the precinct level. A major problem for the vice squad officer is to determine what harm a particular form of vice is causing the community. All too often complaints from members of the community are false or they will not let themselves be involved if a request is made for their testimony. Thus an officer has to resort to either becoming a participant observer in the deviant activity which is personally degrading in most cases or resort to entrapment and/or harassment in order to obtain evidence for a solid arrest.[13]

Administrative Roles

Most large inner city police departments have a few selected officers whose function is to provide analysis of research data. Relatively few suburban departments have the extra manpower and funds for such a task. Only the largest suburban departments gather such data and usually have a parttime criminologist analyze data for them. It is obvious that even in a large metropolitan department there is little or no time to train the patrol officer in other than filling out the most routine of forms let alone analyzing crime and traffic data to be used at the operational level.

Intelligence gathered on organized crime and radical group activities is the task of every patrol officer in theory but usually only the largest municipal departments have a staff for such purposes. Further the data gathered by such units is highly sensitive politically. The patrol officer who inadvertently uncovers the activity of such groups is in no position to deal with such data other than to forward it to the departmental special unit handling such matters or to give information to state and federal agencies that are organized to handle such purposes. The intelligence files of such units at the municipal and county levels are often filled with raw information that is usually heresay since the patrol officer has no way of verifying either the source or accuracy of data while on duty. There must be more coordination of state and federal agents with patrol officers if the intelligence gathering function of any metropolitan police department is to be accurate and up to date on any given group of people.[14]

Police training is an essential part of the socialization process toward becoming an efficient patrol officer. The socialization process consists of a combination of both police academy theory and on the job practice with emphasis on the latter as Kirkham can clearly state from first hand knowledge.[15] According to the Task Force Report on the Police of the President's Commission, most academy training programs prepare an officer to perform police work in a mechanical manner. This training does not give the officer insight into the community in which he works, insight into his role as an officer, and a comprehension of the real problems of the criminal justice system.[16] There is also a certain amount of resistance by administrators concerning the use of sociological methods in the academy. They tend to continue to use "seasoned" or retired officers to train new officers. Lastly there is a continued lack of field observation of street problems that are reviewed back in the classroom. In other words, it is from academy theory to patrol reality without the benefit of classroom orientation on the use of discretionary powers and responsibilities to the public.[17]

Executive Roles

Every police department deals with the problem of citizen complaints and charges of corruption against their officers on the street. Inner city departments usually have internal investigation units which conduct periodic investigations of the conduct of patrol officers, sometimes with or without the knowledge of the precinct commander. Most suburban departments cannot spare the manpower for such units so ask the state police to deal with such matters. Most patrol officers and even some line commanders do not like the integrity of their job performance questioned which leads to a morale problem. There is always the possibility of mass media crusades, crime commission investigations, and grand jury probes, and no officer wants to degrade his status as a law enforcement agent by exposing inept or corrupt departmental policies and practices.[18]

Internal investigation unit officers have a rather difficult time in dealing with fellow officers since most patrolmen often overlook and rationalize the serious misconduct of their partner or fellow precinct colleagues due to either misplaced loyalty, fear of retaliation, loss of chance for promotion, transfer to a less desirable or more dangerous patrol area. Further there is usually no well established procedure to deal with the complaint of one officer against another. On both the formal and informal levels, it is difficult for the patrol officer to inform senior officers at the precinct level or higher of the wrongdoing of a fellow officer or for that matter the wrongdoing of a supervisor. Every department requires that a complaint go through the chain of command before dealing with the problem outside the department (i.e., mayor's office, city council, or resort to the mass media). The author has known of instances where an officer would ask for a transfer or resign his position rather than go through the process of exposing alleged improper or illegal practices of fellow officers to anyone including a member of the internal investigation unit.[19]

A related problem that is not aired in public is the problem of dealing with the patrol officer who is an alcoholic. It is estimated that large inner city police departments may have as many as ten percent of their officers who suffer major drinking problems. The author talked with one sergeant with eighteen years service who readily admitted being an alcoholic and a member of AA. Most fellow officers usually cover for such an individual but the general public would probably be somewhat uneasy in having to deal with an inebriated officer or depend on his judgment for their general welfare.

Each patrol officer is taught in the police academy that he is the best community relations unit that the department can provide the public. Most inner city and large suburban police forces have a special community relations unit but the patrol officer still represents community relations to the average citizen. Poor street police procedures, lax discipline over offending officers, and inefficient procedures to handle citizen complaints all make it difficult for an officer to operate on his beat. All too often the police are ignorant of the community which they serve. Most inner city officers live in the suburbs and are not familiar with the life-styles and problems of their work area. Suburban police officers live in a moderate income type suburb but work in a low or high income type suburb. Further all officers except those working in high income areas come in contact with large numbers of low income non-whites who are traditionally hostile to the criminal justice system in general and the police officer in particular. Thus the patrol officer must be especially conscious and cautious when dealing with clients who have been embittered and frustrated by society and who symbolize the police as a repressive instrument of a racist and class biased society.[20]

Police Attitude Toward Their Role

Internal Image

Like any bureaucratic institution, the police department and its members must follow a large number of impersonal and sometimes unintelligible standard operating procedures. In practice each officer learns that there are boundries to his professional role and tolerance limits are discovered which allow the patrol officer to handle problems that the police bureaucracy have not foreseen or have inadvertently created. Further the patrol officer through experience (i.e., trial and error) on the street finds out what standard operating procedures should be followed and what statutes other than those for major offenses can be enforced. He learns that the dispatcher of his communications network is the final word on authority since all conversations are taped for later analysis if a problem occurs. The patrol officer also learns that his shift supervisor will sometimes say one thing at roll call and another thing on the street in addition to the latest orders of the day. Thus the new officer has to learn to formulate his own policy and modify it if it is in conflict with that of a supervisor. Therefore an officer learns quickly that there are risks involved in his personalized practice of justice on the streets as the existence of unofficial policy will probably be denied when confronted by an official inquiry into why the written procedures were not followed to the letter.[21]

Police administrators are charged with developing policy for dealing with crime and potential crime situations but are also accountable to the public when their internal policy comes into confrontation with the public interest. Thus many police administrators are in conflict with the desire for effective policing and the legal and bureaucratic restrictions placed on the police institution by the state on behalf of society. In practice the administrator does not want to face policy issues directly since he would be faced with the fact that many effective police practices do not conform to the standards set by court, legislature, or the constitution of the jurisdiction. Therefore police administrators avoid difficulty with problem police practices through beneign neglect of them until the effectiveness of the practice is diminished or questioned by legal action of the public. Thus many police administrators allow the courts and/or the mayor and city or county council to decide criminal justice policy in a given jurisdiction.[22]

The basic reluctance of the police administrator to deal clearly and concisely with enforcement policies whether determined by judicial or legislative action leaves a great deal of discretionary power in the hands of the patrolman. The officer knows he will be allowed a great amount of official tolerance for his street practices in the name of crime control as long as no one questions current administrative policy or the lack of it. He also knows the administrator will also be the first to deny the existence of tolerance limits if an officer is "caught" exceeding the law by an enraged citizen, community interest group, or the mass media. Thus each officer has his own conception of the police administrator, the standard operating procedures, and the criminal law itself. The patrol officer knows there is a double standard for himself versus his superiors, rich versus poor, white versus nonwhite, male versus female, young versus old, and straight versus deviant. He knows he can receive an official reprimand that will go in his personnel file for enforcement of the law against the "wrong" person or lack of enforcement of the law against the "right" person.[23] Thus many officers become cynical toward the criminal law and the administrative procedures in general that apply to police work.[24]

Almost all police personnel begin their careers as patrol officers. But it is the ambition of most officers to be assigned to the detective division. It usually takes from one to five years before one is eligible for transfer and the typical patrol officer must perform the mechanical and mundane duties of a beat cop with its high visibility and low status. Thus many ambitious and professionally oriented officers leave their patrol job for a federal or state police position before ever getting promoted to detective. Therefore the patrol officer is envious and jealous of the high status of the detective, and the latter looks at the former with disdain and contempt for his lower status and lack of authority in the police bureaucracy. Further police bureaucracies usually have separate lines of command for patrol and detective bureaus which results in one unit being isolated from the other. Thus there is little contact between patrolman and detective, the latter dealing with criminal investigation after the former has come across the offense. This sometimes leads to resentment and rivalry between the two divisions which results in replication of work that can cause unarticulated field work, loss of a case, and even missing an arrest.[25]

Any patrol officer who expects to be promoted to sergeant or transferred to detective division must think of training beyond the level of the police academy. Since many patrol officers are veterans they can take advantage of their educational benefits. In addition many departments in coordination with the Law Enforcement Assistance Administration of the United States Department of Justice have given aid to officers for taking courses at the community and senior college levels. Some suburban departments require that an officer must possess an associate of arts degree to join the force, a few even require a bachelor's degree. Most inner city departments only require a secondary school diploma but think that some higher education would be useful for promotion purposes. These educational requirements are a great improvement over the old concept that an officer only needs academy and inservice training. Thus younger officers have more formal education than older officers and this is a cause of some resentment. Further most departments give continued formal education greater weight in promotion consideration than just time in service. The traditional route to promotion based on rating by superiors, time in grade, and scores on promotion exams has been adjusted to take into account formal college credits received. Thus a relatively new officer could bypass a more experienced man for transfer or promotion and cause more resentment in the department. The college educated patrol officer also wants a more professionalized department with concomitent benefits that have resulted in police sit-ins, rule enforcement slow-downs, and strikes that have caused problems for administrators of the old school (i.e., time in grade plus practical experience).[26]

The policewoman could be a valuable asset to any police department, inner city or suburban. Unfortunately her role is essentially what it was when the Los Angeles Police Department first hired a female officer 66 years ago. Most suburban departments use women in clerical, communications, community relations, domestic relations, and juvenile division work. Few women are used in patrol work although some are utilized in vice and investigative work. There is still a bias against women patrol officers by their male counterparts. Most women are viewed as unable to perform as effectively in patrol situations as men by both training academy and field supervisors. The Metropolitan Police Department (D.C.) has many women officers on patrol in comparison with the surrounding suburban jurisdictions. Although official reports state that the policewoman is as effective as her male counterpart, unofficial conversations with male patrol partners state that females are in general less dependable in physical confrontations with suspects, shooting accuracy, and driving skills. There are also such problems as police wives negative reactions to their husbands going on midnight shift with a female partner, favoratism in promotions, and some refusal to perform dangerous tasks (i.e., searching of suspects and responding to a partner in trouble).[27] Male officers do admit that some women are good at such tasks as traffic control, domestic relations work, and in handling rape cases.

Alex in his perceptive study of Black officers in the New York City Police Department has spelled out the role of the minority officer in a traditionally white occupation.[28] There are a variety of relationships between Black and white officers in the Washington Metropolitan Area which generally support the findings of Alex. Suburban departments have few Black officers while the inner city police force consists of approximately forty percent Black. There are so few Black officers in the suburbs that it is difficult to gain a good impression of the attitude of most white officers toward their Black counterpart. It is apparent that many white officers relate to their Black fellow officers in stereotypical fashion since there are so few on suburban forces. On the other hand, there are a variety of feelings expressed in a large city department. Some whites view Black officers in a racially negative manner, others are indifferent to Blacks, some deal with the Black officer in the same way they would deal with any law enforcement agent (i.e., in a professional manner), and only a few deal with Blacks as social equals. The majority of Black officers tend to be prejudicial against most white officers. They feel that whites are prejudicial toward the Black cop in particular and members of the Black community in general. As Alex states, white patrolmen are viewed as brutal, incompetent, lazy, ultraconservative, and bigoted.[29]

It is quite apparent even to one who does not work with police that there are racial problems on the force as there are similar problems between Black and white communities within a major metropolitan area. For instance there are two fraternal orders of police in most major inner city police departments, one for whites and one for Blacks. Thus Blacks have been forced to socialize with their own since they tend to get a cool reception at traditionally white social functions where wives and girl friends are present. On the job, Black officers in disproportionate numbers serve in both high crime and nonwhite areas. There are less Blacks in the detective and other specialized divisions and few are sergeant or above in rank. Where a Black watch commander is present (i.e., captain) many whites show disrespect which creates an authority problem in addition to the need for overcompensation on the part of the Black administrator. This disrespect is more obvious than the usual grumbling about superior officers which is common in lockerroom gossip.[30]

Most police departments within a metropolitan area are very conscious of their image vis-a-vis other departments. The peculiarities of the Washington metropolitan area sometimes causes unusual problems in addition to the normal problems of liaison between suburban and inner city departments. Within a given area, there is the problem of cooperation and coordination of services. The city police must deal with county police while the latter deal with both the sheriff's department and state police. Each patrol officer is conscious of the status rivalry between suburban and city police but there is common disdain for the questionable expertise of the deputy sheriff.

There is commonly a certain amount of reciprocity between police jurisdictions. While officers from different jurisdictions are on official business, there is an acceptance of each officer but an inner city officer who is off-duty may be treated with little deference on the way home to suburbia especially if Black by white suburban officers if he offers his assistance in an emergency. In the District of Columbia, there is an overlap of municipal and federal police jurisdictions which has led to squabbles over jurisdiction and a confused citizenry. Many times a guilty speeder will be stopped by a federal officer (i.e., capitol hill police, executive protection agency police, or United States park police) only to see a metropolitan police scout car pull up and challenge the federal officer's right to give the ticket. Sometimes several different police respond to the scene of an incident so that both offender and victim are confused as to who has jurisdiction. One also occasionally notices in traffic accidents on border bridges across the Potomac River several patrol cars from different jurisdictions discussing who should handle the case (i.e., county police, suburban city police, metropolitan police of D.C., United States park police, or state police).

External Image

Patrol officers are usually aware of the political orientation of their department. The chief is usually appointed by the mayor and city council in the inner city and county council in the suburbs. The police officer also learns that politicians make all types of statements concerning what the operations, effectiveness, level of corruption, and police-community relations should be at any given time. Officers learn to relate to politicians very cautiously since the latter often tend to view themselves above the law, especially in traffic cases or public drunkeness situations. Only too often in the District of Columbia, a city council member or congressman (i.e., Wilbur Mills at the Tidal Basin) will be approached or even arrested by an officer on a drunk and disorderly, driving while under the influence of alcohol, or a morals charge (i.e., soliciting a prostitute or possession of drugs) only to find out later that the officer is in trouble due to his "improper" handling of the case. This also happens in suburbia but usually in regards to driving under the influence of alcohol or an arrest involving an immediate member of a politician's family.

Most arrests by inner city and suburban police officers are made prior to consultation with the public prosecutor or United States Attorney's office. Most departments assign a lieutenant or captain to review all "paperwork" done by an officer to determine whether a "good" arrest has been made (i.e., all elements of a crime are present, etc.). This is usually done hurriedly the same day the case is presented to the prosecutor's office. The degree of involvement of the prosecutor with the arresting officer is minimal except in major cases. Usually the patrolman's evidence is reviewed before the prosecutor's presentation in court in order to standardize testimony of the arresting officer, but many times a different assistant prosecutor is assigned to the case without informing the officer of the change in personnel. Often the arresting officer comes into court to give testimony only to find a new assistant prosecutor who is not familiar with the case asking the officer the wrong lead questions. This sometimes results in the officer looking bad or losing the case due to lack of preparation on the part of the prosecutor's office. Further a case may be thrown out, trial or hearing postponed or delayed without informing the officer who waits in the courthouse. Many patrolmen have to come in to testify on a day off especially if their special court time (i.e., time off duty with pay) has elapsed. Many seasoned patrolmen become cynical of the prosecutor's office and his methods of handling cases.[31]

The patrol officer has limited contact with traffic and juvenile court magistrates and criminal court judges although he frequently is called upon to give testimony at a variety of judicial proceedings. Judges are seldom cognizant of police department policy (i.e., standard operating procedures) and do not know whether a given officer has been following such policy. Further each officer learns from experience in giving testimony that a given magistrate or judge will be supportive or biased toward his testimony.[32] Thus many police officers who have made a number of court appearances begin to be critical of judicial behavior and question the authority of the judge as being "pro or anti-police".[33]

Patrol officers have little contact with probation/parole officers although the latter are supposed to theoretically develop close working relationships with patrol officers in order to be better able to control and watch their probationers/parolees.[34] Most often a patrol officer is called upon by the parole officer to arrest a parolee who has committed a serious violation of his parole conditions.

Patrol officers who arrest a suspect have to bring them to some sort of lockup. Thus they come in contact with jailors of various types from deputy sheriffs, United States marshalls, and municipal prison guards. Sine the training, education, and status of such prison personnel is lower than that of the typical patrol officer, these corrections officers are looked upon in a condescending and demeaning manner. This usually results in an exchange of negative comments or jokes. Many patrolmen believe that corrections personnel are rejects from various police academy programs.[35]

Police Contact with the Community

According to the President's Commission, it is not possible for a patrol officer to enforce the law and preserve the peace without creating some problems of hostility and resentment with selective segments of the community (i.e., among juveniles, minorities, and deviants). There are many pressures on a patrol officer, especially in an inner city neighborhood which increase the difficulty of doing a job in a professionally impartial manner. A patrolman maintains order on the street, keeps graft to a minimum, and deals with deviants. Each type of community dictates what kind of order is to be kept (i.e., suburbs have different problems than slums). The officer is potentially challenged by all types of people but especially juveniles who by nature test authority structures. In high crime areas the officer is subjected to all types of verbal and even physical abuse. The patrolman whether inner city or suburban is continually exposed to social deviance. He sees the effects of criminality on the victim, confronts the social deviant, and is witness to both class and racial prejudice. Finally the patrolman is always exposed to the possibility of physical attack without justification whether in suburbia or on skid row.[36]

Despite all the research on the police personality, there are a variety of basic personality types wearing blue uniforms.[37] One must examine the circumstances under which an officer operates in a given community by noting actual behavior on the street in interaction with citizens. Verbal abuse and discourtesy is more a problem in low to moderate income communities whether inner city or suburbs. Citizens who have been stopped for a traffic violation or approach an officer for information may be treated in a demeaning manner or subjected to discriminatory statements.[38] Physical misconduct on the part of a patrol officer is rather infrequent today although many syspects have been subjected to what they perceive as physical abuse on the part of an officer. Discrimination by a patrol officer is still prevalent in the inner city and among minorities and youth in the suburbs. Most officers are still prone not to tolerate deviants such as homosexuals, drunks, and addicts who are not in violation of a given statute at the time of an officer's appearance.[39] The use of field interrogation by police is judicially uncertain but is common in inner city and low income suburban neighborhoods where the method is applied in an indiscriminate, abusive, and unfriendly manner. This method is used as a form of crime/delinquency prevention which often ends in discrimination against the lower class and the nonwhite.[40] Arrests for investigation or on suspicion, although not legally founded, have taken place. So-called dragnet raids have been used by utilizing vagrancy, drunkenness, and loitering statutes to arrest juveniles as well as adults.[41] Patrol officers sometimes use what is called the harassment arrest as a means for bothering those involved in victimless crimes such as prostitution and gambling.[42] All these types of police interference with citizen civil rights leads to charges of false arrest. Many patrolmen have to purchase supplemental liability insurance in addition to increasing the workload of the police department legal counsel. Thus patrol officers who have been sued for false arrest after following department procedures shy away from using this aspect of their arrest power.

Conclusion

The patrolman's role is akin to that of the general practioner in medicine. He has to perform all the general police tasks but has low status and authority in the eyes of both his profession and the police in general. The patrol officer has the most contact with the public and most of his arrests are for minor offenses (i.e., vagrancy, disorderly conduct, use of obscene language, loitering, failure to move on, blocking of street or sidewalk, drunkenness, drinking in public, and curfew violations). Further he has to make so many arrests per month (i.e., quota arrests) which the public is aware of despite departmental denials. All this makes the complex and difficult job of patrolling all the more burdensome for the typical officer who would like to exercise his discretion based on the circumstances of each particular case rather than on some departmental quota.

Some critics of police departments argue that many of the problems of the policing process could be solved by a narrow redefining of the patrol role and function. Domestic relations work is a potentially dangerous part of patrol work and accounts for a high percentage of work response by the police. Crimes without victims also accounts for much police work which can also be degrading and unrewarding for the officer especially if he has to use questionable investigative procedures to apprehend an offender that no complaint has been issued against by the public. Last patrol officers have to deal with a large number of juveniles who have committed both criminal and status offenses. Parents in both inner city and suburbs usually deny their child or adolescent is guilty of any wrongdoing which makes the patrolman's role more uncertain to both superiors and court personnel. Therefore critics want family problems handled by social service agencies, victimless crimes should be legislatively decriminalized, and juvenile problems handled by school, church, and social services agencies.

The proposed changes put forth by critics of the patrolman's role are limited in practice because few efforts have been made to develop alternatives to police involvement in the above areas by inner city and suburban governmental agencies or citizens groups. These proposed patrol role changes do not consider the crime preventive and control functions of the three areas of patrol work just discussed. Thus domestic relations problems often lead to assault or murder of a spouse or even to the responding patrol officer. The person indulging in a socalled victimless crime like prostitution may end up a robbery victim. Finally the juvenile who is allowed to repeatedly break the law may end up an adult criminal or at least someone indifferent to the community standards set for normal behavior.

Notes

1 William Evan (ed.), Law and Society, New York: Free Press, 1962.

2 The President's Commission on Law Enforcement and Administration of Justice, Task Force Report: The Police, Washington, D.C.: U.S. Government Printing Office, 1967, p. 47.

3 Ibid., 13.

4 Jerome Skolnick, Justice Without Trial: Law Enforcement in Democratic Society, New York: John Wiley & Sons, 1975.

5 George Kirkham, "A Professor's Street Lessons," FBI Law Enforcement Bulletin, March, 1974, pp. 4-6.

6 The President's Commission on Law Enforcement and Administration of Justice, Task Force Report: The Police, op. cit., p. 21.

7 Ibid., p. 22.

8 Ibid., p. 24.

9 George Felkenes, The Criminal Justice System: Its Functions and Personnel, Englewood Cliffs, New Jersey: Prentice-Hall, 1973, p. 29.

10 The President's Commission on Law Enforcement and Administration of Justice, op. cit. p. 21.

11 Felkenes, op. cit., p. 29.

12 The President's Commission on Law Enforcement and Administration of Justice, op. cit., pp. 179-180; Felkenes, op. cit., 30.

13 The President's Commission on Law Enforcement and Administration of Justice, _op. cit._, pp. 96-97; Skolnick, _op. cit._, p. 185.

14 The President's Commission on Law Enforcement and Administration of Justice, _op. cit._, p. 80.

15 Kirkham, _op. cit._, pp. 3-6.

16 The President's Commission on Law Enforcement and Administration of Justice, _op. cit._, p. 138.

17 _Ibid._, p. 75, 139; Arthur Niederhoffer, _Behind the Shield: The Police in Urban Society_, Garden City, New York: Doubleday and Company, 1969, pp. 43-54.

18 Lawrence Sherman, _Police Corruption: A Sociological Perspective_, Garden City, New York: Doubleday and Company, 1974, pp. 246-267.

19 The President's Commission on Law Enforcement and Administration of Justice, _op. cit._, 81, 194.

20 _Ibid._, pp. 149-150.

21 _Ibid._, pp. 52-53.

22 _Ibid._, pp. 16-17; Niederhoffer, _op. cit._, pp. 89-92.

23 Skolnick, _op. cit._, 182-199.

24 Niederhoffer, _op. cit._, pp. 95-108.

25 _Ibid._, pp. 81-85; The President's Commission on Law Enforcement and Administration of Justice, _op. cit._, pp. 53, 141-142.

26 Niederhoffer, _op_. _cit_., pp. 27-33; The President's Commission on Law Enforcement and Administration of Justice, _op_. _cit_., pp. 126-218, 140-142.

27 The President's Commission on Law Enforcement and Administration of Justice, _op_. _cit_., p.125.

28 Nicholas Alex, _Black in Blue: A Study of the Negro Policeman_, New York: Appleton-Century-Crofts, 1969, pp. 85-113.

29 _Ibid_., p. 97.

30 _Ibid_., pp. 104-113.

31 The President's Commission on Law Enforcement and Administration of Justice, _op_. _cit_., pp. 30-31; Skolnick, _op_. _cit_., pp. 199-202.

32 The President's Commission on Law Enforcement and Administration of Justice, _op_. _cit_., p. 31.

33 Skolnick, _op_. _cit_., pp. 225-226.

34 The President's Commission on Law Enforcement and Administration of Justice, _Task Force Report: Corrections_, Washington, D.C.: U.S. Government Printing Office, 1967, pp. 69-70.

35 _Ibid_., pp. 94-95.

36 The President's Commission on Law Enforcement and Administration of Justice, _Task Force Report: The Police_, Washington, D.C.: U.S. Government Printing Office, 1967, p. 179.

37 Skolnick, _op_. _cit_., 42-66; Niederhoffer, _op_. _cit_., pp. 109-160.

38 The President's Commission on Law Enforcement and Administration of Justice, _Task Force Report_: The Police, Washington, D.C.: U.S. Government Printing Office, 1967, pp. 180-181.

39 _Ibid_., p. 183.

40 _Ibid_., pp. 183-185.

41 _Ibid_., p. 186.

42 _Ibid_., p. 187.

Prosecutors' Role in Plea Bargaining: Reasons Related to Actions

Mary S. Knudten

Plea bargaining has been the focus of considerable attention within the criminal justice process. In spite of recommendations on the part of some groups that plea bargaining should be eliminated, it is conceded by many that this practice is likely to continue. The American Bar Association regards it as sufficiently important to have issued a report on Standards Relating to the Prosecution and Defense Function (1971) which highlights the standards and practices which should be followed by prosecutors and defense attorneys while engaging in such activity. In spite of numerous case studies of prosecutors' offices, little systematic or comparative research has been carried out regarding the reasons for plea bargaining or the relation of these reasons to actual practice. Analysis of these issues is important to an understanding of the practical realities of the criminal justice process.

The various case studies of prosecutors' offices have led to suggestions of a number of reasons for the prominence of plea bargaining. Alschuler (1968:51) and others (Blumberg, 1967:21; Yale Law Journal 1972:286) have stressed the heavy case loads of prosecutors and the limited resources which are available to actually prosecute cases in court as a primary reason for plea bargaining. On the other hand, Heumann (1975:515-528) has shown that case pressure or work load is not a "causal" factor associated with plea bargaining. Using data on Connecticut courts from 1880 to 1954 and comparing the mean ratio of trials to total cases disposed in low volume and high volume courts, Heumann shows that there is very little difference either over time or from one type of court to another in the use of trials. Nevertheless, prosecutors may indicate that work load is a factor in their thinking when engaging in negotiations.

However, work load and limited resources is not recognized as the only valid reason to invoke negotiations. Another reason which is consistently cited is the need to ameliorate legislative overcriminalization. Legislators tend to make a crime of everything that people are against without regard for administrative convenience or potential enforceability. Thus a prosecutor may decide that some laws are outdated, and others no longer reflect society's interest by specifying penalties that go beyond acceptability.

Taking account of the defendant's social situation or the peculiar circumstances of a particular case is usually thought of as a means to individualize justice. Laws must be written for the general case and specific variations can only be accounted for by the actions of men. Therefore, prosecutors may need to act through negotiating to insure that defendants with unique characteristics or situations are not unfairly categorized with others whose circumstances differ.

A variety of legal problems may arise in a case which would cause a prosecutor to search for a less demanding form of prosecution. Finding errors in the arrest or search procedures, levying a statute of limitations, the death, disappearance or unwillingness to testify of a witness, and other types of legal problems are potential reasons for negotiation as well.

Kress (1976) cites three factors as commonly involved in the charging decision which, of course, precedes any negotiation decision. Those are: whether there is sufficient evidence (legal decision); whether prosecution is in the public interest (systemic factor) including such considerations as the reality of limited system resources, the cost to society of prosecution, and the cooperation of the suspect; and whether alternatives are available (Kress, 1976:110-111). Similar factors may be considered in deciding whether to plea bargain.

This paper examines which reasons are indicated by prosecutors as important in plea bargaining, determines the extent to which these reasons are associated with actual plea negotiation, and specifies the conditions under which one reason or another is associated with plea bargaining.

METHODOLOGY AND FINDINGS

The findings presented here come from a survey of county prosecutors in the states of Wisconsin and Michigan. The data reported are based upon the responses of 77 prosecutors, 50 percent of the total number available in the two states. Only the elected prosecutor in each county, no appointed assistants or deputies, are included.

Each prosecutor was asked to respond, using a Likert-type scale to rate importance, to a series of reasons which may be important in causing the prosecutor to enter into negotiations with a defendant. A factor analysis of these reasons for negotiating reveals that the reasons group themselves into patterns which coincide with those generally acknowledged.

Reasons for Plea Bargaining

The principal-factor orthogonal solution yields four factors which may be titled, F1:Legal Problems, F2:Limited Resources Rationalized, F3:Individualize Justice, and F4:Overcriminalization. Factor loadings are presented in Table 1. Loadings of .30 and over are highlighted by boxing. There is very little overlap in the loadings on the several factors, the two exceptions being a positive loading of work load on F2:Limited Resources Rationalized and negative loading of work load on F3:Individualize Justice; and an overlap of personal sympathy on both F2:Limited Resources Rationalized and F4:Overcriminalization. The first factor, Legal Problems, explains 38 percent of the variance, Limited Resources Rationalized explains 33 percent, and the last two factors explain 16 and 12 percent of the variance each.

Factors Associated with Reasons for Plea Bargaining

To specify the conditions under which these reasons are given a number of other factors were controlled for and correlation coefficients were calculated. The factors used as controls include the socioeconomic background of the prosecutor, measured by combining the educational achievement of both mother and father; the numbers of years the individual has been an attorney; the number of years experience as a prosecutor; the urbanness of the prosecutor, combining both the individual's background with location of current practice and considering county size of 50,000 or greater as urban; whether the prosecutor is full-time or part-time; whether the individual expects to seek further political office; the prosecutor's response to items measuring the Packer Crime Control-Due Process Models; the political liberalism-conservatism of the prosecutor; whether more or less felony arrestees are charged; and whether the defense attorney or another person generally initiates negotiation discussions.

The factors relating to the background and experience of the prosecutor were chosen for control because each of them, theoretically, could influence the thinking of the prosecutor relative to reasons for negotiations. The attitudinal factors, each of which is elaborated in the following paragraphs, were also chosen because of theoretical relevancy.

Herbert Packer first suggested that the criminal process may be viewed as a continuum which emphasizes at the limits either the rights of society or the rights of the individual. His two models, Crime Control and Due Process, have been elaborated in THE LIMITS OF THE CRIMINAL SANCTION (Packer, 1968). Basically, crime control values focus on the proposition that repression of criminal conduct is the most important function of the criminal process and that it is important for the system to be efficient and produce a high rate of apprehension and conviction. A premium is placed on speed which requires a good deal of informality and uniformity, and on finality, which encourages the minimization of challenges. These values legitimize the use of extra-judicial processes in preference to judicial processes, and various forms of informal operation as opposed to formal are encouraged, especially the use of the guilty plea. Due process values, on the other hand, emphasize that the determination of guilty is made not only on the basis of evidence presented, but also on whether the evidence is presented in regular procedural fashion. It assumes that the use of discretion by the prosecutor is a substantial abandonment of the adversary system.

Prosecutor views regarding Packer's Models were measured with Likert-like items which incorporated either crime control or due process values. The responses to these items were combined in an index, with a high score indicating Crime Control. The range for this variable is between 7 and 20 with a mean of 15.2 and a standard deviation of 2.34.

A second attitudinal dimension, political liberalism-conservatism was measured by asking prosecutors to rank a series of terminal values (Rokeach, 1971:21-39). Rokeach has found that the relative ranking of freedom and equality within a series of 18 values served to differentiate persons with liberal and conservative political perspectives. In fact, the relative rankings are associated with behavior (Rokeach, 1968:171-172). According to their rankings on these measures, 60 percent of prosecutors in Wisconsin and Michigan are liberal, 40 percent are conservative.

The reason for controlling for who initiates the negotiation is that this factor is clearly one which could have an effect on the reason a prosecutor would plea bargain. Among the respondents in this study, most, 93 percent, indicated the defense attorney was most likely to initiate negotiations.

To describe the expected relations which were anticipated between these factors and the reasons for plea bargaining several hypotheses were developed.

Hypothesis 1: None of the control variables will be associated with F1: Legal Problems as a reason for negotiation.

When legal problems arise in a case, there is little a prosecutor can do, especially if she/he does not want to dismiss the case, but to plea bargain. Thus, one would not expect any single type of prosecutor to cite this reason more often than other types.

Hypothesis 2: Urban prosecutors with a Crime Control and/or liberal political perspective will cite F2: Limited Resources Rationalized as a reason for negotiation.

Most studies of urban prosecutors offices have spoken of the heavy work load and the pressures on prosecutors to expedite cases. This perspective is also characteristic of the crime control approach. Being politically liberal may cause a prosecutor to cite this reason, primarily because of the rationalization reasons associated with this factor. As was indicated in Table 1, personal sympathy, a feeling that public opinion would support negotiation and a cooperative attitude on the part of the defendant also loaded on this factor. These perspectives may be typically ascribed to persons with a liberal political perspective. A conservative is more likely to take a hard line approach and ignore personal feelings and those of the public oriented to letting the defendant off easier.

Hypothesis 3: Rural, part-time, more experienced attorneys will indicate the need to individualize justice as a reason for negotiating.

The ability and consciousness of the need to individualize justice by considering each case unique rather than to develop general categories for the processing of cases (Sudnow, 1968:255-276) is more likely to exist among prosecutors in rural settings, those who are also more likely to be part-time. Knowledge of the individual and more extensive background information about the case is more likely to be available in that type of setting. It may take some experience to know quite how to do this, however. It is easier to think in terms of predetermined categories than to take account of the particular circumstances of the situation and the defendant. More experienced attorneys may be able to do this better.

Hypothesis 4: Urban prosecutors and those with a liberal political perspective will be most sensitive to overcriminalization through legislation and will cite F4:Overcriminalization as a reason to bargain.

Associated with the work load issue, urban prosecutors will think in terms of overcriminalization, especially as it is reflected in the penalties specified for various criminal activities. Liberals are noted for their desire to decriminalize certain statutes and at the very least to remove harsh penalties. Thus both these factors can be expected to be related to having indicated overcriminalization as a reason for negotiation.

The findings which test these hypotheses consist of correlation coefficients for each of the control variables with the factor scores developed on the basis of the factor analysis (see Table 2). While it was expected that none of the control variables would be significantly related to F1:Legal Problems, one is, namely the initiation of negotiation by someone other than the defense attorney. This is understandable in that when legal problems arise, it may be in the interest of the prosecutor to plea bargain rather than have a case dismissed.

The fact that no other variable is associated with this factor confirms the ideas stated in the hypothesis that legal problems as a reason for negotiation are not unique for one group or type of prosecutors, whether considering background variables or attitudinal perspectives.

It was expected that urban prosecutors, those with a Crime Control perspective, and the liberals would indicate F2:Limited Resources Rationalized as a reason for negotiation. Actually the urbanness of the prosecutor, and his/her having a Crime Control perspective is not associated, while being liberal is. In addition, part-timeness and more experience as an attorney are significantly associated with this reason. It is interesting that the urbanness of the prosecutor is not correlated with this reason. Both the media and the literature suggest that prosecutors offices in large metropolitan communities are overburdened with heavy work loads. Lack of association does not mean this is not a problem, it simply means that limited resources is equally a problem in rural areas. In fact, the negative sign on this coefficient indicates that to a slight extent, rural prosecutors are more likely to feel that limited resources and work load cause them to plea bargain. This is reinforced by the finding that part-timeness is significantly correlated with this reason. In fact it helps to explain why both urban and rural prosecutors have such a heavy work load. Being able to devote only part of work time to prosecutorial duties effects work load just as the crush of cases does in urban areas. Being part-time and rural are associated (r - .42).

Why those prosecutors with a Crime Control viewpoint do not indicate this reason to bargain more than those with a Due Process perspective is not clear. One would expect those who put a premium on efficiency and informality to be more likely to cite this reason than those concerned for the legal procedures being followed. However, as is reported elsewhere (Knudten, 1977), these prosecutors do not distribute themselves equally on the Crime Control-Due Process continuum, but rather concentrate toward the crime control end. Lack of sufficient variability on this variable may contribute to the lack of association.

The association of experience as an attorney with the Limited Rescurces Rationalized reason is more difficult to understand. It may occur because of the rationalization items which are part of this reason, rather than because of the work load item.

Experience was expected to be associated with F3:Individualize Justice but did not turn out to be. However, the other two expected relationships are both correlated. Rural, part-time prosecutors seem to be more concerned for the defendant's prior criminal record and the particular situation of the crime than their urban counterparts. As indicated in the explanation of the hypothesis, it is reasonable to expect prosecutors in this framework to be able to consider individual variations to a greater extent than those in urban settings.

Regarding the last reason for negotiation F4:Overcriminalization, it was expected that prosecutors and liberals would likely favor this reason for bargaining. Urban, full-time prosecutors are significantly more likely to do so. The extent to which urbanness is associated is indicated by the fact that this relationship remains relatively strong (.22) even when full- or part-timeness is controlled. However, liberals are not more likely to cite this reason than conservatives. In fact, the positive sign for this correlation indicates that conservatives more than liberals indicate overcriminalization as a reason, although the relationship is low.

Reasons Related to Actions

Each prosecutor was also asked what percentage of all guilty pleas handled through his office was a negotiated plea. Zero-order correlations of the factors with this variable reveal that only F1:Legal Problems is significantly correlated with actual negotiation (see Table 3). In fact, while the correlation values are very low, F3:Individualized Justice and F4:Overcriminalization are negatively associated with actual negotiation.

While the direct correlation of bargaining reasons with actions yielded the finding that only F1:Legal Problems is significantly associated with plea bargaining, the fact that other variables are associated with the reasons suggests that controlling for them may elaborate the relationships between reasons and actions. For example, Legal Problems as a reason for negotiation is positively associated with actual plea bargaining particularly among more experienced, rural, part-time prosecutors with high socioeconomic background and a due process perspective who indicate fewer than 10 percent of felony arrestees are not charged and who do not expect to run for further political office (see Table 4).

On the other hand, F2:Limited Resources Rationalized, which was not significantly correlated with actual plea bargaining under uncontrolled conditions, still is not correlated, even when controlling for a variety of other variables. What this means is that while work load and the other conditions which load on this factor are mentioned by prosecutors as being somewhat important, under none of the tested conditions is this reason associated with actually engaging in plea bargaining. In other words, those who give this reason do not necessarily plea bargain that much.

The correlations that exist for F3:Individualize Justice are all negative meaning that within all of the groupings where a significant association is noted, the prosecutors who give this as a reason for plea bargaining actually do not engage in negotiation to any great extent. Additionally, the prosecutors within these groupings who do plea bargain, do so for other reasons. More experienced, rural, part-time attorneys with low socioeconomic background and a due process perspective and those who indicate less than 10 percent of felony arrestees are not charged, and do not expect to run for political office again fall into this category. These persons also indicate the defense attorney is likely to initiate the negotiations. It must be noted that these are pretty much the same categories of prosecutors who indicated plea bargaining because of legal problems. What this means is that when these persons plea bargain it is more because of legal problems. Those within these categories who cite individualizing justice as a reason for negotiation do much less of it.

To some extent, the same situation is evident in relation to F4:Overcriminalization except that here negative significant correlations are apparent for those with both limited experience as an attorney and a prosecutor and those who are rural and part-time. These findings can be interpreted to mean that although some of these types of prosecutors will cite overcriminalization as a reason to negotiate, when they do, they plea bargain less in actuality. This conforms to the earlier reported finding that urban, full-time prosecutors were more likely to cite this as a reason to begin with.

SUMMARY AND CONCLUSIONS

The reasons Wisconsin and Michigan prosecutors give as important for plea bargaining group themselves into patterns that conform to those cited in the literature. The most important reason cited is that there are legal problems with a case. Somewhat less important are work load and limited resources problems, those which have been frequently emphasized elsewhere. The work of Milton Heumann (1975) supports a finding that work load is not as important as might have been suspected. Other reasons, the need to individualize justice or to counteract overcriminalization, are somewhat less important.

Different types of prosecutors vary on the reasons they indicate are important. No one single type emphasizes legal problems. This highlights the universality of this reason. The more experienced, part-time prosecutors with liberal political perspectives are most likely to say work load and other rationalizing reasons are important for plea bargaining. Rural, part-time attorneys focus on individualizing justice while overcriminalization is most often mentioned by urban, full-time prosecutors.

The only reason which is associated with actual plea bargaining at a statistically significant level is legal problems. However, when controls are used, other correlations of reasons with actions become apparent. Legal problems is correlated especially among experienced, rural, part-time prosecutors with high socioeconomic background who exhibit a due process perspective, and among those who charge most felony arrestees and do not expect to run for office again.

Experienced, rural, part-time attorneys with low socioeconomic status background, who have a due process perspective, charge most arrestees and who do not expect to run for office again and who cite the need to individualize justice do less plea bargaining. Similarly, less experienced attorneys and prosecutors in a rural, part-time setting who espouse overcriminalization as a reason for plea bargaining do less of it.

Limited resources rationalized is not associated with actual bargaining even among subgroups of prosecutors. Giving this as a reason and actually engaging in negotiation simply do not coincide.

The net result of this study is the finding that situations vary for prosecutors just as they do for defendants. Where the prosecutor holds office, how much experience she/he has, and his/her viewpoints may affect the reasons cited for plea bargaining as well as the extent to which these reasons are linked to actions. The fact of plea bargaining remains, however. This study merely examines some of the conditions which may be related to it.

References

Advisory Committee on the Prosecution and Defense Functions, Standards Relating to the Prosecution and Defense Function. American Bar Association Project on Minimum Standards for Criminal Justice, Approved draft. 1971.

Alschuler, Albert. "The Prosecutor's Role in Plea Bargaining," University of Chicago Law Review, 36:50-112, 1968.

Blumberg, Abraham S. Criminal Justice. Chicago: Quadrangle Books, 1967.

Heumann, Milton. "A Note on Plea Bargaining and Case Pressure," Law and Society Review 9:515-528, 1975.

Knudten, Mary S. "A Test of Packer's Two Models: Do They Define Prosecutors' Attitudes or Influence Their Behavior?" Unpublished paper, 1977.

Kress, Jack. "Progress and Prosecution," The Annals of the American Academy of Political and Social Science 423 (January):99-116, 1976.

Packer, Herbert. The Limits of the Criminal Sanction. Stanford: Stanford University Press, 1968.

Rokeach, Milton. Beliefs, Attitudes and Values: A Theory of Organization and Change. San Francisco: Jossey-Bass, 1968.

______________. "The Measurement of Values and Value Systems," Social Psychology and Political Behavior, eds. Gilbert Abcarian and John W. Soule. Columbus, Ohio: Charles E. Merrill, pp. 21-39, 1971.

Sudnow, David. "Normal Crimes: Sociological Features of the Criminal Code in a Public Defender Office," Social Problems 12 (Winter): 255-276, 1965.

Yale Law Journal. "Restructuring Plea Bargaining," Yale Law Journal, 82:286-312, 1972.

TABLE 1

FACTOR ANALYSIS
Principal-factor Orthogonal Solution with Iteration

Reason for Negotiation	F1 Legal Problems	F2 Limited Resources Rationalized	F3 Indivi- dualize Justice	F4 Over criminal- ization	h^2
Witness not willing to continue	78	-05	-14	15	66
Weak case	60	06	14	-06	38
Repetitious counts	41	24	-14	-12	26
New plea provides adequate punishment	36	-21	-09	-04	18
Workload	06	63	-30	05	49
Personal sympathy	-22	60	07	64	82
Popular sentiment or public opinion	-01	58	04	-17	37
Cooperative attitude of defendant	01	32	25	10	18
Defendant's prior criminal record	-08	-03	57	04	33
Particular crime charged	-01	-01	34	-06	12
Penalties of law too harsh	01	-05	-02	34	12

FACTOR	H	% Variance
1	1.51	38.4
2	1.31	33.4
3	.62	15.8
4	.49	12.4

TABLE 2

Zero-order Correlations
Control Variables and Reason for Negotiation Factor Scores

Control Variable	Reason for Negotiation FACTOR SCORES 1 (Legal Prob.)	2 (Re-sources)	3 (Indiv. Justice)	4 (Over-crim.)
Socioeconomic Background	-04	-10	-15	01
Experience as an Attorney	-15	20*	11	05
Experience as a Prosecutor	-11	18	06	09
Urbanness of Prosecutor (Positive = Urban)	09	-09	-20*	28*
Full-timeness (Positive = Part-time)	-14	29**	22*	-19*
Expect to Seek Political Office (Positive = Yes or Maybe)	07	-11	07	16
Crime Control-Due Process Perspective (Positive = Crime Control)	01	-09	-14	07
Political Liberalism-Conservatism (Positive = Conservative)	-06	-26*	13	11
Percent Felony Arrestees Not Charged	-10	-04	-01	-02
Who Initiates Negotiation (Positive = Defense Attorney)	-28*	-04	-14	04

* statistically significant at the .05 level
** statistically significant at the .005 level

TABLE 3

Zero-order Correlation Matrix
Reason for Negotiation Factor Scores
and Percent Guilty Pleas Negotiated

	X_1	X_2	X_3	X_4
X_1 Factor 1 (Legal Problem)				
X_2 Factor 2 (Resources)	-04			
X_3 Factor 3 (Individ. Justice)	-10	-03		
X_4 Factor 4 (Overcriminalization)	-10	03	05	
Y Percent Guilty Pleas Negotiated	23*	07	-18	-12

* statistically significant at the .05 level

TABLE 4

Zero-order Correlation of Factor Scores with Percent Negotiated Pleas, Controlling Other Independent Variables

Number of Cases	Variable - Value	FACTOR SCORES 1 (Legal Prob.)	2 (Re-sources)	3 (Indiv. Justice)	4 (Over-Crim.)
37	Socioeconomic Background -- Low	18	04	-37*	-16
39	Socioeconomic Background -- High	27*	04	01	-10
40	Experience as an Attorney 0-9 Years	21	02	-02	-34*
36	Experience as an Attorney 10 years plus	26	14	-34*	10
34	Experience as a Prosecutor 0-2 years	06	12	-08	-38*
42	Experience as a Prosecutor 2.5 years plus	38*	03	-24	06
55	Urbanness - Rural	26*	05	-36*	-28*
20	Urbanness - Urban	13	02	17	13
32	Full-timeness -- Full-time	18	14	-04	15
44	Full-timeness -- Part-time	27*	02	-32*	-33*
33	Expect to Seek Political Office No	32*	08	-31*	-22
42	Expect to Seek Political Office Yes or Maybe	22	03	-06	01
38	Due Process Perspective	36*	11	-29*	-07
38	Crime Control Perspective	08	02	-08	-18
45	Political Liberal	20	01	-16	-05
28	Political Conservative	25	02	-17	-15
49	Percent Felony Arrestees Not Charged Less than 10%	23*	10	-30*	-20

TABLE 4 (continued)

Number of Cases	Variable - Value	FACTOR SCORES 1 (Legal Prob.)	2 (Re-sources)	3 (Indiv. Justice	4 (Over-Crim.)
27	Percent Felony Arrestees Not Charged 10% plus	22	-01	07	01
66	Who Initiates Negotiation Defense Attorney	15	-05	-21*	-12
5	Who Initiates Negotiation Other	79	28	17	-45
	UNCONTROLLED CORRELATION	23*	07	-18	-12

* statistically significant at the .05 level

The Bus Driver and the Management of Deviance

Gordon E. Misner and
William F. McDonald

While social pressure is a force for social order on buses, and in spite of the fact that passengers do occasionally aid in controlling troubled situations on buses, the greatest amount of active management of deviance on buses is conducted by the drivers. Their ability to manage deviance, however, is not learned overnight. It is one of the two major skills which a driver learns over a period of time, namely, handling the equipment and handling the public. Of the two, the latter seems to take longer to master.

In this section, the problem of how drivers deal with deviance is examined. Since the management of deviance is a skill that is learned, it is important to examine how drivers learn it. Also, since different drivers use different strategies, a review of the different strategies will be made for the purpose of assessing their relative frequency of use. Certain common problems on buses will be examined in detail; furthermore, the reasons for the differential employment of these strategies for dealing with deviance will be offered. Finally, an estimate of the success of these methods, as given by the drivers surveyed, will be presented.

"Meeting the Public"

Any driver will tell you that if you don't like to deal with the public you shouldn't be a bus driver. "Meeting the public," as it is known to drivers, is a requirement of the job and a demanding one. Even under "normal" circumstances, i.e., when passengers are not engaging in deviant behavior, handling passengers is a source of strain on drivers, as the following typology of "normal," every day passengers suggests. This typology was developed by a delightfully humorous driver who, in the opinion of certain management personnel was one of the "worst" drivers in the division. His difficulty was with passengers! He was always arguing with them and they often complained about him. His difficulty is our gain!

His typology is composed of four classifications of passengers:

Congenial type - the nice guy - "the girl you wouldn't mind waiting for."
These people have their change ready, smile at the driver, speak to him. They could be male or female. They say things like "good morning," "pardon me," or "will you let me know where I get off?"

Chip-on-the-shoulder type - henpecked - moody - discontented. This type could be either male or female, between the ages of 30 and 40. He (she) is usually dressed nicely, lives in a "good area" but is discontent for some reason. If he (she) asks for a transfer, he (she) grabs it, uses abusive language, offends the ladies, and then sits down like a sheep because he (she) realizes he (she) did wrong and because his (her) friends have seen him (her). A typical interchange between driver and this type of passenger is the following: "Won't you please step up?" (said in a highly stylized politeness). Response: "Where do you want me to go goddamit?"

Also, this is the lady who complains because the driver wasn't over to the curb or calls out to him, "Why are you driving so fast?" or "Didn't you see that lady running for the bus?" This is the inconsiderate type who forgets the driver's humanity, has no respect for him, cusses him and asks unnecessary questions. These people have ridden the same line for years, but they always ignore the signs and whenever they hear another passenger ask a question, they ask the same question.

Senior-citizen or older. These passengers are male or female. They need extra help boarding or de-boarding and are often critical of the driver's "impatience." (Actually, many drivers are more annoyed by this type of passenger than any others.) Because of age, they are less responsive to the social pressures on the bus and hence are less restrained with their criticism of drivers. While most passengers grin and bear petty annoyances, the elderly passengers are often vociferous in their complaints about driving too fast, or too jerkily, or not pulling to the curb, or about the tardiness of the service. (Many drivers complained about the medicard arrangements in some cities which allow senior citizens to ride for reduced fare during certain times of the day, e.g. 9 A.M. to 3 P.M. The drivers' complaints were two-fold. They don't like driving elderly people, generally, because of the associated safety, time, and nuisance problems. Secondly, many complaints about fares arise as a result of the special hours. Elderly people either don't know the hours, or pretend not to know the hours or argue with drivers that the special hours are unfair and that senior citizens should get reduced rates any time of the day.

The dollar-bill type. This type may be male or female, any age. No matter how many times he rides the bus, he never has the correct change. If the driver tries to point out the inconvenience he causes, this type gets upset. This often happens in low-income areas. This type runs the driver out of change, which for some drivers is seen as a form of harassment. This type also slows the service down, forces the driver to get behind schedule, and thereby puts a strain on him because the driver must then speed up and drive recklessly to catch up to schedule.

Various lengths of time have been suggested by different drivers regarding how long it takes and what is involved in learning to deal with the public. One driver suggested that it took three years of "adjusting;" another suggested that the process is better titled "rehabilitation;" still another suggested that after he had worked two months and was called into the "old man's" office about a complaint from one of the passengers, he knew from then on how to deal with passengers, namely, "say nothing, hear nothing, do nothing." Still another driver discussing the "breaking-in" period said, "During the first couple years, you are always fighting, arguing, taking things out on your wife. Then you either learn to get along with the public or quit." Several drivers mentioned the cultural differences that exist among the riding public in different areas of the city and the necessity for the driver to be flexible enough to "meet his environment," i.e. change his style according to the people for whom he is driving. Many Negro drivers cited their ability to get along with Negroes, especially youths, better than non-Negro drivers.

One Negro driver described how when he first worked on a morning run in a Negro district he tried to be a "nice guy." He smiled at his passengers and said, "good morning." However, he found this usually annoyed them and often brought snaps like, "Why yo' smilin' like that?" So he began feigning depression and discontent, and found he got along with his morning Negro passengers much better. But, he could not use the frown for his afternoon Caucasian office-worker passengers who preferred to joke and banter with him.

One driver expressed the opinion that meeting the public should be as automatic as driving the bus. He notes that driving is only a semi-conscious (i.e. guided by reflex and muscle memory) process once it has been mastered. Similarly, he felt, meeting the public can be another semi-conscious reflex. It includes putting on a half smile, at least, and perhaps saying, "hello."

Inadequacy of Existing Training Programs

In searching for the ways in which drivers are socialized into their profession and learn to meet the public, one negative finding was clear. Drivers do not adequately learn about dealing with the public through the initial training program which the companies give them. Instructors in these programs were aware of the difficulty of teaching "psychology," i.e. how to deal with the public. Their only advice to their trainees is to "use common sense." However, this advice is tantamount to no advice and is perhaps misleading and demoralizing in a way. Management does have a way of dealing with the public that it wants its drivers to observe which is not accurately indicated in the advice to use "common sense." Rather, a more appropriate admonition would be "exercise more personal restraint than you ever thought you had." Management does not want its drivers to become involved in arguments, much less fights, with customers. However, many drivers seem not to know about this policy, or if they do know, then do not fully appreciate it, until they have violated it and been reported. Then, when they learn about it, they are demoralized. Previously, they thought of themselves as "captains of their ships." They feel stripped of a power which, in fact as far as management is concerned, they never had. Their response to this is often the response described above, namely, apathy and indifference toward any events on the buses. As one driver said, "...you can't enforce the rules because you will end up in the office with a reprimand or whatever, and this is why a lot of guys give up...."

It can be seen that the most frequent response was that drivers felt their training programs were adequate! Of those improvements which drivers did mention, the area most often mentioned was that of "dealing with the public." Another topic often mentioned was really a subtopic of dealing with the public, namely, more training on how to deal with disturbances on buses.

It is interesting that drivers should request this type of training while training instructors who were interviewed felt that the subject could not be taught; it could only be learned through the ubiquitous "school of hard knocks." Perhaps this difference in opinion pin-points the limitations of some of the current trainers. They may be competent to teach the use of the equipment, but less skilled at teaching the art of manipulating people. This particular art can be taught, and is regularly a part of the curriculum of schools that train salesmen and business men. It is also already being done in an informal way in the transit companies. Sometimes the informality with which it is taught is more structured than at other times. That is, some drivers known for being able to get along with passengers are sought out by other drivers and asked for advice. In other cases, the skills of dealing with the public are transmitted to the new driver through episodes related by drivers in the gilley room and through <u>ex post facto</u> instruction from the superintendent after the driver has made a mistake. A portion of the driver questionnaire was devoted to the adequacy of training in the art of dealing with people. Two criteria of "adequacy" were used: (1) If a training program is adequate, then most drivers who go through it would know how to handle most situations it is designed to teach them how to handle, (2) and most drivers would, in practice, follow the methods they were taught for dealing with such situations. These criteria were incorporated in the design of a question which presented the drivers with six situations involving people-problems which occur on or in connection with operating buses. The drivers were asked to indicate whether the company would agree with or disagree with how each would handle the situation. If he was not sure, what the company's opinion would be, he was to indicate that. Thus, fewer drivers feel the company would disagree with how they would deal with event #6, a regular passenger who does not have a fare, than event #1, a bus load of school kids getting on without paying fares. Most significant is that a substantial minority of the drivers are either handling situations in ways that the company would not agree with or are not sure of how the company wants the situation handled. Thus, by both criteria of adequacy employed, it can be said that training programs are not accomplishing their goals.

It is obvious that greater attention should be given to teaching drivers how to deal with the public. More use should be made of drivers with known skills in this area. Also, professional consultants in the management of people should be brought in on a periodic basis as part of a continuing in-service training program. These consultants should conduct short clinics demonstrating techniques for managing people-problems. There is no reason to think that the techniques being taught in other fields involved in dealing with the public would be inappropriate to the problems faced by drivers.

The Problematic Nature of Meeting the Public

Even after many years of meeting the public and developing techniques for minimizing problems and learning to restrain oneself, the handling of problems with people on the bus remains problematic for most drivers. The difficulty of dealing with the public is evident in much of the advice that drivers said they would give to a new driver.

Implicit in such advice as "understand human nature," "not let yourself be carried to extremes," "keep calm," "not let what people say bother you," is that dealing with people as the company requires, i.e. with restraint, is a burdensome undertaking. The driver who is able to do so is a person who has to be able to manipulate a huge, awkward piece of equipment through crowded streets without hitting anything, while simultaneously answering questions, and collecting fares as well as listen to a half a dozen people pull the buzzer for the same stop. He is a person who is harassed by youths, and harassed by adults, and threatened by both. Under these conditions, it is not surprising to find drivers occasionally "explode." Also, it would be misleading to suggest to a new recruit that meeting the public will be an easy job.

Problems and "Solutions"

There are a variety of human problems and disturbances which occur on buses and constitute, in part, the work of "meeting the public." To determine the relative saliency of these problems drivers were asked in an open-ended question, what type of criminal or disruptive behavior on their buses -- excluding serious crimes such as robbery and assault -- bothers them the most.

The most frequently mentioned disturbance which bothers drivers is profanity. Other types of disturbances which were mentioned frequently by drivers were dealing with drunks and with youths, vandalism and fare cheating. Other disturbances which are common enough that respondents thought to mention them on the questionnaire included smoking and playing radios; fighting and fooling around; poor dispositions of passengers; harassing and insulting the driver; and physical abuse of passengers, including bothering women and pocket-picking.

Drivers were also asked what it was about these disturbances that bothered them. Their answers were reduced to six categories: First, role strain on the driver. He feels he must act as a norm enforcer or feels he has a special responsibility for what is happening on his bus beyond simply being embarrassed for everyone, e.g. "I feel I have to do something about the situation." "Passengers expect me to stop the trouble." Second, Social offensiveness: it violates the norms of appropriate conduct including: (a) embarrasses and/or irritates driver or passenger; (b) inappropriateness, e.g. "there's a place for everything;" violates time-place-manner rules on buses, e.g., silence, no smoking, no fooling around; (c) lack of respect for elders, women, others, property; (d) "offensive," "disgusting," "I don't like it." Third, Uncertainty: This use of the word, "uncertainty," is in its broadest sense including "danger," "uncontrollability" and "unpredictability" e.g. "you don't know what a drunk will do." "You can't reason with them." Fourth, Psychological strain on driver, e.g. "gives you ulcers;" "gets to me," "upsets me." Fifth, Frustration: Not being allowed by the company to take action or the situation precludes action. Sixth, Other.

The most frequently mentioned reason why disturbances bother drivers is the "social offensiveness" of the distrubance. Next most frequently mentioned reason was the uncertainty which these disturbances create. The next most often cited reasons are the demands that these disturbances place on drivers and the frustration drivers feel at their inability to respond to situations.

Drivers were also asked in an open-ended question what should be done about disturbances on buses. Their responses were reduced to nine categories: first, drivers should have the authority to act e.g., refuse service, eject passengers, be able to call police and remove passengers; second, offenders should be made to pay restitution; third, nothing can or should be done; fourth, intervene in situation -- stop fight or review rules for passengers; fifth, stronger laws or more enforcement of laws; sixth, educate public to the possible dangerous consequences of their behavior on buses; seventh, don't know; eighth, give driver protection, e.g. shields or police escort; and ninth, other.

Drivers would like to take a more active role in dealing with trouble but they are prevented from doing so by company rules. Drivers are apparently more interested in taking an active rather than a passive role, i.e. seated securely behind a shield, in dealing with troublemakers.

Having been asked in an unstructured way what they felt should be done to deal with trouble on buses, drivers were then presented with a list of strategies for dealing with problems on buses which had been compiled on the basis of interviews in the first two study cities. For each strategy drivers were asked to indicate whether they had ever employed it. Calling the supervisor to deal with problems, which is the officially sanctioned means of handling problems, is frequently used. Many drivers also use a technique which does not meet with official approval, namely, refusing to drive the bus until the problem is solved. Other methods widely used are reasoning with the disturbers; ejecting them from the bus; and getting out of the driver's seat and quelling the disturbance himself. These findings suggest that drivers are already taking an active role in the management of deviance, despite company policies against such actions.

Because of their prevalence two types of problems were given special attention in the driver survey: viz. cheating on fares and dealing with youths. Regarding the former, drivers were asked what they recommend doing when a passenger refuses to pay his fare. Their answers were reduced to three major categories: (1) allow to ride free, (2) refuse to let ride, and (3) other. These categories were then subdivided according to the qualification and conditions the respondents attached to their recommendations.

The most frequently recommended means of dealing with fare cheaters is to allow them to ride free. The next most frequently recommended means is to call the supervisor or police. Refusing to let passengers ride was only recommended by a small minority of the drivers. If it can be assumed that what the drivers recommend is what they, themselves, have found to be the best way of dealing with the problem (not necessarily the way they do in fact handle the problem,) then it appears that the proper advice to give new drivers in training or older drivers in re-training, on how to deal with this common and inflammatory problem is either to allow the person to ride free or to call a supervisor. This, in fact, is the advice that the company gives.[1]

In addition to indicating what most drivers feel is the best way to handle the fare cheaters, the data provides a glimpse of another problem which has been mentioned before, viz., demoralization. As noted above, in interviews some drivers expressed the view that they and others do not enforce company rules because the company "doesn't care." Several drivers suggested that the demoralizing effect of seeing management's unwillingness to deal with fare cheaters and drivers who in turn do not bother to collect fares. The question dealing with fare cheats, elicited responses that had a cynical, "demoralized," tone to them. All of these responses recommended that the driver let the fare cheater ride for nothing. And, all of them seemed to be recommending this strategy as a result of an attitude of indifference to company interests that had developed out of observances of management's non-prosecution policy on passenger rule violators. This unsolicited cynicism on the part of the drivers suggests that management's *laissez-faire* policy has taken its toll in low morale.

Youth Problems

The second problem given special attention in the questionnaire is the problem of dealing with youths. Drivers were presented with a list of nine different methods of dealing with youth problems on buses. They were asked to pick which of the nine best characterized the way they usually deal with youngsters who cause trouble on the bus.

Most drivers report that they deal with youthful troublemakers by trying to reason with them. Unfortunately, the next most frequently cited category was "other." Strategies which the drivers say they use infrequently include trying to scare youths by sounding tough, trying to joke with them or forcing them off the bus. These data suggest that although youth problems on buses may be common, they are of the sort that one usually deals with not be means of force or armed intervention, but by rational persuasion. This suggests that for the most part the youth problem, at least, does not demand heavy defensive shielding or police escorts.

After indicating what method they usually use in dealing with youths, drivers were asked to evaluate the success of their methods.

<u>Drunks</u>

Although not given special attention in the questionnaire, the manner in which drivers deal with the problem of drunks was the topic of many interviews with drivers. The procedure for dealing with them that emerged from these interviews is as follows.

Drunks are viewed by drivers as a constant nuisance and as a highly undesirable category of passengers. Drunks are unstable and this can result in their being easily knocked down and injured. Hence, like elderly people, they are a prime source of accidents and civil suits. They are often obnoxious, belligerent, boisterous, obscene, foul smelling, and unpredictable in their behavior; they make overtures toward women. The "loud drunk" is particularly disliked by drivers, because his misconduct puts a "role strain" on the driver. Some drivers try to convince themselves that their only responsibility as a driver is to operate the equipment and to collect the fares -- and "that is it!" They insist that they are not "policemen." They argue that they have no more obligation to deal with any problems on the bus than anyone else on board. But, maintaining this detachment is difficult because there is <u>no</u> way of avoiding the demands made by passengers to be more than just a driver, i.e., to be a policeman. Many more drivers than not seem to have succumbed to the role demands placed upon them by the passengers, i.e. they agree that they should be the policemen on their buses. They are caught, however, in a role conflict because management is against such activity. For either type of driver, the willing or unwilling "policemen," the loud drunk is a problem because his presence <u>demands</u> policing by the driver.

One common way of dealing with a drunk is a method used by drivers for a variety of problems, namely, selective service. Drivers will often avoid picking up a drunk, if at all possible. But, because there are other passengers at the stop or on board and waiting to get off, this strategy is not always possible. In such a situation, the driver may ask the drunk where he is going and no matter what the reply tell him he is on the wrong bus. This strategy occasionally back-fires when an eavesdropping passenger speaks up and corrects the driver's misinformation! This sometimes results in either the passenger or the drunk or both becoming irate. Since not every drunk is as bad as the next, drivers usually try to avoid only the more "dangerous" ones. Drivers judge who is a dangerous drunk on the basis of the drunk's approach, his dress, his voice, demeanor, and attitude.

The method of avoiding trouble by "breezing" the stop, is used by most drivers under certain conditions. Unless he is lazy, a driver will not deliberately "breeze" a stop if any one of the following conditions are present: there is a group present and women are in it, or if the group is composed of all males, but they are between the ages of 40 to 50. He will breeze the stop if it is a suspicious group of teenagers.

This practice of passing up "fares" who look suspicious is one of the dilemmas and injustices of urban public transportation systems. Taxi drivers and bus drivers have both been robbed, assaulted and killed and, consequently, should be allowed to take precautions to protect themselves. The precaution often used, *viz.*, selecting which passengers will be given service, results in the exclusion from public transportation facilities large numbers of people only a few of whom may intend to commit criminal acts. This results from the fact that the criteria used by drivers for evaluating a "fare's" dangerousness are vague. For example, the manager of the Yellow Cab Company of

Tampa, Florida, reported that his taxi drivers are "told that the best means of defense (against being victimized by criminals) is to 'size up your fare -- if you don't like the looks of him, don't pick him up.'"[2] A similar lack of specificity of criteria was evident in another taxi driver's account of how he determines the danger potential of people looking for rides. He said, "...I play it my own way. If a customer looks at me funny, I don't pick him up."[3]

It is the vagueness of these criteria that leads to the injustice of the practice. The criteria are so general that "classes" of people and whole communities rather than "individuals," are being either under-serviced or totally denied service. In Tampa, Florida, for example, the Yellow Cab Company manager reported that "unfortunately there are several areas of Tampa that our drivers simply do not want to go into some hours and days of the week -- and I can't blame them too much."[4] He went on to say that high density Negro areas fell into this category of areas drivers want to avoid.

Because of the nature of their work, taxi drivers are much more at liberty to engage in this practice of "discretionary rendering of service" than are bus drivers.[5] Bus drivers, because of their scheduled routes and because of the monitoring by company supervisors, cannot as easily avoid servicing whole communities. However, bus drivers do use this technique of discretionary service, and it was reported (by residents of a community -- not drivers) that some drivers do avoid servicing whole communities which they are scheduled to serve.

<u>Pickpocketing and Jack-rolling</u>

While there does not seem to be any crimes which occur exclusively on urban transportation, that is, there are no special transit crimes that occur on transportation and nowhere else, there are certain categories of crime which require for their perpetration certain conditions which are supplied by the environment of urban mass transportation. They are supplied elsewhere in society also, but, they are most accessible in urban transportation. One such crime is pickpocketing. Others are jack-rolling and sexual deviance related to body apposition.

The conditions necessary for these kinds of crimes include the following: 1) crowded situations; 2) a quick, rapid entrance and exit; 3) anonymity; 4) standing-in-line behavior or stable groupings of people which will remain stable long enough to allow the criminal to perpetrate his crime. Pockets are picked and drunks are rolled on sidewalks, in large crowds of people, and in other situations besides transit. However, a popular site for this kind of behavior is the urban transit system.

Pickpockets work in downtown buses especially during the Christmas season when passengers have large sums of cash on them. Sometimes, the perpetrator waits for a passenger to come out of a bank, follows him into the bus and then picks his pocket. There is a very definite and standard type of procedure for picking pockets, although the skill with which it is done and the ease depends on the "professionalism" of the pickpocket. Reports from the drivers are that kids who are pickpocketing today do not have the finesse nor the skill of the professional pickpocket of the past. Pickpocketing has really become another form of strongarm robbery.

The usual procedure for pickpocketers is to work in groups of twos or threes. The lead man gets in front of the victim and gets on the bus, he drops his money and bends down to pick it up and put it in the machine. In the process, he crowds into the victim, known as the "goat." The middle man is behind the goat and pushes on, irritated at the delay caused by the first man. In pushing into the victim, he picks his pocket and passes the valuables to the third man who is behind the middle man. Variations of this basic procedure are to have a woman in the lead who helps to distract the victim a little more, or to have a raincoat over the arm if you are the middle man.

Once a pickpocket is on the bus, he usually tries to walk up and down the aisle under the guise of asking the driver for information and in the process, he picks out his target. One technique is to sit next to sleeping people and to reach over against them and take their wallets, but the pickpocket has to first be sure that the person is actually asleep. Generally, the pickpockets leave the drivers alone because they know that the drivers know what's up. They look down the bus to see if there is anyone sleeping and then sit down next to that person, nudging him slightly to see how deeply asleep he is. The bus could be entirely empty except for a few people sleeping or one person sleeping and the pickpocket will sit next to the sleeping person. This is an almost unmistakable sign that he is going to pick the pockets. When this happens, drivers would have to go to some lengths to deny to themselves the man is a pickpocket. However, the driver is in a bind because he cannot make an accusation which he cannot back up. Frequently, drivers have found passengers simply will not back them up nor will the company, nor will the unsuspecting victim.

Almost all drivers, in all cities, are aware of the problem of pickpocketing on their buses, but they are not unanimous as to how they should deal with it. Those drivers who feel that they have no "policing" obligations ignore the problem. However, some drivers do any one of a range of things to try to avoid or thwart the problem. One common technique is to simply do as drivers will do and tell the victim to "step up" (and hence out of the way). Thereby, the driver gets him away from the middle man under the legitimate pretext of simply trying to get the man on the bus quicker. The other method that some drivers use when they see a pickpocket group (some of them know the pickpockets by sight, others know them by the way in which they are standing or carrying their raincoats on their arms on a sunny day) is that they will make an announcement on the bus before reaching the stop to protect their pocketbooks and their wallets. Making the announcement <u>after</u> the door has been opened is dangerous from the point of view of the possibility of revenge. If the pickpockets knew that the driver was trying to warn passengers, they (according to the beliefs of the drivers) would lay and wait for the driver and take revenge upon him. One driver reports that he makes everyone get off the bus without saying why.

The difficulty in trying to make an arrest with a pickpocket is that you cannot find the evidence on the man who actually committed the crime. If you arrest the lead man, he has done nothing. If you arrest the middle man, he wouldn't have the valuables on him because he gives the valuables to the man behind him. Another problem is that pickpockets do not remain on the bus long enough to call the police. They ride one stop beyond where they get on, cross the street and go back down on the other side.

The Chicago Transit Authority (C.T.A.) has printed on the back of its transfers little notes to their passengers about various aspects of C.T.A. operations. It might be helpful in terms of larceny from the person, i.e. pickpocketing, if the

C.T.A. and other companies printed notices to their passengers warning them to be careful of pick-pocketing and to describe the type of procedures used by pickpockets. This would relieve the driver of the police function and of the threat of revenge in performing that function. The C.T.A. also apparently makes announcements during the Christmas season, warning people about pickpocketing. These efforts might be increased and copied by other cities.

The Problem of Women Molesters

Another kind of situational crime in which the urban mass transportation provides the necessary conditions for is women molestation. The necessary conditions are, of course, that there be women and that they be in some kind of captive arrangement so that they can be molested. Another condition is that the molestation can be done in a semi-legitimate fashion. These three conditions are met by urban mass transportation and the pattern of behavior on it. It is perfectly legitimate for anyone to sit next to anyone else on a bus. Under crowded conditions, people are thrown into fairly intimate personal contact with each other. From there, it is only a matter of degree and to some extent as to whether or not a woman is molested. The peak hours for women molestation on buses is in the afternoon and evening between 2:00 p.m. and 8:00 p.m. when there is a considerable number of women riders. Many of the molesters have been drinking and are riding either from work or simply between bars. According to one driver, it is rare that a drunk will try to molest a woman during the late evening or early morning hours. It is also rare, according to him, that teenagers try to molest women on an individual basis. If they do approach women, it is usually only in a group.

Again, because of the difficulty of proving any accusations he may make, the driver generally does not get involved in attempting to control this kind of behavior.

Profanity

The use of obscene language on the bus is common and is seen as a problem by many drivers. The problem is not that the language is shocking to the drivers, many of whom hear or use language as bad or worse around the gilley room. It is that the language is being used in a social context where, according to them, it should not be used. This is at the heart of the problem. Some people are simply against any use of profanity. But, many people including drivers and passengers, male and female, are not entirely opposed to profanity, itself, but only to its use in certain social context.[6] Drivers, for example, may join in the rough talk around the gilley room, but will tell you that they would never bring their wives in there. This dual standard of the appropriateness of profanity is usually the issue which causes problems on the buses. Drivers do not mind profanity unless there are women on board, and then the standards change. Drivers who hold this norm feel they must quiet the profane person. If the driver does not happen to adhere to this standard, the women passengers or another male passenger may insist that the driver do something. When this occurs each driver relies on his characteristic way of dealing with problems, e.g. reasoning with the person, ejecting him, or calling for help.

Summary and Conclusions

An examination of the social and situational conditions on buses reveals that a considerable amount of social control is exercised in various ways on buses. Passengers, by their presence alone, supply a pressure to conform or risk the penalty of public humiliation. The relatively small space on the bus and the orientation of the seats toward the front increase the effectiveness of this force for control. At the same time this seating arrangement creates an area of low visibility at the rear of the bus. People sitting in the rear -- usually youths -- therefore feel less conspicuous and freer to fool around or to violate various rules of deportment. This may eventuate into more serious misbehavior if the driver attempts to control it. For another thing, the high visibility at the front of the bus may result in pressures towards deviance in those cases where a passenger feels he has been publicly humiliated, fairly or otherwise, by a driver. This is especially true of youths who, because of peer group pressures, are sensitive to any criticism by authority figures.

In addition to their indirect influence for control, passengers also engage in direct intervention as agents for control in certain circumstances. A small minority (eleven percent) of the drivers surveyed reported that direct intervention by passengers occurs "frequently" (almost every time there is a problem) on their buses. Three times as many drivers (33 percent) reported that this type of aid occurs "sometimes." There seems to be only a slight difference in the frequency with which "regular" passengers, in contrast to passengers whom the drivers do not know supply this type of aid.

Many drivers as well as several school officials reported that there are advantages in having drivers work the same run and serve the same group of people over a long period of time. One advantage is that it allows drivers to establish a consistent standard of authority on the bus so that passengers -- especially, but not only youths -- will know what rules they are expected to obey and what they can and cannot get away with in terms of misbehavior. Another advantage is that it allows drivers to establish social relations with some passengers. These social ties, although frequently of a very superficial sort, are useful to drivers. They supply him with allies in times of conflict on the bus. They also reduce his sense of being an alien in certain areas of the city which he is scheduled to drive in but which do not reflect his own cultural background. Because of these advantages it is recommended that efforts be made to increase the number of drivers who work the same runs or pieces of work (such as "school trippers" and other "extra board" work). Drivers should be made aware of the advantage of driving the same passengers and management should make efforts to ensure that extra work assignments are arranged in such fashion that this goal can be approached as closely as possible.

Drivers learn how to manage the deviance which occurs on their buses as part of acquiring the skill of "meeting the public." The major task of this occupational skill is learning self-control. The learning process involved in acquiring the necessary self-control is long, taxing, and never fully completed. Apparently, company training programs are of virtually no help in acquiring this skill of meeting the public. Current training-program instructors feel they cannot teach this skill, but many drivers feel otherwise. As it is, the skill is taught informally through gilley room conversations and in some cases through direct advice from older drivers at the request of younger drivers. A third way in which this skill is learned appears to have an undesirable effect. This way is the *ex post facto* method of waiting for drivers to be complained about and then having the superintendent reprimand them and explain either explicitly or implicitly how a driver is supposed to deal with the public. The approach fosters cynicism and poor management-labor relations. It could be avoided and the process of learning to meet the public could be made less taxing if companies would develop training programs specifically designed to help the driver attain this skill. Conceivably such programs would incorporate the experience and wisdom of older drivers, some of the findings of this study, and the talents of professional instructors in the art of dealing with people. Among the latter are professionals who are skilled at conducting "sensitivity" groups and/or those people who are now employed in teaching businessmen and salesmen the techniques of dealing with people. The goal of such a training program would be to minimize driver-passenger conflict by making drivers aware of how they are dealing with these problems now, and by supplying them with alternative means of dealing with problems so that when necessary, drivers can exercise flexibility in handling deviance.

Excluding robbery and associated assaults or murder, the deviance which occurs on buses and which drivers must deal with is of a relatively minor sort. These types of deviance -- listed in the order of decreasing frequency -- include the following: profanity, drunks, problems with youths, vandalism, fare cheating, smoking, playing radios; also mentioned were deportment (rowdiness), passenger disposition (meanness), harassing the driver, physical abuse of passengers (molesting women of harassing passengers) and pocket picking. The most frequently cited (43 percent) thing about these disturbances that bothers drivers is their "social offensiveness," ie.., the fact that they entail one of the following: 2) embarrass the driver, b) they are inappropriate to the bus, c) they show lack of respect, d) they are "disgusting" or simply "offensive." The second most frequently cited (14 percent) reason why these disruptions bother drivers is the "uncertainty" they create, i.e. the uncontrolability and unpredictability of the situation into which they put the driver.

Other reasons why drivers are disturbed by these problems refer to the personal strain they place on the driver either in the form of role strain (four percent), i.e. the demand to act as a policeman, and psychological strain (three percent) in terms of "nervousness" the situations engender. Some drivers (four percent) also mentioned that what bothered them about these problems is that theythey could not actively deal with them because of company policy restricting driver behavior.

Most drivers use a variety of different methods for dealing with deviance on their buses. Only a few of these methods are officially sanctioned by management. A minority of drivers (16 to 31 percent depending on the type of problem) are managing problems on buses in ways which they know management would disapprove of. Another larger minority of drivers (y to 38 percent depending on the problem) are currently using methods of handling problems with the public which they are not sure the company would approve of or not. This again suggests the need for more adequate training. It also suggests that perhaps, even with training, part of the conflict between management and drivers over the appropriate means of meeting the public will not and cannot be resolved.

Two particularly prevalent problems on buses are fare cheating and youth problems. The two ways of dealing with the former problem most frequently cited by drivers are to allow the fare cheater to ride (41 percent) and to call for a supervisor or policeman (38 percent). Very few drivers (16 percent) force the person off the bus in these circumstances. The most frequently cited (38 percent) "usual method of dealing with youth problems" is to reason with the youths involved.

Notes

1 Perhaps drivers responding to our questionnaire may simply have been giving the "official line." However, the variety and quality of the answers and the wording of the question lead us to the conclusion that they were not. The exact wording was, "What would you recommend a driver do if a passenger refuses to pay his fare?" There was no mention of what the driver "must do" "is supposed to do" according to management.

2 Tampa Tribune, "Murders, Robberies, Shake Taxi Drivers: Wary of Suspicious Looking Fares," 2/1/70, pp. 1-B, 6-B.

3 Ibid., p. 6-B.

4 Ibid., p. 6-B.

5 Many cab drivers go a step further and use this practice not just for self-protection but for self-aggrandizement, and the exercise of their prejudices as well. Some drivers try to select only fares which look "lucrative." Some refuse to transport classes of people such as Negroes. The latter case seemed to be involved in the New Year's Eve (1970) incident in which a Negro comedian, Godfrey Cambridge, was dragged several blocks in New York City by a cabbie who apparently did not want to provide service to Negroes.

6 In addition some object to the substantive variety of the profanity. A high school principal discussing some of the evils of the racial transfer program was upset that his students would learn some new profanities and regarded this as one of the more serious faults of the program.